WHEN NO ONE IS WATCHING

WHEN NO ONE IS WATCHING

Preventing suicide and avoiding lawsuits:
Insights from a correctional expert of 25 years

Forensic Psychiatrist • Correctional Expert

Author of *Suicide in Jails and Prisons: Preventive and Legal Perspectives* (2022)

ANASSERIL E. DANIEL, MD

When No One Is Watching: Preventing Suicide and Avoiding Lawsuits: Insights from a Correctional Expert of 25 Years

For information about this title or to order other books and/or electronic media, contact the publisher:

Anasseril E. Daniel, MD
www.Prisonsuicideexpert.org
anasserildaniel@gmail.com

ISBNs:
979-8-9852048-3-4 (hardcover)
979-8-9852048-4-1 (softcover)
979-8-9852048-5-8 (eBook)

Printed in the United States of America

Cover and interior design: 1106 Design

To the families who have lost loved ones in custody,
whose pain reminds us why prevention must always
remain at the center of correctional practice. And to the
correctional professionals who, when properly trained and
supported, hold the power to make a difference—often
unseen, often unrecognized, but never unimportant.

TABLE OF CONTENTS

Note on Case Vignettes . . . xiii
Keywords . . . xv
Preface . . . xvii
Introduction . . . 1

CHAPTER 1: Suicide in Corrections—Scope, Scrutiny, and Responsibility . . . 5
- Scope of the Problem . . . 7
- Recent Uptick in Suicide Rates . . . 8
- Media Attention and Public Accountability . . . 9
- Historical Background . . . 11
- Suicide Prevention Programs . . . 14
- Role of Staff in Suicide Prevention . . . 16
- Staff Reactions to Suicide . . . 17
- Family Reactions to Suicide . . . 19
- Due Diligence and Training in Suicide Prevention . . . 20
- Ethics in Suicide Prevention . . . 22
- Conclusion—The Challenge Ahead . . . 23

CHAPTER 2: When Tragedy Becomes Litigation—Anatomy of a Legal Complaint . . . 27
- Introduction . . . 29

- Legal Representation 29
- Personal Representative 30
- Features of a Legal Complaint 30
- Causes of Action 32
- Claims for Relief 33
- Filing the Complaint 34
- What Happens after Filing 34
- Causes of Action in Legal Complaints Identified in Lawsuits 35
- Conclusion 38

CHAPTER 3: Exposed in Court—Screening Failures, Ignored Records, and False Logs Become Lawsuits 41
- Introduction 41
- Identification and Screening 42
- Assessment 46
- Mental Health and Psychiatric Care 48
- Documentation and Communication 54
- Conclusion 62

CHAPTER 4: Defining and Identifying Suicidal Behaviors . . 65
- Introduction 65
- Definitions 66
- Suicidal Ideation and Intentionality 68
- Assessing the Seriousness of Suicidal Thoughts and Behaviors 72
- Non-Suicidal Self-Injury 72
- Denial of Suicidal Ideation 76
- Manner of Communicating Suicidal Ideation 77
- Method of Choice 78
- Staff Attitudes 80
- Conclusion 81

CHAPTER 5: The Vulnerable Detainee/Inmate—Predictable Risk, Preventable Tragedy . . . 85
- Introduction . . . 85
- Who Are the Most Vulnerable? . . . 86
- Risk Factors of Suicidal Behavior and Suicide . . . 86
- Protective Factors . . . 115
- Critical Risk Factors . . . 116
- Conclusion . . . 117

CHAPTER 6: Screening and Suicide Risk Assessment—Gateways and Pitfalls . . . 121
- Introduction . . . 121
- Screening: The First Step . . . 122
- Problems Identified in Lawsuits (Screening) . . . 124
- Do's and Don'ts of Suicide Screening . . . 128
- Suicide Risk Assessment (SRA) . . . 128
- Core Elements of Suicide Risk Assessment . . . 130
- Problems Identified in Litigation in Suicide Risk Assessment (SRA) . . . 133
- Conclusion . . . 141

CHAPTER 7: Staying Ahead of Crisis—Monitoring, Treatment, and Emergency Management . . . 143
- Introduction . . . 143
- Arrest and Booking . . . 144
- Monitoring . . . 147
- Medical Services Requests ("Kites"): Missed Warnings and Litigation Risks . . . 152
- Solitary Confinement . . . 154
- Video Surveillance: Merits and Pitfalls . . . 155
- Intervention and Treatment . . . 157

- Empathy and Understanding 160
- Emergency Medical Management 161
- Conclusion 164

CHAPTER 8: Housing, Cell Fixtures, and Supplies—Often Overlooked Factors 167

- Introduction 167
- Ligature Materials and Tie-Off Points 170
- Facility-Issued Razors 171
- Cell Design, Visibility, and Sight Lines 173
- Intercoms and Suicide Prevention 174
- Keep-on-Person (KOP) Medications 176
- Telephone Cords and Suicide 181
- Conclusion 185

CHAPTER 9: The Critical First Two Weeks of Incarceration—Risks, Realities, and Lessons 189

- Introduction 189
- Profiles of High-Risk Detainees 190
- Psychological Reactions to Arrest and Detention 191
- Lockups: High-Risk Settings for Suicide 192
- U.S. Marshals Service 196
- Drug-Intoxication and -Withdrawal Related Suicide . . 200
- Conclusion 204

CHAPTER 10: Policies, Procedures, and Practice 207

- Introduction 207
- History of Suicide Prevention Development and the Standard of Care 208
- Policies on Paper Versus Practice on the Ground 210
- Problems in Policy Development across the Country . . 212

- Suicide Prevention Policy Framework 214
- Legal Defensibility of the Suicide Prevention Policy Framework 227
- Building Legally Defensible Systems 228
- Conclusion 230

CHAPTER 11: Training—A Case Law-Based Approach 233
- Introduction 233
- Objectives of Suicide Prevention Training 235
- Who Should Receive Training? 235
- Traditional Training Approaches 236
- Why Traditional Approaches Fail 239
- Case Law as a Training Tool 241
- Key Legal Precedents and Failures 243
- Twenty Critical Action Items to Prevent Suicide and Avoid Liability 245
- Methodology of Training Execution 248
- Drawbacks of Case Law-Based Training 249
- Toward a Hybrid, Legally Defensible Training Model . . 251
- Governance, CQI, and Sustainability 255
- Conclusion 256

CHAPTER 12: Legal Liability and Risk Management 259
- Introduction 259
- Estate of *Ryan Clark v. County of Green Lake*—(later appealed as *Clark v. Walker*) 260
- Broader Implications of *Ryan Clark*: Risk Management Strategies 261
- Risk Management Strategies from Case Law and Clinical Practice 264
- Road Map for Facility Implementation 267

- Documentation 269
- Training as Risk Management 270
- Leadership and Oversight 271
- Accountability 273
- Integrating Risk Management into Daily Operations . . 274
- Conclusion 275

CONCLUSION—The Duty That Never Ends 277

APPENDICES 279

- Suicide Prevention Checklists 280
- Risk Factors: Static and Dynamic 285
- Suicide Prevention Policy Checklist 287
- Risk Management Checklist 291

Acknowledgments 295

About the Author 297

Index 299

NOTE ON CASE VIGNETTES

This book includes real-world case vignettes drawn from more than twenty-five years of correctional mental health practice and litigation review. Each has been de-identified and adapted to protect confidentiality while preserving key facts and lessons. Together, these forty cases highlight recurring risks, system breakdowns, and legal exposure to guide prevention, strengthen policy, and promote a culture of safety and accountability.

The chapters that follow integrate these lessons into a comprehensive framework for suicide prevention and legal-risk management in correctional settings.

NOTE ON TERMINOLOGY

In correctional settings, multiple terms are used to describe individuals in custody. For clarity and consistency, this book adopts the following usage:

- **Inmate**—Refers to individuals serving criminal sentences in jails or prisons. This is the term most widely used in correctional practice and will be applied throughout discussions of operations, housing, supervision, and policy.

- **Detainee**—Refers to individuals held in custody pending trial, sentencing, immigration, or other civil proceedings. This distinction is especially important in intake, screening, and the early stages of confinement, when vulnerability to suicide is often heightened.
- **Prisoner**—Retained when citing case law, statutes, or legal decisions, in order to reflect the language used by the courts.

While terms such as *incarcerated person* or *resident* are increasingly used in academic and advocacy contexts to emphasize personhood, this book employs the terminology most commonly found in correctional operations and legal proceedings. The goal is to maintain professional accuracy, legal precision, and readability for diverse audiences engaged in suicide prevention and risk management.

A WORD ABOUT CROSS REFERENCES

As you move through the chapters, you will occasionally see references to related case vignettes elsewhere in the book. These connections are included to help readers ***recognize patterns of failure that recur across different stages of custody****—from screening and housing to monitoring, emergency response, and policy execution. They are especially valuable for* ***trainers, administrators, and legal reviewers*** *who wish to study systemic issues and design prevention strategies. Readers focused on narrative flow may skip these links without losing the main thread of the discussion.*

10 KEYWORDS/PHRASES

- Suicide prevention in jails and prisons
- Correctional mental health care
- Legal-risk management in corrections
- Deliberate indifference lawsuits
- Suicide risk assessment (SRA) in custody
- Correctional policy and national standards
- Case law-based staff training
- Liability avoidance for correctional facilities
- Monitoring and emergency response in detention
- Best practices for correctional suicide prevention

PREFACE

On a quiet evening in a county jail, a young man was discovered hanging in his cell. The officers on duty had passed by his door earlier, but the signs of acute withdrawal and agitation had not been recognized. His cries for help were dismissed as disruptive behavior. By the time staff entered the cell, it was too late. The case would later become the subject of a lawsuit—one of hundreds across the nation alleging negligence, inadequate training, and deliberate indifference.

For more than twenty-five years, I have reviewed cases like this—more than one hundred suicides in jails, prisons, and police lockups. As an expert witness and correctional psychiatrist, I have been called upon to explain what went wrong: the missed warning signs, the failures in supervision, the poorly designed policies, and the lack of timely medical or mental health intervention. Each case has taught me that suicide in correctional settings is rarely the result of a single factor. Instead, it reflects systemic weaknesses—failures of policy, practice, and accountability—that converge with the vulnerabilities of the incarcerated individual.

This book grew out of my conviction that these deaths are not inevitable. Suicides in custody are preventable when correctional institutions take seriously their constitutional and moral obligation to provide a safe environment, adequate medical and mental health care, and properly trained staff. The lessons learned from litigation, consultation, and clinical experience must be transformed into practical strategies for prevention and risk management.

When No One Is Watching is not an abstract review of theories. It is grounded in forty real cases I consulted, as well as landmark legal rulings that define the obligations of correctional institutions. These cases reveal recurring patterns of failure—poor screening, inadequate monitoring, communication breakdowns, and neglect of known risk factors. But they also highlight opportunities for reform, from suicide-resistant housing to collaborative staff responsibility, case law-based training, and legally defensible policies.

My hope is that this book will serve both as a resource and a call to action: a resource for correctional administrators, staff, attorneys, and clinicians seeking to understand the complexity of suicide in custody and a call to action for institutions to recognize that every missed opportunity can cost a life—and that every preventable death can become a lawsuit.

"Every missed warning sign carries two shadows:
the loss of a life and the weight of legal accountability."

INTRODUCTION

When No One Is Watching

S*uicide in correctional facilities* is a multifaceted and deeply troubling phenomenon that continues to command the attention of policy-makers, administrators, clinicians, custody staff, and the public. The high prevalence of suicides in lockups, jails, and prisons across the United States—and the resulting lawsuits filed by surviving family members—demand a serious examination of the adequacy of mental health care, staffing, training, policies, procedures, and the correctional environment itself.

As a correctional and forensic psychiatric consultant, I have drawn on my technical expertise and knowledge of penal systems to advise attorneys on whether facilities fulfilled their duty of care and whether constitutionally guaranteed rights to adequate medical and mental health treatment were violated. The legal foundations of suicide-related lawsuits are complex: survivors often pursue negligence claims against correctional officers and healthcare professionals, as well as civil-rights claims when mental health care is inadequate or when staff fail to protect individuals from self-harm.

From a pragmatic standpoint, expert consultation can drive systemic change. My evaluations over the last twenty-five years have fostered improvements in correctional practices designed to reduce the risk of suicide. In more than 110 suicide-related lawsuits, I have critically examined whether facilities violated established standards of care and whether professionals deviated from accepted clinical practice. My case reviews, research-based analysis, and testimony have highlighted areas of liability while also offering strategies for prevention and defense.

My approach has always been guided by sensitivity to the profound loss experienced by families, balanced with professional objectivity in evaluating institutional practices. This blend of analysis, critique, and advocacy has not only influenced litigation outcomes but has also supported positive reforms in suicide prevention within correctional facilities.

During my tenure as Director of Psychiatric Services for the Missouri Department of Corrections in the early 2000s, I developed a sustained interest in inmate suicide—its causes, risk factors, and methods of prevention. My retrospective review of all suicides in Missouri prisons between 1992 and 2001 revealed that most were preventable if staff had recognized behavioral warning signs and followed existing suicide prevention policies. Clinical experience and research both confirm that staff training is a critical factor in ensuring timely intervention during suicidal crises.

Through my consultation work, I have studied the constellation of factors that contribute to suicide risk in custody, as well as the adequacy and accuracy of staff responses. While each case is unique, three risk factors consistently stand out across both clinical literature and litigation:

1. **Active mental disorder**
2. **Substance withdrawal**
3. **Prior near-lethal suicide attempt**

Failure to identify and address these elements has repeatedly led to preventable deaths. Beyond these factors, three recurring systemic problems are often cited in successful lawsuits:

- **Inadequate screening and assessment**
- **Poor communication and coordination among staff**
- **Insufficient staff training**

While issues such as overcrowding, budget shortages, and staffing deficits shape the correctional environment, they are rarely as central to individual suicides as these core failures. Plaintiffs' attorneys consistently attempt to link suicides to deficiencies in screening, assessment, communication, and training, while defense attorneys argue the opposite.

In my previous book, *Suicide in Jails and Prisons: Preventive and Legal Perspectives*, I provided a comprehensive review of suicide in custody, examining prevention strategies and legal issues based on literature, clinical practice, and case law. In this new book, *When No One Is Watching*, I turn to real cases from my consulting work, presenting my perspective on the factors most directly linked to suicide attempts and completed suicides. I also explore practical steps for prevention and strategies for avoiding liability.

Throughout this book, some case vignettes include cross references to other chapters. These connections are intentional: they highlight recurring themes and systemic failures across different facilities, policies, and legal outcomes. By linking cases in this way, the reader can better appreciate how similar risk factors and institutional shortcomings appear in multiple contexts, reinforcing the lessons for prevention and liability-risk management.

The book consists of three components:

1. **Understanding Suicide in Corrections**—prevalence, risk factors, and systemic challenges.
2. **Legal Dimensions**—how lawsuits are framed, litigated, and defended.
3. **Pathways to Prevention**—lessons from case consultation, training, and policy reforms that can save lives and reduce liability.

Although systemic problems shape the overall environment, my consultations have shown that suicides often turn on case-level failures: missed warning signs, inadequate assessments, and breakdowns in policy implementation. Chapters 10, 11, and 12 bring the discussion full circle by examining how policy frameworks can be made legally defensible, how case law-based training can transform staff practice, and how risk management strategies can help institutions prevent suicide and reduce liability.

This book focuses on those failures and the lessons they hold for correctional staff, clinicians, administrators, and legal professionals.

"Most suicides behind bars are not mysterious or unforeseeable—they are preventable tragedies that expose where systems fail, and where accountability must begin."

CHAPTER 1

SUICIDE IN CORRECTIONS: SCOPE, SCRUTINY, AND RESPONSIBILITY

"In correctional settings, it is the silence between policy and practice that too often leads to preventable deaths."
—Anasseril E. Daniel

CASE VIGNETTE 1.1—SEVERE MENTAL ILLNESS, IGNORED WARNINGS, AND FALSIFIED WATCH LOGS

A *thirty-six-year-old White male* incarcerated in a state prison died by hanging using a torn piece of mattress as a ligature in a single cell. He had a high-school education, was unmarried, and had no children. His history revealed long-standing psychiatric disturbance characterized by anxiety, paranoia, aggressiveness, and impulsivity. He carried a diagnosis of schizophrenia and had been treated intermittently with antipsychotic medications. His symptoms included auditory hallucinations and persecutory delusions, such as believing a device had been implanted in his ear to read his thoughts.

He had previously expressed suicidal ideation on multiple occasions and had been placed on suicide watch at least twice. In the days before his death, his mother reported to prison staff that he was acting strangely and warned that he was at risk of taking his life. Despite this warning, he received only a cursory assessment by an unlicensed mental health provider. Though briefly placed in a specialized cell, he was not properly monitored. A correctional officer later admitted he had failed to conduct the required every-fifteen-minutes suicide checks and, instead, falsified records to suggest compliance.

Risk and Contributory Factors

- Severe mental illness (schizophrenia with hallucinations and delusions).
- History of suicidal ideation and prior suicide-watch placement.
- Acute decompensation three days before death.
- Poor medication compliance.
- Loss of stabilizing influence (mother's concern not acted upon).
- Inadequate professional assessment.
- Failure of monitoring and falsified records.

This case illustrates multiple layers of institutional failure: disregard of family warnings, use of unlicensed staff for suicide risk assessment, and falsification of suicide-watch logs. Each element compounded liability, reflecting both **deliberate indifference** and violation of accepted correctional standards of care.

"A false log can be as deadly as a tightened noose."

This tragic case is not an isolated incident but a window into a systemic crisis. Behind every individual story lies a pattern of institutional gaps, missed opportunities, and failures in recognition, monitoring, and care. To understand why suicides like this continue to occur in jails and prisons across the world, we must examine both the broader context and the recurring vulnerabilities that correctional systems struggle to address.

SCOPE OF THE PROBLEM

The alarming rise in suicide within correctional facilities in recent years has reached a critical inflection point. With the deinstitutionalization of the mentally ill from state hospitals and the dwindling number of psychiatric beds, correctional institutions have become the de facto mental healthcare providers. As a result, facilities are now managing increasingly complex populations with histories of mental illness, newly arrested or detained, and the stakes are higher than ever.

Structural vulnerabilities—overcrowding, inadequate mental health support, and isolation—intersect with the psychology of inmates to create a scenario where suicide is tragically predictable, not spontaneous. Legal scrutiny and the proliferation of lawsuits in response to preventable deaths underscore the urgency of understanding and addressing these compounding factors.

Recent research confirms this trend. Swartz and McDonald (2024) documented suicide in correctional settings as a growing public-health crisis shaped by structural, environmental, and clinical factors. Their work highlights that incarceration significantly increases the risk of suicide, especially in solitary confinement and among those with untreated psychiatric illness. Kaba *et al.* (2014) previously found that inmates assigned to solitary confinement were nearly seven times more likely to commit self-harm than those not in isolation.

Emerging evidence stresses the importance of preventive measures such as systematic screening upon intake, ongoing monitoring, supportive housing, and comprehensive staff training. Interventions such as restricting access to means, improving mental health services, and integrating trauma-informed care have shown promise—yet systemic barriers remain.

RECENT UPTICK IN SUICIDE RATES

Overall, incarcerated people remain at high risk for suicide. In U.S. jails, suicide is the leading cause of death, while, in prisons, it ranks as the third-leading cause.

The *National Institute of Justice (NIJ)* issued a report in February 2024 documenting that, between 2013 and 2021, 187 inmates died by suicide in federal prisons—accounting for 54 percent of all unnatural deaths during that period (187 of 344). Federal prisons collectively house approximately 155,000 prisoners, underscoring the scale of the crisis (NIJ, 2024)

Trends in local jails have been equally concerning. The *Bureau of Justice Statistics (BJS)*, analyzed by E. Carson (2021), showed that suicide rates in jails have increased steadily since 2015 after a period of relative stability following the introduction of suicide prevention initiatives in the early 2000s. Over the 20-year period from 2000 to 2019, more than 6,200 jail inmates died by suicide, with deaths increasing by 13 percent. Carson reported that those who died by suicide were most often male, non-Hispanic White, incarcerated for violent crimes, and most frequently died by self-strangulation.

According to BJS statistical tables, suicide accounted for nearly one-third of all deaths in local jails and 8 percent of deaths in state and federal prisons in 2019. Nearly one-fifth of the nation's 1,161 state and federal prisons and one-tenth of the 3,234 local jails reported at least one suicide that year.

A particularly troubling finding is that more than three-quarters of jail inmates who died by suicide between 2000 and 2019 had not yet been convicted but were awaiting adjudication of their charges (Carson, 2021). This underscores the acute vulnerability of pretrial detainees, whose uncertainty about sentencing and lack of mental health support place them at elevated risk.

MEDIA ATTENTION AND PUBLIC ACCOUNTABILITY

The increasing suicide rate in correctional facilities has captured the attention of national and international media, raising alarm among the public, lawmakers, and correctional policymakers. Media reports not only highlight tragic deaths but also expose systemic failures, often serving as a catalyst for reform, litigation, and policy revision.

The New York Times reported in November 2022 that "jail is a death sentence for Americans," underscoring the pervasive nature of the crisis. Across the country, local outlets have amplified this concern: the **Bristol County Jail** in Massachusetts has faced repeated criticism for inmate suicides, all seven since 2017 involving bunkbeds; in **South Mississippi**, a man became another casualty in a growing number of suicides in the jail; in **Milwaukee County**, a twenty-year-old woman's suicide by hanging reignited public debate; and in **North Carolina**, suicides in 2024 reached historic highs, with eight of thirteen deaths occurring in solitary confinement. Similar headlines appeared in **Hawaii**, where seven suicides since 2022 prompted litigation and large settlements, and in **Alaska**, where eighteen in-custody deaths in 2022 were described by officials as "too many."

High-profile cases have drawn particularly sharp scrutiny. On August 25, 2022, **Michael Nieves**, a forty-year old pretrial detainee at Rikers Island, slit his throat with a shaving razor issued under Department of Corrections policy. Officers allegedly watched him bleed for nearly 10 minutes without providing aid. The incident provoked outrage from the New York Attorney General and was cited in the *NYC Department of Corrections In-Custody Death Report*, which noted multiple suicides in 2022–24. Cases such as this underscore how media coverage can magnify public outrage, galvanize oversight, and pressure city or state officials to act.

The *Department of Justice* has also intervened, suing states such as Hawaii and Pennsylvania for inadequate mental healthcare and high suicide rates. Federal courts have at times appointed special masters to oversee remedial measures.

Media scrutiny is not confined to the U.S. In **Italy**, severe prison overcrowding, understaffing, and heat were linked to record numbers of suicides in 2024. Reports prompted the Italian parliament to enact reforms, including early release of 15 percent of prisoners. Ninety suicides were reported in 2024—the highest since 1992. Other European countries, including **France**, **Romania**, **Cyprus**, and **Greece**, have also recorded high rates. In **Scotland**, BBC quoted criminologist Sarah Armstrong, who criticized reliance on superficial assessments by mental health non-professionals that failed to identify high-risk inmates despite obvious markers, such as past attempts and recent life stressors.

In **India**, suicide has emerged as a leading cause of unnatural death in prisons. The *National Crime Records Bureau* reported that, in 2022, 119 prisoners died by suicide. A 2021 handbook by the *National Institute of Mental Health and Neurosciences (NIMHANS)* revealed that 23.8 to 81 percent of prisoners had mental illness, yet psychiatric-staffing levels remain critically low compared to Europe and the United States. Reports emphasize that inadequate screening and lack of treatment are major contributors to rising suicide rates.

Constructive or Counterproductive?

While some coverage is sensationalistic, media attention has generally been constructive in spurring reforms. Reports often lead to:

- **Policy revisions**, such as changes in housing design (removing bunkbed tie-off points) or intake-screening procedures.
- **Budget reallocations** to improve staffing ratios, add suicide-resistant fixtures, and expand mental health programs.
- **Litigation pressure**, resulting in costly settlements and court-ordered oversight.
- **Training reforms**, as facilities recognize the need to prepare staff to identify and respond to risk.

At the same time, sensational headlines without context risk demoralizing staff, inflaming public distrust, and overshadowing genuine efforts at reform. The challenge for correctional leaders is to harness media scrutiny as a driver of accountability rather than view it as a purely adversarial force.

HISTORICAL BACKGROUND

Over the last four decades, the scope and quality of medical and mental healthcare in U.S. jails and prisons have substantially improved, approaching parity with community standards. Focused research has delineated the causes and contexts of inmate suicide, identifying correction-specific risk factors and shaping intervention strategies to mitigate risk. Class-action lawsuits initiated by prisoners have played a vital role in expanding access to healthcare and establishing enforceable rights.

Privatization and Shifts in Care Delivery

Beginning in the late 1990s, privatization of correctional healthcare became the norm, replacing institution-governed systems with for-profit medical providers. This shift represented a significant departure in philosophy and delivery, with mixed results regarding continuity of care and suicide prevention.

Key Legal Foundations

The legal framework for suicide prevention in correctional settings was built largely through federal-court decisions. In *Estelle v. Gamble* (1976), the Supreme Court ruled that prisoners have a constitutional right under the Eighth Amendment to receive adequate medical care, establishing that deliberate indifference to serious medical needs constitutes cruel and unusual punishment. This right was soon expanded to include mental healthcare, making suicide prevention an essential element of correctional responsibility.

The courts further clarified the duty of facilities to provide evaluation and treatment. In *Bowring v. Godwin* (1977), the Fourth Circuit held that inmates are entitled to psychiatric and psychological treatment when needed, requiring systems of screening and evaluation. The concept of "serious medical need" became central to suicide-related lawsuits: when correctional staff recklessly disregard or show gross indifference to suicide risk, they may be found in violation of constitutional rights.

Later, in *Farmer v. Brennan* (1994), Justice David Souter articulated the standard for liability: prison officials are culpable when they know of and disregard an excessive risk to inmate health or safety. This "deliberate indifference" standard remains the bedrock of modern suicide litigation.

Legislation and Oversight

The Civil Rights of Institutionalized Persons Act (CRIPA, 1980) gave the Department of Justice authority to investigate systemic abuses in state and local correctional facilities. Suicide prevention became a recurring focus of CRIPA investigations, which often culminated in consent decrees requiring reforms such as improved intake screening, timely mental health assessments, and enhanced supervision. While implementation has sometimes been hindered by bureaucratic inertia and resource constraints, CRIPA reinforced suicide prevention as a federal-oversight priority.

Professional Guidelines and Standards

Court rulings also prompted professional organizations to formalize suicide prevention standards. The American Psychiatric Association (APA), American Correctional Association (ACA), and the National Commission on Correctional Health Care (NCCHC) all issued guidelines mandating suicide screening, watch procedures, and staff training. By the 1990s, many state statutes required suicide prevention programs, though they rarely specified exact screening tools or procedures, leaving implementation uneven.

Training and Institutional Liability

Since the Supreme Court's decision in *Monell v. Department of Social Services of the City of New York* (1978), municipalities can be held liable when constitutional violations result from official policy or custom. Applied to suicide litigation, this has meant that inadequate staff training is often treated as evidence of deliberate indifference. In nearly every lawsuit I have consulted, plaintiffs alleged that correctional staff and medical providers lacked adequate training in suicide prevention.

Courts have accepted arguments that poor or absent training on risk factors, prevention policies, and monitoring procedures contributed directly to inmate deaths. This argument is particularly strong in "cluster suicide" cases, where multiple suicides occur in the same facility over a short period. Plaintiffs often argue that such clusters reflect not only systemic negligence but also a pervasive lack of staff preparedness.

SUICIDE PREVENTION PROGRAMS

An adequate suicide prevention program is essential in every correctional facility to ensure inmate safety, security, health, and well-being. State statutes and accreditation agencies such as the *National Commission on Correctional Health Care (NCCHC) Standards for Health Services in Correctional Facilities* (2018) provide guidelines for development of such programs.

Core Requirements

A comprehensive suicide prevention program depends on the availability of mental health services, timely substance-abuse interventions, sufficient staffing, and a supportive treatment environment. Yet many lockups and small county jails operate with only limited suicide prevention policies rather than full programs aligned with NCCHC standards. In such settings, administrators often cite financial constraints, limited staffing, or the relative rarity of suicide in their facilities as reasons for underdeveloped prevention systems.

Components of a Program

According to NCCHC standards, a complete suicide prevention program should include:

1. **Training**—regular and mandatory for all staff.
2. **Identification**—of at-risk individuals through screening and observation.
3. **Referral for Evaluation**—ensuring timely mental health assessments.
4. **Treatment**—individualized clinical interventions.
5. **Housing and Monitoring**—appropriate placement, with close supervision.
6. **Communication**—clear and ongoing information exchange among staff.
7. **Intervention**—immediate-response protocols during crises.
8. **Notification**—of supervisors, families, and investigative bodies as required.
9. **Review**—structured mortality and morbidity reviews following incidents.
10. **Debriefing**—support for staff and inmates after a suicide or attempt.

Evaluation and Quality Improvement

Periodic evaluation—preferably annual—is critical but often neglected. Facilities should track data on suicide attempts and deaths through continuous quality-improvement (CQI) programs. Reviewing incident reports, assessment tools, and staff-training outcomes allows administrators to adapt prevention efforts to the changing needs of the inmate population. In this way, data collection becomes not a bureaucratic exercise but a vital safeguard, enabling facilities to evaluate effectiveness and make strategic adjustments.

The Importance of a Written Manual

A comprehensive suicide prevention manual is a crucial tool for any correctional facility. It sets forth policies and procedures, implementation guidelines, and training requirements. In litigation, attorneys frequently highlight the absence of such a manual—or the failure to implement its provisions—as evidence of negligence. Courts have repeatedly treated lapses in policy, inadequate training, or disregard of written procedures as strong indicators of liability. This underscores the practical and legal necessity of developing, updating, and faithfully implementing a comprehensive suicide prevention program.

ROLE OF STAFF IN SUICIDE PREVENTION

Preventing suicide in correctional facilities is not the responsibility of one professional group alone—it must be embraced collectively. Whether custodial or clinical, every staff member plays a critical role in recognizing suicidal risk and taking timely action.

Collaborative Responsibility

In a previous article of mine, "Preventing Suicide in Prison: A Collaborative Responsibility of Administrative, Custodial, and Clinical Staff." (*Journal of the American Academy of Psychiatry and the Law Online* 34, no. 2 (2006): 165–17), I have articulated that an effective prevention program depends on *administrative, custodial, and clinical collaboration*—with each group fulfilling its unique role and administration serving as a facilitator.

From a legal standpoint, adherence to policies and competent professional judgment help demonstrate that staff members took reasonable steps to protect at-risk inmates, which can be a critical safeguard against liability claims.

Communication and Coordination

Effective prevention critically depends on seamless information sharing. Custodial staff are often first to notice subtle changes in inmate demeanor or behavior, such as agitation or attempts to hide materials—signals that, when relayed promptly, can trigger assessment and intervention by mental health staff. Administrators must ensure protocols do not obstruct this exchange, even while respecting privacy laws like HIPAA. Clear communication pathways are fundamental to creating a responsive and unified approach.

Guidance and Checklists

Operational tools—like checklists for notification, housing adjustments, referral for evaluation, and follow-up—provide legal and clinical structure to staff roles. As detailed in *Suicide in Jails and Prisons: Preventive and Legal Perspectives*, these structured instruments help guide staff actions and serve as a record of procedural compliance during litigation.

STAFF REACTIONS TO SUICIDE

When an inmate dies by suicide, the effects ripple far beyond the individual cell. Correctional officers, healthcare staff, and administrators often experience profound personal and professional consequences. For many officers, discovering a hanging or otherwise self-injured inmate is a traumatic event that leaves lasting impressions of guilt, helplessness, or anger.

Emotional and Psychological Impact

Correctional staff are frequently the first responders to suicide attempts, expected to act quickly in situations where every second counts. The shock of encountering a lifeless body, combined with the pressure of performing emergency measures, can lead to acute stress reactions. Over time, these experiences may contribute to post-traumatic stress symptoms, depression, or burnout. Some officers have reported recurring nightmares, intrusive recollections, and difficulty returning to their duties after such incidents.

Healthcare professionals within correctional systems are not immune. Nurses, psychologists, and psychiatrists often struggle with feelings of failure when a patient under their care dies by suicide. Even when they followed procedures, the question of whether more could have been done lingers, eroding confidence and contributing to compassion fatigue.

Institutional Consequences

At the institutional level, suicides often trigger immediate internal investigations, external reviews, and sometimes litigation. Staff may feel that they are "under the microscope," with their decisions, actions, and even omissions dissected in depositions or courtrooms. This scrutiny can create a climate of defensiveness, mistrust, and lowered morale.

Moreover, suicide incidents frequently lead to changes in policies, intensified audits, or additional layers of supervision—measures that staff may perceive as punitive rather than supportive. Without adequate debriefing or organizational support, correctional staff may become resentful, detached, or less engaged in suicide prevention efforts.

The Need for Support Systems

Structured debriefings after suicides can help staff process the event, share their experiences, and reduce stigma associated with emotional distress. Critical-incident stress-management programs, peer-support teams, and access to confidential counseling have all been shown to mitigate long-term psychological harm. In facilities where administrators emphasize care for both staff and inmates, suicides are more likely to be viewed as opportunities for systemic improvement rather than solely as individual failures.

FAMILY REACTIONS TO SUICIDE

The death of an incarcerated loved one by suicide sends devastating shockwaves through families. For many, the anguish is compounded by the fact that their loved one was in the custody of the state, which carries a constitutional duty to protect life. Families often struggle with overwhelming grief, anger, and a sense of betrayal, believing that the system failed in its obligation to keep their son, daughter, spouse, or parent safe.

Emotional and Practical Consequences

Family members commonly experience guilt—questioning whether they could have done more to prevent the suicide—or anger at correctional officials for ignoring warning signs. The trauma is deepened when families learn that concerns were raised in advance, only to find those warnings dismissed or unheeded. Some families find themselves permanently fractured, carrying unresolved grief and resentment for years.

Beyond emotional devastation, practical burdens often emerge. Parents and spouses may face medical debt from hospitalizations preceding death, funeral costs, and the lifelong financial impact of losing a loved one. The emotional distress can evolve into prolonged grief disorder, depression, or secondary trauma, particularly when families replay the circumstances of neglect or missed opportunities for prevention.

Legal and Advocacy Responses

Many families turn their grief into advocacy, pursuing litigation not only for financial redress but also to hold institutions accountable and prevent future tragedies. Civil-rights lawsuits filed under **42 U.S.C.**

§1983 often cite correctional negligence, deliberate indifference, or systemic failures in suicide prevention programs. For families, legal action is often less about money and more about truth, accountability, and the hope that no other family will suffer a similar loss.

Others channel their grief into activism—testifying before legislatures, participating in watchdog organizations, or pressing for reforms in jail- and prison-suicide prevention. These efforts have contributed to systemic changes, including improved intake screening, mandatory staff training, and revisions to suicide prevention protocols in multiple states.

DUE DILIGENCE AND TRAINING IN SUICIDE PREVENTION

Correctional facilities carry both a constitutional duty and an ethical obligation to protect inmates from self-harm. Traditionally, suicide prevention training for correctional officers and healthcare staff has relied on manuals, policy reviews, and generalized awareness programs. Yet despite these efforts—and despite improvements in intake screening and intervention protocols—suicide rates in U.S. jails have risen steadily since 2015. This paradox underscores a sobering truth: *existing training models by themselves are not enough.*

A case law-based approach to training offers a more powerful and realistic complement to traditional methods. Rather than relying solely on abstract guidelines, staff are confronted with the real-world lessons of litigation. Court decisions reveal exactly where failures in supervision, communication, documentation, or professional judgment resulted in liability. When correctional and healthcare staff see how seemingly small lapses—such as skipping a welfare check, ignoring a family warning, or falsifying a log—translate into multimillion-dollar settlements and findings of deliberate indifference, the message resonates more deeply than theoretical instruction.

The combined hybrid-training approach reframes training as more than a compliance exercise: it becomes both an ethical mandate and a legal safeguard. By integrating the lessons of case law with the foundational elements of traditional training, facilities can create programs that not only promote best practices but also reinforce accountability. Chapter 11 will expand this concept into a structured training model, demonstrating how case law can be systematically incorporated into correctional education, policy, and daily practice.

Suicide prevention in correctional facilities is not simply a matter of policy—it is a matter of duty. Both the legal framework of due diligence and the ethical obligations of humane treatment define how institutions and staff must act when confronted with suicide risk. When these duties are neglected, tragedy often follows, and litigation becomes inevitable.

Due Diligence

The concept of *due diligence* is widely recognized in finance and business but extends far beyond those spheres. In correctional settings, it represents the level of care and attention required to reasonably protect inmates from known or foreseeable risks. The Legal Information Institute defines due diligence as "care or attention to a matter that is sufficient to avoid liability."

In practice, responsibility for inmate suicide rarely falls on the "institution" as an abstract entity. Instead, accountability attaches to individuals: wardens, sheriffs, jailers, correctional officers, contracted medical groups, physicians, nurses, and mental health staff. Any staff member who interacted with the inmate or participated in decisions surrounding their care may be scrutinized in court.

For institutions, remedial actions often take the form of financial settlements. For individual professionals, consequences may include loss of licensure, reputational damage, and, in some cases, criminal liability.

Defending Due Diligence

Establishing a due-diligence defense requires evidence that staff reasonably discharged their duties and that documentation supports compliance with policy. Even the best suicide prevention programs cannot guarantee zero suicides. However, due diligence demonstrates that the facility took reasonable steps to mitigate risk, which can shift a court's perspective from "deliberate indifference" to "tragic but unforeseeable."

Risk management in suicide prevention includes two core strategies:

1. **Managing the Risk of Occurrence.** Sound practice requires staff training to recognize warning signs, regular review of policies, and updating procedures as new risk factors emerge.
2. **Managing the Risk of Litigation.** Documentation of all preventive actions—screenings, housing decisions, mental health referrals, suicide-watch logs—provides the strongest legal defense. Courts consistently treat accurate documentation as evidence of professionalism and accountability.

ETHICS IN SUICIDE PREVENTION

Ethical obligations in suicide prevention extend beyond legal requirements. They reflect a fundamental respect for the dignity and worth of all incarcerated individuals.

Staff Competence and Preparedness

Correctional officers are often the first line of defense, yet many lack sufficient training in mental health and suicide prevention. Ethically, correctional systems must ensure comprehensive training for all staff, since a program's success depends on the administration's commitment to competence and preparedness.

Confidentiality and Information Sharing

Balancing inmate privacy with safety remains an enduring challenge. Professional ethics demand confidentiality, yet failure to share critical information may endanger lives. HIPAA allows for the disclosure of essential safety information, and, ethically, facilities must ensure that correctional staff are equipped with the knowledge necessary to monitor high-risk inmates effectively.

Human Dignity and Compassion

Suicide prevention must never be reduced to a purely custodial task. Even when restrictive measures such as suicide smocks or safety cells are necessary, staff must conduct themselves with professionalism and respect. Humane treatment, rather than punitive attitudes, is central to ethical correctional care.

Ethical Treatment and Medication

Medication management raises questions of autonomy, beneficence, and harm avoidance. While inmates have the right to refuse treatment, clinicians and staff must weigh this against the risks of untreated illness. Ethical training ensures that staff understand how to balance autonomy with safety in ways that preserve dignity.

CONCLUSION: THE CHALLENGE AHEAD

Suicide in correctional facilities is neither random nor unforeseeable. As demonstrated in the opening case, it is often the predictable outcome of unaddressed vulnerabilities, missed warning signs, inadequate monitoring, and fragmented communication. The rising rates of suicide—documented by federal reports and amplified by national media—have intensified public scrutiny and forced lawmakers, administrators, and practitioners to confront the scope of the crisis.

Litigation has both exposed systemic shortcomings and driven reform. Court decisions, beginning with *Estelle v. Gamble* and strengthened by *Farmer v. Brennan* and subsequent rulings, have established the constitutional principle that incarcerated individuals are entitled to adequate medical and mental health care. This legal framework places suicide prevention not only in the realm of good practice but also within the constitutional duty of correctional institutions.

At the same time, history demonstrates how class-action lawsuits, federal oversight, and accreditation standards have shaped suicide prevention programs. The development of screening procedures, staff-training mandates, and comprehensive prevention manuals reflects progress—but implementation remains uneven. Small jails and underfunded facilities often struggle to meet even basic requirements.

Staff and family reactions underscore the human dimension of these tragedies. Officers, nurses, and administrators often carry the weight of loss, while families grieve and sometimes turn to litigation to seek accountability. Their voices, whether expressed in testimony, complaints, or public protest, remind us that suicide behind bars reverberates far beyond the walls of a facility.

Ultimately, suicide prevention in corrections requires more than compliance with checklists. It calls for a culture of **due diligence**, where policies are consistently implemented, documentation is accurate, and staff training is reinforced with real-world lessons from case law. It also demands adherence to **ethical principles** that emphasize dignity, compassion, and collaborative responsibility. Only when legal obligations and ethical commitments converge can correctional systems hope to reduce suicide, protect vulnerable individuals, and avoid costly and preventable litigation.

This chapter establishes the foundation for the rest of the book. The following chapters will examine how legal complaints are filed, how lawsuits expose systemic failures, and how correctional professionals can learn from these cases to build safer environments. The challenge is clear: correctional suicide is preventable, but only when vigilance, training, collaboration, and accountability are made non-negotiable.

> *"Correctional suicide is preventable—when vigilance, training, collaboration, and accountability are made non-negotiable."*

REFERENCES

1. Carlson, E. *Suicide in Local Jails and State and Federal Prisons, 2000–2019.* Bureau of Justice Statistics, October 2021.
2. *Bowring v. Godwin*, 551 F.2d 44 (4th Cir. 1977).
3. Civil Rights of Institutionalized Persons Act (CRIPA), 42 U.S.C. §1997 (1980).
4. Cornell Law School, Legal Information Institute. "Due Diligence." Last modified April 14, 2023. https://www.law.cornell.edu/wex/due_diligence
5. Daniel, A. E. "Preventing Suicide in Prison: A Collaborative Responsibility of Administrative, Custodial, and Clinical Staff." *Journal of the American Academy of Psychiatry and the Law Online* 34, no. 2 (2006): 165–17
6. Daniel, Anasseril E. *Suicide in Jails and Prisons: Preventive and Legal Perspectives.* Phoenix, AZ: 1106 Design, Inc., 2022.
7. *Estelle v. Gamble*, 429 U.S. 97 (1976).
8. *Farmer v. Brennan*, 511 U.S. 825 (1994).

9. Kaba, Fatos, Andrea Lewis, Sarah Glowa-Kollisch, James Hadler, David Lee, Howard Alper, Daniel Selling, Ross MacDonald, Angela Solimo, Amanda Parsons, and Homer Venters. "Solitary Confinement and Risk of Self-Harm Among Jail Inmates." *American Journal of Public Health* 104, no. 3 (2014): 442–447. https://doi.org/10.2105/AJPH.2013.301742
10. *Monell v. Department of Social Services of the City of New York*, 436 U.S. 658 (1978).
11. National Commission on Correctional Health Care (NCCHC). *Standards for Health Services in Correctional Facilities*. Chicago: NCCHC, 2018.
12. National Institute of Justice (NIJ). *Evaluation of Issues Surrounding Inmate Deaths in Federal Bureau of Prisons Institutions, 2013–2021*. Report no. 24-041, February 15, 2024.
13. Piel, Jennifer L. "Suicide in Correctional Settings: Trends, Prevention, and Intervention." *Journal of Correctional Health Care* 30, no. 2 (2024): 85–94.
14. Swartz, Glenn L., and Rebecca McDonald. "Solitary Confinement and Suicide Risk: A Public Health Crisis in U.S. Prisons." *American Journal of Public Health* 114, no. 4 (2024): 414–422. https://doi.org/10.2105/AJPH.2023.307528
15. Spina, Matthew. "County to Pay $900,000 in Death of Inmate Denied Medicine." *Buffalo News*, March 5, 2020
16. Shenefelt, Mark. "Former Weber Jail Doctor Once on Suicide Watch Has Lawsuit Dismissed." *Standard-Examiner*, March 22, 2022.

CHAPTER 2

WHEN TRAGEDY BECOMES LITIGATION—ANATOMY OF A LEGAL COMPLAINT

CASE VIGNETTE 2.1: FAILURE TO PROVIDE LIFESAVING MEASURES

T*o illustrate how litigation unfolds* following a custodial suicide, consider the following case. It demonstrates how early clinical decisions, documentation, and staff responses—or the lack thereof—can shape the foundation of a legal complaint.

A twenty-nine-year-old white male was arrested on multiple charges, including drug possession, and booked into a county jail. He reported daily fentanyl use, with his last dose occurring on the day of his detention. At intake, he disclosed a prior suicide attempt, ongoing uncontrolled anxiety, and intermittent suicidal ideation. Despite these risk factors, he was placed in the general population rather than the infirmary, where medical supervision for withdrawal and psychiatric instability could have been provided.

Within a day, the detainee showed visible withdrawal symptoms, including tremors, sweating, and agitation. Officers reported that he complained of being "dope sick." Despite this, he was given only over-the-counter medications such as acetaminophen and ibuprofen. No medication-assisted treatment was initiated. Importantly, while the Clinical Opiate Withdrawal Scale (COWS) score showed moderately high, staff did not escalate his level of monitoring.

On the third day of his detention, he was found unresponsive in his cell, seated on the floor with a T-shirt wrapped around his neck and anchored to the bunk. Nurse Todd, who was first on the scene, noted no signs of life and chose not to initiate CPR or other life-saving measures. The detainee was later pronounced dead, with the autopsy listing the cause of death as asphyxiation and the manner of death as suicide. Toxicology revealed the presence of fentanyl metabolites, consistent with his history of heavy use.

This case highlights critical failures in **screening, withdrawal management, and emergency response**. Each lapse—placement in general population despite risk, failure to provide appropriate treatment, and the decision not to initiate resuscitation—was cited in the subsequent lawsuit filed by the decedent's estate.

"Doing nothing in the face of crisis is itself a fatal act."

Cases like this demonstrate how the legal system scrutinizes every stage of correctional care—from intake screening to staff responses in moments of crisis. A single failure, whether clinical, custodial, or procedural, can form the foundation of a lawsuit alleging negligence or deliberate indifference. To understand how these claims are structured, it is necessary to examine the legal complaint itself—the document that initiates litigation and frames the alleged failures of correctional facilities and staff.

INTRODUCTION

A **legal complaint** marks the beginning of litigation after a suicide in custody. Filed by attorneys on behalf of a personal representative, it sets the stage by establishing jurisdiction, presenting facts, outlining causes of action, and requesting relief. Supported by evidence gathering, the complaint frames the facility's and staff's alleged failures.

Suicide-related litigation often holds mental health professionals, correctional officers, and facilities accountable when negligence or deliberate indifference is suspected in causing or contributing to wrongful death. As Fred Cohen emphasizes in *The Mentally Disordered Inmate and the Law*, litigation plays a central role in shaping correctional practices and ensuring accountability for constitutional obligations. Similarly, in my own work, *Suicide in Jails and Prisons: Preventive and Legal Perspectives*, I documented how legal complaints often expose the precise failings that also serve as pathways to prevention if addressed systemically.

LEGAL REPRESENTATION

Survivors typically begin by seeking **legal representation**. Attorneys specializing in personal injury, wrongful death, or civil rights evaluate the facts and determine whether a viable claim exists. Experienced attorneys help families navigate the trauma of litigation, gather critical records, and assess whether facility actions or omissions contributed to suicide.

Sometimes, grieving families decide not to pursue a lawsuit due to the emotional burden. In my experience, I have seen families withdraw after contacting me for consultation, recognizing that the process of reliving their trauma was too painful.

PERSONAL REPRESENTATIVE

In many cases, a **personal representative** is appointed by the probate court to act on behalf of the decedent's estate. Typically a parent or spouse, the representative is tasked with initiating litigation, overseeing settlements, and protecting the estate's legal interests.

The personal representative must act in the estate's best interest and file within the **statute of limitations**. This ensures that the deceased's rights, which do not expire at death, are fully protected.

FEATURES OF A LEGAL COMPLAINT

Identification of Parties

The complaint must name the plaintiff (family or representative) and the defendants (correctional officers, medical staff, contractors, or counties). Sometimes hospitals or outside providers are also included. Unidentified defendants are often listed as **John/Jane Does** until discovery confirms their identities.

Jurisdiction and Venue

Jurisdiction is established in state or federal court, depending on the claim. Violations of constitutional rights are typically brought under **42 U.S.C. §1983**, while negligence or wrongful-death claims are filed under state law. Some cases proceed in both.

Evidence Gathering

Attorneys gather extensive records, including:

- Mental health records
- Logs of suicide watch or welfare checks
- Prior suicide attempts
- Criminal history

- Incident reports and staff statements
- Postmortem and toxicology reports
- Facility policies and training records

This evidence demonstrates whether staff complied with standards of care and whether systemic failures existed.

Statement of Facts

The **statement of facts** presents the chronology of events in plain language, describing encounters between staff and the inmate, communications, and observed behaviors. It links failures—such as ignoring risk factors or failing to monitor—to the suicide.

In **Case Vignette 2.1**, for example, the facts would emphasize:

- Placement in general population despite known risk
- Failure to treat withdrawal adequately
- Lack of escalation despite moderately high COWS score
- Failure to initiate CPR

The statement typically concludes with an **impact statement** describing the emotional, financial, and psychological harm suffered by the family. For example, one attorney wrote,

"As a result of the negligent acts of the defendants and their conscious disregard of the decedent's serious medical needs, the estate sustained irreparable harm, including emotional distress and suffering by the plaintiff and family, and financial loss from this preventable tragedy." This final element connects the factual narrative to the human consequences of the suicide, setting the stage for the legal claims that follow.

Attorneys frequently cite national statistics to underscore the high risk of suicide in custody. For example, the Bureau of Justice Statistics (BJS) has repeatedly reported that suicide is the leading cause of death in jails and the third-leading cause in prisons. Hanging remains the most common method, and most deaths occur in isolation or segregation units.

If a particular state or facility has experienced a cluster of suicides, or if a contractor has a litigation history of suicide-related cases, attorneys often reference these patterns to argue that systemic deficiencies in suicide prevention policies and mental health care contributed to the death in question.

CAUSES OF ACTION

Medical Malpractice

Healthcare defendants are alleged to have failed in assessment, diagnosis, treatment, or monitoring. Complaints argue that these failures proximately caused or contributed to suicide.

Negligence

Correctional officers have a special duty to protect inmates from self-harm. Complaints highlight failures to monitor, document, and report suicidal behaviors.

Negligent Supervision

Administrators and supervisors may be accused of failing to create or enforce adequate policies, train staff, and ensure compliance.

42 U.S.C. §1983—Deliberate Indifference

This constitutional claim alleges violations of the **Eighth Amendment** (cruel and unusual punishment) and **Fourteenth Amendment** (due process). Plaintiffs must show:

1. The inmate had a serious medical need
2. Defendants knew or should have known of the risk
3. Defendants deliberately disregarded it

The standard requires proof of **recklessness**, not mere negligence (*Estelle v. Gamble*, 429 U.S. 97, 1976; *Farmer v. Brennan*, 511 U.S. 825, 1994). Defense counsel frequently argue that staff lacked knowledge of the inmate's suicide vulnerability. More often than not, however, such lack of knowledge stems from inadequate training or failure to implement policies designed to detect and address suicide risk. Courts have repeatedly underscored that those institutional deficiencies in training and policy can sustain a deliberate-indifference claim.

Monell *Claims*

Under *Monell v. Department of Social Services*, municipalities and contractors can be held liable when policies, customs, or practices are the "moving force" behind a constitutional violation. Failures to train staff, enforce suicide prevention policies, or design safe cells are often cited.

Wrongful Death and Survivorship

Filed under state law, these claims compensate families for financial losses, pain and suffering, and loss of companionship. Survivorship claims focus on the decedent's suffering prior to death.

CLAIMS FOR RELIEF

Plaintiffs usually seek:

- **Compensatory damages** (economic and emotional losses)
- **Punitive damages** (for reckless disregard of inmate safety)

- **Attorney's fees and costs**
- Any relief deemed just and equitable

Most complaints demand a **jury trial.**

FILING THE COMPLAINT

After the complaint is meticulously drafted and thoroughly reviewed for clarity and accuracy, the next step involves submitting the complaint to the court clerk, paying the necessary filing fees, and ensuring that the defendants receive a copy of the complaint, usually through a process server or certified mail.

WHAT HAPPENS AFTER FILING

Once filed, cases move to **discovery**, where both sides gather evidence through interrogatories, document requests, and depositions. Records often include:

- Suicide-watch logs
- Mental health assessments
- Facility training schedules
- Video surveillance
- Incident reports

Both sides use **expert witnesses** to argue whether staff actions met standards of care. These experts may offer their insights on mental health practices, negligence, or the officials violating the constitutional rights of the inmate. The impact of these expert analyses on the case can be substantial, potentially establishing that correctional officials either took appropriate preventive measures or failed to do so. Similarly, defendants may engage their own experts to challenge the basis of any claims. Discovery often exposes systemic flaws in policy and training.

One potential challenge in the discovery is the facility's apparent resistance to disclosing relevant information and records. The facility and staff may claim immunity for their actions during their line of work to avoid liability. In addition, concerns about institutional confidentiality may arise that would hamper access to sensitive information. In this context, the plaintiff has to file motions to compel disclosure of such information by subsequent discovery or proven at trials.

CAUSES OF ACTION IN LEGAL COMPLAINTS IDENTIFIED IN LAWSUITS

Analysis of **110 suicide-related lawsuits** I consulted reveals that attorneys consistently pursue claims under several recurring theories of liability. These claims typically fall into three broad categories: (1) medical and mental health negligence, (2) custodial negligence, and (3) deliberate indifference, including ***Monell* claims** targeting systemic failures. Together, these categories illustrate how litigation frames suicide in custody as both an individual failure of care and a broader institutional breakdown.

1. *Negligence by Healthcare Professionals*

Attorneys frequently allege that clinicians **deviated from the standard of care**, resulting in preventable suicides. Common claims include:

- Failure to diagnose mental disorders accurately and promptly
- Inadequate or absent suicide screening at booking, with no follow-up questioning
- Failure to communicate screening findings to mental health staff

- Failure to place at-risk inmates on appropriate watch levels (constant, 15-minute, or observation)
- Failure to assess prior suicide attempts and their predictive value
- Ignoring or minimizing expressed suicidal ideation
- Accepting denial of suicidal ideation at face value, leading to premature release from watch
- Failure to recognize alcohol or drug withdrawal as critical risk factors and to place inmates on withdrawal protocols/ medication-assisted treatment
- Failure to identify deteriorating mental states (acute depression, agitation, psychosis)
- Inadequate development and implementation of treatment plans
- Delays in prescribing/dispensing medications or failure to address medication refusal
- Failure to admit suicidal inmates to crisis stabilization or transfer to an outside facility
- Failure to address stressors related to family, legal proceedings, or confinement
- Failure to respond to family warnings about imminent risk

2. *Negligence by Correctional Staff*

Correctional officers have a constitutional duty to protect inmates from harm, including self-harm. Alleged failures by custodial staff include:

- Failure to place a suicidal inmate on suicide watch
- Failure to monitor inmates on watch consistent with policy
- Failure to recognize suicidal behaviors such as isolation, withdrawal, refusal of food, or refusal of medication

- Failure to act on warnings from family members
- Failure to respond after observed suicide attempts (e.g., no referral, no watch placement)
- Failure to conduct welfare checks as required by policy
- Improper classification and housing of at-risk inmates
- Failure to inspect suicide-watch cells for anchor points or dangerous items
- Failure to notify mental health staff of concerning behaviors (e.g., fashioning a noose)
- Failure to initiate life-saving measures when suicide attempts were discovered

These allegations reflect how lapses in **basic custodial responsibility**—observation, reporting, and emergency response—often form the basis of negligence claims.

3. *Deliberate Indifference and* Monell *Claims*

Beyond individual negligence, many lawsuits allege **constitutional violations** under the **Eighth and Fourteenth Amendments**, arguing that facilities and staff acted with **deliberate indifference** to inmates' serious medical needs, including suicide risk. Attorneys claim defendants knew of an inmate's vulnerability but **recklessly disregarded it**, failing to provide adequate protection or treatment.

Alleged acts of deliberate indifference include:

- Inadequate psychiatric care and mental health treatment
- Inadequate or absent screening and monitoring of suicidal inmates
- Failure to provide appropriate supervision of inmates on suicide watch

- Failure to supervise employees assigned to suicide-watch duties
- Failure to conduct routine rounds to monitor at-risk inmates
- Inadequate communication among staff regarding mental health status
- Failure to ensure tier walkers or camera monitors were present and attentive
- False logging of rounds that were not performed

In addition, ***Monell*** **claims** target **systemic failures** by counties, state agencies, or private contractors operating correctional facilities. These lawsuits allege that the **institution itself** was the "moving force" behind the constitutional violation due to:

- Negligent hiring and retention of unqualified staff
- Failure to train staff supervising suicidal or mentally ill inmates
- Failure to develop, implement, or enforce suicide prevention policies
- Failure to adequately staff mental health units or provide crisis services
- Patterns or customs of ignoring suicide prevention protocols

By linking individual acts of negligence to **systemic deficiencies**, *Monell* claims highlight how inadequate policies, staffing shortages, and training lapses expose facilities to substantial liability.

CONCLUSION

The legal complaint is the **gateway to litigation** in suicide cases. It transforms a tragic death into a structured legal claim, identifying failures in care, monitoring, training, or policy enforcement.

From my decades of consultation, one truth is clear: **every misstep can become a legal allegation**. Inadequate screening, poor communication, failures in monitoring, and disregard of obvious risk factors all open the door to liability.

For correctional facilities, the path forward is equally clear. Only through **robust policies, comprehensive training, rigorous documentation, and transparent communication** can they protect both the lives of inmates and their own legal standing. As Fred Cohen observes, litigation serves as both a corrective and preventive force in correctional psychiatry, and, as I argued in my own book, systemic reform and adherence to established preventive standards are essential if suicides—and lawsuits—are to be reduced.

REFERENCES

1. Fred Cohen, *The Mentally Disordered Inmate and the Law.* Kingston, NJ: Civic Research Institute, 1998–2023.
2. Daniel, Anasseril E. *Suicide in Jails and Prisons: Preventive and Legal Perspectives.* 1106 Design, Inc., Phoenix, AZ, 2022.
3. *Estelle v. Gamble*, 429 U.S. 97 (1976).
4. *Farmer v. Brennan*, 511 U.S. 825 (1994).
5. *Monell v. Department of Social Services of the City of New York*, 436 U.S. 658 (1978).

CHAPTER 3

EXPOSED IN COURT: SCREENING FAILURES, IGNORED RECORDS, AND FALSE LOGS BECOME LAWSUITS

"What is hidden in practice becomes exposed in litigation."
—Anasseril E. Daniel

INTRODUCTION

Lawsuits arising from suicides in custody expose a consistent pattern of preventable failures. Courts and juries rarely view these deaths as isolated tragedies. Instead, they interpret them as the result of systemic lapses in screening, evaluation, record review, monitoring, documentation, and communication.

This chapter explores these recurring problems through case stories drawn from my consulting experience. Failures include superficial screenings that miss critical risk factors, ignored or unreviewed records that conceal known suicide attempts, and falsified watch logs that devastate staff credibility. Equally troubling are communication breakdowns between officers and mental health staff, as well as between families and jailers, where warnings go unheeded and vital information never reaches those who could intervene.

By examining these failures through both a clinical and legal lens, this chapter demonstrates how everyday lapses become the foundation of lawsuits—and how the same problems repeat across institutions. Knowledge of the most common failures identified in litigation can be instrumental in properly training staff to prevent suicide in correctional facilities.

Research and litigation reviews show that problems most often cited in lawsuits fall into six domains (Daniel, 2021):

1. **Identification and screening of at-risk detainees**
2. **Suicide risk assessment**
3. **Mental health/psychiatric care**
4. **Documentation and communication**
5. **Classification and housing**
6. **Policy development and implementation**

This chapter focuses on the first four domains—identification and screening, assessment and treatment planning, mental health care, and documentation and communication. The remaining domains will be discussed in later chapters.

1. IDENTIFICATION AND SCREENING

Timely and accurate identification of suicide risk at every point during incarceration—from arrest through release—is a cornerstone of suicide prevention. Yet many facilities fail at this most basic step. Recognition of suicidal inmates largely depends on diligent implementation of standardized screening procedures.

Screening questionnaires can yield valuable information when properly administered, but no instrument captures every risk factor. Too often, the screener—whether a mental health professional, nurse, or correctional officer—asks questions mechanically and accepts simple "yes" or "no" answers without clarifying or probing for context. This superficial approach fails to uncover nuanced risk factors such as prior attempts, recent losses, or concealed ideation (Hayes, 2010).

When screening is treated as a bureaucratic exercise rather than a clinical safeguard, tragedies follow.

CASE VIGNETTE 3.1: SUPERFICIAL SCREENING AND A MISSED RISK

In a large urban jail, a sixty-year-old detainee of high socioeconomic and educational status was brought in on criminal charges. At intake, he was screened by a correctional intake officer rather than a trained mental health professional.

The screening form consisted of standardized yes/no questions about suicidal ideation, past attempts, and mental health history. The detainee denied suicidal thoughts and answered "no" to other relevant questions. The officer accepted these answers at face value, made no effort to clarify responses, and did not probe further, despite observing that the man appeared anxious and withdrawn.

No collateral information was obtained. No review of prior medical or psychiatric records was undertaken. Family members later testified that he had been severely depressed in the weeks prior to his arrest, had spoken about feeling hopeless, and had a documented history of psychiatric care.

Within forty-eight hours, the detainee was found hanging in his cell, dead from suicide. The subsequent lawsuit alleged deliberate indifference, pointing to the facility's failure to implement meaningful screening procedures and the officer's failure to probe obvious warning signs. The plaintiffs argued that the man's risk would have been apparent had the screening been conducted thoroughly or by qualified mental health staff.

This case underscores how **superficial screening, without clarification or record review, fails to identify risk and exposes both staff and the facility to liability.**

The key issue in this case was the **failure to probe beyond a superficial denial of suicidal thoughts** at intake. The detainee's history of suicide attempts and psychiatric hospitalization could have been uncovered with basic follow-up questioning. The absence of probing, reliance on a checklist, and lack of professional judgment allowed risk factors to go unrecognized, leading to preventable death and liability exposure.

"A missed risk at intake is often the first chapter of a lawsuit."

Group Screening

Suicide screening must be conducted in a **private, face-to-face interview** that respects the dignity of the detainee and allows for meaningful disclosure. Group screenings—where multiple arrestees are processed together—violate best practices and create an atmosphere of intimidation, shame, and silence. In such settings, detainees are far less likely to admit to past suicide attempts, current ideation, or psychiatric symptoms for fear of ridicule, stigma, or repercussions from peers.

Professional guidelines emphasize that screening is not merely a clerical step but a clinical safeguard. When facilities reduce screening to a group questionnaire, they compromise accuracy, undercut confidentiality, and increase liability (Hayes, 2010; Daniel, 2021).

CASE VIGNETTE 3.2: GROUP SCREENING IN A LARGE URBAN JAIL

At a large urban jail, a twenty-seven-year-old African-American male underwent intake screening in a **group setting with approximately ten other detainees**. The intake officer distributed questionnaires and asked detainees to respond aloud to a series of yes/no questions.

During the group session, the man denied suicidal ideation, past attempts, or psychiatric history. No one-on-one interview was conducted, and no effort was made to review his prior-incarceration records.

Two days later, he was found hanging in his cell with a bedsheet tied to the upper bunk. Family members later testified that he had attempted suicide three times in the past year, including a serious near-lethal overdose. Medical records obtained during litigation confirmed a history of depression and substance-use disorder.

The lawsuit alleged that the **group-screening process discouraged disclosure**, directly contributing to the failure to identify a high-risk detainee. The plaintiffs argued that group intake created stigma and pressure to deny vulnerability in front of peers. Expert testimony emphasized that proper, confidential, one-on-one screening would likely have revealed his history and triggered preventive measures.

This case illustrates how **group screenings compromise validity, obscure known risk factors, and expose facilities to liability for preventable deaths**.

The central issue was the **use of a group intake-screening process**, which suppressed disclosure of suicidal ideation. Conducting suicide screening in a non-confidential, public setting discouraged honesty, particularly given stigma and fear of judgment. The failure to cross-check prior records compounded the error. The key problems were **breach of confidentiality, missed history, and inadequate policy safeguards.**

"Group screenings don't reveal suicide risk—they bury it."

Screening Instruments

The use of a **standardized, evidence-informed screening instrument** is fundamental to suicide prevention in correctional facilities. When facilities rely on informal questioning or hastily designed checklists, critical warning signs are often overlooked. Failure to ask about the **timing, method, and lethality of prior suicide attempts**, the presence of active ideation, past psychiatric hospitalizations, psychotropic-medication use, and recent substance use—particularly opioid or alcohol withdrawal—may result in a false sense of security.

More importantly, inadequate screening often leads to the **failure to place genuinely suicidal inmates on suicide watch** or refer them for timely mental health evaluation. Research emphasizes that standardized instruments provide a structured approach, improve reliability across staff, and ensure that essential domains are not skipped (Hayes, 2010; Daniel, 2021).

2. ASSESSMENT

One of the most significant findings in many inmate suicides is the **absence of a comprehensive mental health assessment** following screening. A proper assessment should include:

- A detailed **mental-status examination**
- A psychiatric diagnosis aligned with **DSM-5 criteria**
- Development of an individualized **treatment and safety plan**

Yet, in practice, such assessments are frequently superficial or absent altogether. Mental health professionals are typically tasked with treatment planning, safety-plan development, and aftercare; however, many facilities lack consistent implementation.

Equally problematic is the prevalence of **inadequate suicide risk assessments (SRA)**, often limited to a single inquiry—"Are you suicidal?"—rather than a thorough exploration of both **risk and protective factors** in context. These omissions deprive clinicians of crucial information and leave inmates vulnerable.

Critical Times of Screening and Evaluation

The National Commission on Correctional Health Care (NCCHC) emphasizes that adherence to specific clinical time frames is essential to suicide prevention. Intake screening must be conducted on the day of arrival to a jail or prison, and a mental health and suicide screening should occur within the first twenty-four hours of detention. A comprehensive mental health evaluation should be completed within fourteen days, unless emergent needs dictate more immediate action. Psychiatric evaluations are expected within this same fourteen-day period, and follow-up psychiatric contact generally occurs within thirty days. Delays in meeting these time frames can increase vulnerability to deterioration of mental health and may precipitate suicidal behaviors (NCCHC, 2018).

In addition to these formal time frames, detainees often initiate contact with mental health professionals by submitting a Medical Services Request (MSR), commonly referred to as a "kite." These written requests may express acute concerns such as suicidal thoughts, feelings of depression or anxiety, or requests for medication adjustment. Some explicitly state, *"I can't take it anymore."* According to NCCHC standards, MSRs should be responded to within three business days under routine circumstances, but emergencies—especially those involving suicidal statements—require immediate intervention.

Despite these standards, my consulting experience has shown that some jails delay responses to MSRs for up to seven days. Such lapses not only place detainees at grave risk but also expose facilities and staff to significant liability for failing to act on clear warning signs of self-harm.

Cross References

Cross-case analysis from my caseload underscores the consequences of failing to honor these time frames:

- **Chapter 2 (Legal Complaints):** The family of the deceased alleged that the facility ignored repeated warnings and requests for urgent mental health care, creating the basis for wrongful-death and deliberate-indifference claims.
- **Chapter 6 (Suicide Risk Assessment):** In Case 6.2, a fifty-eight-year-old man was prematurely discharged from acute care after vague denials of suicidal intent. The psychiatrist admitted under oath that he failed to review past records—an omission that would have been avoided by timely, comprehensive evaluation.
- **Chapter 7 (Emergency Management):** In Case 7.5, a twenty-seven-year-old male requested psychiatric medication but was left unseen for days. His escalating crisis culminated in self-inflicted vascular injury and death, highlighting the lethal impact of delayed psychiatric attention.

These examples illustrate how breaches in timeliness—whether ignoring an intake red flag, disregarding an MSR, or failing to follow up within mandated windows—convert foreseeable risks into preventable tragedies and litigation.

3. MENTAL HEALTH AND PSYCHIATRIC CARE

Deficiencies in ongoing mental health and psychiatric care are recurrent themes in cases of custodial suicide. Common failures include:

- **Not consulting prior psychiatric or medical records** to understand the inmate's history

- **Failure to initiate appropriate psychiatric medications**
- **Delays in the initiation of psychiatric care**
- **Failure to implement detoxification protocols**, particularly in the presence of opioid or alcohol withdrawal.

Such lapses are often cited in litigation as evidence of both negligence and deliberate indifference (Cohen, 2014).

Records

A frequent systemic failure is the **failure to obtain or review medical and psychiatric records**. Community medical providers, prior-incarceration records, and previous suicide-watch notes are valuable resources that can inform both treatment and supervision strategies.

Yet, facilities often neglect these resources. A particularly damaging oversight is the failure to review **internal records from the same jail**, which may document recent suicide attempts or risk factors. Ignoring this information has repeatedly resulted in preventable deaths and subsequent liability for correctional facilities.

CASE VIGNETTE 3.3: IGNORED RECORDS IN A REPEAT DETAINEE

A fifty-eight-year-old male died by suicide during his **third detention in the same county jail within a year**. The facility—a medium-sized jail—had previously documented a **serious suicide attempt by hanging** during an earlier stay. At that time, he was placed on suicide watch, treated in the infirmary, and eventually stabilized before release.

Despite these clear warnings, during his most recent detention, he was screened with only a cursory intake form. The screener failed to review prior jail records, including the documented attempt. He was housed in a general-population cell with access to ligature points.

Within days, he was found hanging and unresponsive. Litigation revealed that the facility had **ample prior knowledge of his suicide risk**, yet this information was never incorporated into current screening or treatment planning.

The lawsuit argued that the **failure to review internal records constituted deliberate indifference**, as staff were aware—or should have been aware—of his particular vulnerability to suicide. Expert testimony highlighted that even minimal effort to review prior files would have placed him on watch and likely prevented his death.

This case underscores how **institutional memory lapses translate into legal liability** when prior, documented risk is ignored.

The key issue was the **failure to review and integrate prior institutional records** during risk assessment. The detainee had attempted suicide in the same jail during previous detentions, yet this history was ignored. The absence of a systematic process to flag repeat detainees, coupled with inadequate record review by the psychiatrist, represented **foreseeable negligence** and a breach of professional standards.

"A suicide attempt ignored is a suicide repeated."

Medication

Many detainees enter jails or prisons already prescribed essential medications, including psychotropic agents, antihypertensives, antidiabetic drugs, and antianginal medications. In correctional settings, abrupt discontinuation of such medications can trigger severe withdrawal symptoms, destabilize underlying conditions, and heighten distress. When psychotropics are stopped suddenly, inmates may experience agitation, confusion, insomnia, or exacerbation of psychiatric illness—all of which can precipitate suicidal ideation and behaviors.

One instructive example is *Steele v. Shah*, where abrupt discontinuation of an inmate's psychiatric medication was central to the plaintiff's claim of deliberate indifference. The court emphasized that failing to provide continuity of essential treatment—even during the intake and verification processes—can expose staff and facilities to liability for reckless disregard of serious medical needs.

Failure to Provide "Bridge" Medications

It is understandable that time is required to verify prior prescriptions or obtain outside records. However, best practice—and, increasingly, the legal expectation—is to prescribe "bridge" medications. These are temporary prescriptions based on the inmate's self-report, collateral information, or immediate clinical assessment, designed to sustain psychiatric stability until full documentation becomes available. Failure to provide such interim treatment not only prolongs suffering but can also precipitate withdrawal syndromes, recurrence of psychotic or depressive symptoms, and suicidal thoughts. Courts have scrutinized delays in providing bridge medications as evidence of systemic neglect, particularly when the risk of harm was obvious.

Delay in Psychiatric Care

Delayed mental health and psychiatric evaluation is another recurrent failure identified in suicide litigation. Inadequate staffing, poor triage systems, or neglectful scheduling can result in inmates waiting days—or even weeks—before being seen by a qualified professional. These delays often leave high-risk detainees untreated during the very period of greatest vulnerability, which plaintiffs' attorneys argue demonstrates deliberate indifference to serious medical needs.

CASE VIGNETTE 3.4—DELAY IN PSYCHIATRIC CARE: MISSED FOLLOW-UP FOR A HIGH-RISK INMATE

In a county jail, a detainee was evaluated by the facility psychiatrist after repeated reports of persistent distress. During the assessment, the psychiatrist diagnosed depressive disorder and determined the inmate was at moderate risk of suicide. Despite this finding, initiation of psychiatric treatment was delayed while the facility attempted to verify outside records. No bridge medications were provided. Within days, the inmate decompensated further, exhibiting hopelessness, agitation, and withdrawal. He died by suicide shortly afterward. The case highlighted how gaps in continuity of care—including medication management—can transform clinical oversight into a preventable tragedy and a legally indefensible position for both medical staff and the jail.

The central issue was the **unreasonable delay in psychiatric follow-up** for an inmate already identified with depressive disorder and suicide risk. Scheduling reassessment twelve weeks later ignored the immediacy of the danger. The key problems were **inadequate continuity of care, failure to match follow-up to risk level, and disregard of the dangers associated with antidepressant initiation without close monitoring.**

"In suicide care, delay is as dangerous as denial."

Failure to Implement Detoxification Protocol

Failure to recognize an inmate's state of intoxication and initiate a detoxification protocol is a recurring systemic gap that has devastating consequences. Untreated withdrawal from substances such as alcohol, opioids, or benzodiazepines can precipitate agitation, confusion, anxiety, psychosis, or severe physical symptoms. These, in turn, elevate suicide risk, either through impulsive self-harm or the exacerbation of underlying psychiatric vulnerabilities. The critical role of detoxification protocols is thus twofold: to manage medical safety during withdrawal and to reduce psychiatric distress that may fuel suicidal ideation and behaviors.

When correctional staff or medical professionals fail to implement timely detoxification measures, litigation often follows. Plaintiffs argue that the absence of a protocol or its improper application demonstrates deliberate indifference to an inmate's serious medical needs, in violation of both constitutional protections and correctional health standards. The National Commission on Correctional Health Care (NCCHC) emphasizes that withdrawal management is a **medical emergency,** requiring structured protocols and close observation, particularly within the first seventy-two hours of detention (NCCHC, 2018).

CASE VIGNETTE 3.5—FAILURE TO INITIATE WITHDRAWAL PROTOCOL: TWENTY-THREE-YEAR-OLD MALE IN A RURAL JAIL

In a small rural jail, a twenty-three-year-old White male was taken into custody and screened at intake. He disclosed a recent history of opioid and benzodiazepine use, with his most significant use occurring within twenty-four hours of detention. Despite these disclosures, staff did not initiate a detoxification protocol or conduct any structured-withdrawal assessment.

Within hours, the inmate began exhibiting early-withdrawal symptoms: profuse sweating, tremors, and visible agitation. Instead of being referred for medical or psychiatric evaluation, he was placed in a general-housing unit without closer monitoring. Over the next two days, his symptoms worsened. He was described by peers and officers as restless, increasingly distressed, and withdrawn.

On the third day of his detention, he was found unresponsive in his cell, having hanged himself with a bedsheet tied to a vent. The autopsy confirmed suicide by hanging, and toxicology was negative except for residual traces of benzodiazepines and opioids, consistent with early withdrawal.

The plaintiff's estate filed suit, alleging deliberate indifference and wrongful death, emphasizing that the jail's failure to recognize acute intoxication and implement a detox protocol constituted reckless disregard for his serious medical needs. During depositions, jail officials admitted that no formal detoxification policy existed and that officers lacked training on the medical and psychiatric risks of withdrawal.

This case illustrates the dangerous convergence of untreated withdrawal, inadequate screening follow-up, and failure to apply established protocols. From a legal perspective, it underscores how even small, resource-limited facilities are held accountable for omissions in basic medical and mental health safeguards.

The critical issue was the **failure to implement a withdrawal protocol** despite the detainee's disclosure of recent opioid and benzodiazepine use. Staff ignored clear signs of withdrawal and placed the inmate in general housing without heightened monitoring. The absence of structured-withdrawal assessment, lack of medical referral, and poor custody medical communication created **foreseeable risk for suicide and direct liability for negligence.**

*"Ignoring withdrawal is ignoring suicide risk—
protocols save lives and protect institutions."*

4. DOCUMENTATION AND COMMUNICATION

Accurate and timely documentation—whether electronic or on paper—is the backbone of effective suicide prevention in correctional settings. Documentation ensures that essential information about an inmate's custody, medical needs, and suicide risk is available to all relevant staff. Conversely, incorrect, inadequate, or delayed records compromise the adequacy of care and place both inmates and institutions at risk.

Training staff in **proper, consistent documentation practices** is, therefore, fundamental. Without clear communication between **mental health professionals and custody staff**, supervisors, healthcare providers, and line officers may miss critical cues, leaving inmates vulnerable and facilities exposed to liability.

Equally important is **effective communication**. Suicide prevention depends on a seamless flow of information between all staff:

- From **arresting officer to booking officer**
- From **booking officer to mental health professional**
- From **nursing staff to physicians and psychiatrists**
- From **schedulers to psychiatric providers**
- From **administration to line staff**

Every link in this chain matters. Clear and timely communication is often the difference between identifying a potentially suicidal inmate and overlooking imminent danger.

Yet communication is too often undermined by **compartmentalization of medical, mental health, and custody records**. When silos exist, vital information is not shared between healthcare providers and correctional officers. Although HIPAA regulations protect private health information, they do not prohibit sharing essential safety-related details. Reasonable information exchange—such as suicide-watch status, initiation of withdrawal protocols, or level of supervision—is both permissible and necessary.

The exchange of information must be **two-way**. Mental health professionals can share risk-related guidance with custody staff, while correctional officers must report observable warning signs to clinical teams. Subtle-but-critical inmate behaviors—such as tearing bedsheets and hiding the pieces, hoarding medication, or expressing suicidal thoughts to others—must be **documented and communicated immediately**. Too often, these seemingly minor details foreshadow suicide attempts. When staff communicate these observations promptly, they provide clinicians with essential context to refine suicide risk assessments (SRAs) and initiate appropriate preventive measures.

In short, **documentation and communication are not administrative tasks—they are frontline suicide prevention tools.**

Key Practice Points: Documentation and Communication

- **Document promptly and accurately**—delays or errors weaken suicide prevention and expose liability.
- **Ensure two-way communication**—custody staff share observations; clinicians share suicide risk status and supervision needs.
- **Avoid silos**—medical, mental health, and custody information must be accessible and shared when safety is at stake.
- **Know what HIPAA allows**—sharing risk-related information is permissible and often essential for inmate safety.
- **Report warning behaviors immediately**—torn sheets, hoarding medications, and verbalized suicidal intent must trigger documentation and communication.
- **Train continuously**—staff must learn that documentation and communication are suicide prevention tools, not paperwork.

CASE VIGNETTE 3.6—IGNORE FAMILY WARNING: NINETEEN-YEAR-OLD MALE IN A COUNTY JAIL

The mother of a nineteen-year-old incarcerated male with a severe mental disorder and frequent episodes of suicidal ideation and behavior called the jail directly, warning that her son was at immediate risk of harming himself. She spoke with the sergeant on duty, who assured her that *"we will take care of it."* Despite this explicit warning, no action was taken—no medical referral, no suicide watch, and no communication with mental health staff.

Within twenty-four hours, her son attempted suicide by hanging. Although he was resuscitated, he survived in a vegetative state, requiring long-term care. Litigation followed, and the case was eventually settled out of court for a substantial sum, reflecting both the seriousness of the harm and the facility's failure to act on direct information provided by family.

Cross References

- **Chapter 5 (Vulnerable Inmate):** family members often recognize vulnerability and acute risk more clearly than correctional staff or screening tools.
- **Chapter 6 (Screening and Evaluation):** external information from family must be incorporated into suicide risk assessments.
- **Chapter 10 (Policy, Procedures, and Practice):** policies should require documenting and escalating family reports of suicide risk.
- **Chapter 12 (Legal Liability and Risk Management):** ignoring family warnings is frequently reframed in litigation as deliberate indifference.

This case highlights the failure to act on explicit warnings from family members. The inmate's mother communicated direct and urgent suicide risk, yet custody staff neither referred him for care nor communicated with mental health providers. The critical issues were **failure to document and recognize escalated family concerns, absence of referral to medical/mental health staff, and lack of accountability for custody responses.**

"When families sound the alarm, ignoring them is both a moral failure and a legal liability."

Family Fails to Inform the jail

Research demonstrates that fewer than half of incarcerated individuals communicate their suicidal intent to family members or others. Daniel and Fleming reported that only **less than 50% of inmates disclose suicidal thoughts** to those close to them. Even when risk is disclosed, family members do not always communicate the warning to correctional staff.

At the same time, communication failures are not limited to families. Officers themselves may be unaware of an inmate's efforts to gain attention due to the **noise level in overcrowded and understaffed housing units.** In such environments, detainees often resort to **banging on cell doors or shouting** to signal an emergency. If officers ignore these distress calls, lives may be lost. Courts have found that officers who disregard **inmate-generated alarms** may be held liable when suicide or other adverse events occur.

CASE VIGNETTE 3.7—FAMILY WITHHELD SUICIDE RISK INFORMATION: MALE DETAINEE

A detainee expressed **acute suicidal intent** to his family before entering custody. Despite knowing the seriousness of his statements, the family did not inform jail staff of his risk. While in custody, the detainee made a serious suicide attempt that resulted in his death.

In the litigation that followed, plaintiffs argued that the facility failed to protect a vulnerable inmate. However, court review established that **officers and medical staff were never made aware of the detainee's suicidal threats.** Without knowledge of this risk, they could not reasonably have been expected to implement preventive measures. The court ultimately ruled that the **facility and its staff were not liable,** since the critical information was withheld by the family.

This case illustrates the **limits of liability** when suicide risk information is not disclosed to correctional staff. Families may withhold or fail to share critical warnings, leaving staff unaware of imminent risk. The key issues here were **the absence of information-sharing from family to jail staff, reliance on incomplete knowledge, and the legal principle that liability hinges on foreseeability and notice.**

> *"Correctional staff can't act on risks they are never told—but facilities must make it easy for families to share concerns."*

CASE VIGNETTE 3.8—COMMUNICATION AND MONITORING FAILURE: THIRTY-TWO-YEAR-OLD IN CITY LOCKUP

In a city lockup, a thirty-two-year-old male fashioned a noose from his bedsheet and anchored it to the ventilation grate above his bunk. At the time, he was supposed to be monitored by an officer assigned to watch the housing area via camera. Instead, the officer spent the shift surfing the internet and failed to observe either the noose or the detainee's escalating actions.

The officer's failure to perform his assigned duty meant that critical warning signs went unnoticed until the man was discovered with the bedsheet tightened around his neck. Although staff eventually responded, the lapse had already sealed the outcome. Litigation followed, and the failure of communication and monitoring became central to the determination of liability. The officer had not alerted mental health staff, supervisors, or other personnel at any point during the crisis, and the breakdown in observation and communication was a decisive factor in establishing facility responsibility.

Cross References

- **Chapter 7 (Monitoring and Supervision):** underscores that observation duties are active, not passive, and require vigilance.
- **Chapter 10 (Policy, Procedures, and Practice):** highlights the importance of policies mandating communication of risk behaviors to supervisors and clinical staff.
- **Chapter 11 (Training):** emphasizes training custody staff to recognize warning behaviors and communicate them promptly.
- **Chapter 12 (Legal Liability and Risk Management):** shows how courts view failure to monitor and communicate as evidence of deliberate indifference.

This case highlights the dangers of neglecting assigned monitoring duties and failing to communicate observed risks. The officer's inattention to camera surveillance, compounded by the absence of timely communication with mental health staff, created conditions in which a preventable suicide attempt occurred. The key issues were **failure of monitoring, failure of communication, and breach of policy and professional duty.**

"Failure to watch is failure to protect."

Falsification of Records

Willful falsification of records is among the most egregious errors in correctional suicide cases. Even if every other aspect of supervision and care is provided, falsification of records at critical times is often decisive in litigation, leading to large settlements or adverse judgments. False documentation directly linked to a suicide attempt or completed suicide almost guarantees an unfavorable outcome.

For example, when daily suicide assessments are required, if a mental health professional records a note for a visit that never occurred, and the detainee subsequently kills himself, such falsified documentation becomes **key evidence** against the defense. A frequent problem is falsification of **suicide-watch logs**—which must be completed every fifteen minutes at staggered intervals. Plaintiffs' attorneys frequently highlight logs showing straight-line entries, demonstrating lack of accuracy. In many lawsuits, falsified suicide-watch records become the single-most-damaging piece of evidence for the defense.

CASE VIGNETTE 3.9—FALSIFIED SUICIDE WATCH RECORDS: TWENTY-EIGHT-YEAR-OLD HISPANIC MALE IN A COUNTY JAIL

In a medium-sized county jail, a twenty-eight-year-old Hispanic male with a history of serious mental illness, prior suicide attempts, and psychotropic-medication use was placed on suicide watch in accordance with facility policy. He was supposed to be observed every fifteen minutes for an extended period.

The monitoring requirement was documented as being performed without incident. However, contemporaneous video recordings of the unit revealed that the assigned officer did not enter the housing area for several hours. Despite this, the officer had filled out the log to reflect that all checks were completed on schedule. After the inmate was later found dead by suicide, deposition testimony confirmed that the officer had knowingly **falsified the suicide-watch records.**

Cross References

- **Chapter 7 (Monitoring and Supervision):** stresses the importance of direct, verifiable observation of inmates on suicide watch.
- **Chapter 10 (Policy, Procedures, and Practice):** underscores that falsification of records undermines institutional integrity and magnifies liability.
- **Chapter 11 (Training):** highlights the need for staff education on both performance of suicide watches and ethical documentation.
- **Chapter 12 (Legal Liability and Risk Management):** illustrates how falsified records are almost always interpreted by courts as deliberate indifference, often determining case outcomes.

This case demonstrates how falsification of suicide-watch records undermines both suicide prevention efforts and legal defense. Even when policies exist on paper, their credibility collapses when documentation is false. The critical issues were **failure to conduct required checks, falsification of official records, and institutional lack of supervision to detect and prevent false reporting.**

"Falsified logs don't protect staff—they convict them."

CONCLUSION

The cases and analyses in this chapter demonstrate that suicides in correctional settings rarely result from a single failure. Instead, they emerge from **repeated and predictable breakdowns**—superficial screening, reliance on group intakes, failure to review past records, delays in psychiatric care, neglect of withdrawal protocols, ignored family warnings, poor communication among staff, and, the most damaging of all, falsification of records. Each of these lapses, when exposed in litigation, is reframed as **negligence, deliberate indifference, or systemic failure.**

Courts and juries consistently recognize that suicide prevention is a matter of both **clinical care and operational diligence**. The failure to document accurately, to communicate promptly, or to act on known risks undermines not only inmate safety but also the credibility of correctional institutions. In lawsuits, what may appear as minor oversights inside the facility often become the **central evidence** that determines liability.

The lesson is clear: correctional leaders and staff must understand that **screening, monitoring, documentation, and communication are not administrative tasks—they are lifesaving interventions.** When faithfully carried out, they protect vulnerable inmates and provide a strong defense in litigation. When neglected or falsified, they expose both staff and institutions to devastating outcomes in court.

REFERENCES

1. Cohen, Fred. *The Mentally Disordered Inmate and the Law.* Kingston, NJ: Civic Research Institute, 1998–2023
2. Daniel, Anasseril E. "A Multidisciplinary Approach to Suicide Prevention in Jails and Prisons: The Best Defense against Liability Lawsuits." *Open Journal of Psychiatry* 11, no. 4 (2021): 248–264.
3. Daniel, Anasseril E., and Fleming, Jennifer G. "Suicide in a State Correctional System, 1992–2001: A Review." *Journal of Correctional Health Care* 12, no. 1 (2006): 24–35.

4. Hayes, Lindsay M. *National Study of Jail Suicide: 20 Years Later.* Washington, DC: U.S. Department of Justice, National Institute of Corrections, 2010.
5. National Commission on Correctional Health Care (NCCHC). *Standards for Mental Health Services in Correctional Facilities.* Chicago: NCCHC, 2018.
6. *Steele v. Shah*, 87 F.3d 1266 (11th Cir. 1996).

CHAPTER 4

DEFINING AND IDENTIFYING SUICIDAL BEHAVIORS

INTRODUCTION

Effective suicide prevention in corrections begins with a **clear understanding of what suicidal behavior actually looks like.** Before risk factors can be evaluated or interventions applied, staff must be able to **define, identify, and distinguish the various forms of suicidal expression** encountered in correctional settings. This task is especially challenging: some individuals openly voice suicidal thoughts, while others deny them until an attempt is made. Behaviors may range from serious, sustained expressions of intent to **expressions of suicidal distress that may appear attention-seeking but still carry life-threatening potential.**

This chapter examines the **definitions and categories of suicidal behavior**—including suicidal ideation, suicide attempt, suicide, and non-suicidal self-injury (NSSI). It explores how detainees may **communicate or conceal their distress**, the methods they choose, and how the **perceptions and attitudes of staff** influence the seriousness with which such behaviors are addressed.

Key points for recognition and differentiation are outlined, so that correctional staff can better distinguish between **ideation, intent, and attention-seeking expressions of distress** without overlooking the danger inherent in each.

By clarifying these definitions and patterns of expression, this chapter provides the **foundation for recognition**, upon which the later chapters on **risk assessment (Chapter 6)** and **intervention strategies** are built.

DEFINITIONS

As an introduction to the discussion of the characteristics of those who may consider taking their lives, an understanding of what constitutes **suicidal ideation, suicidal behavior, suicide attempt, and suicide** is essential.

The **National Institutes of Health (NIH)** classifies suicidal thoughts and behaviors into three categories:

1. **Suicidal ideation**—thoughts of engaging in behavior intended to end one's life
2. **Suicide plan**—the formulation of a specific method through which one intends to die
3. **Suicide attempt**—engagement in potentially self-injurious behavior in which there is at least some intent to die.

The **Centers for Disease Control and Prevention (CDC)** further define these concepts. **Suicidal ideation** is "thinking about, considering, or planning suicide." Inmates may express ideation explicitly and directly, for example, by stating: *"I want to kill myself," "I am suicidal," "I want to die,"* or *"There is no point in living."*

The CDC defines a **suicide attempt** as "a non-fatal, self-directed, potentially injurious behavior with an intent to die as a result of the behavior." Essentially, a suicide attempt is a **self-destructive act that failed to cause death.** For instance, a revived hanging inmate is known to have made a suicide attempt.

The concept of a suicide attempt is significant because it provides a **predictive window into future behavior.** A survivor is at heightened risk of repeating the act, often along similar lines. An attempt has two major components: **intent and outcome.** If intent to die is present, the act qualifies as an attempt, regardless of whether death occurs. The prevention perspective is clear: an individual who attempts suicide has already **given up on life.** The fact that the outcome was unsuccessful—due to outside intervention, technical failure, or chance (e.g., a broken rope, a misfire, or timely rescue)—does not lessen the seriousness of the act.

Suicide is an intentional, self-destructive act that begins with the idea of harming oneself, develops into a plan, identifies a means, and culminates in an attempt. Intent is not always explicitly stated, but it is usually assumed when a person creates a plan and seeks the means to carry it out.

From the perspective of prevention, **intent has profound implications.** An individual who attempts suicide has already **abandoned life.** For the general population, research found that **81.8% of suicide survivors eventually completed suicide within one year of their initial attempt (Bostwick, Pabbati, Geske, and McKean).** The act of "giving up on life" often manifests in behaviors such as giving away possessions, isolating from others, or engaging in extremely violent actions that signal an increased likelihood of death.

Intent and manipulative motives may coexist in the same individual. Some inmates may express suicidal ideation or behaviors in an effort to be transferred out of a highly regimented or stressful environment. Yet even when secondary motives appear, ideation and behavior often reflect a **high degree of genuine suicidal intent.**

SUICIDAL IDEATION AND INTENTIONALITY

Clinical experience and extensive expert consultations suggest that the following **characteristics of suicidal thoughts** strongly indicate suicidal intent:

1. **Specificity of statements**—e.g., *"I will kill myself," "I will hang myself," "You will not see me in the morning."*
2. **Repetition of statements**—genuinely suicidal inmates often repeat their thoughts with increasing urgency.
3. **Statements with a specific plan**—e.g., *"I will hang myself tonight"* or *"I will hang myself if I am not allowed to contact my family."*
4. **Association with hopelessness or helplessness**—suicidal statements tied to despair, loneliness, or severe anxiety are highly correlated with serious attempts or death.
5. **Accompanied by preparatory behaviors**—such as packing belongings, wrapping sheets around the neck, displaying a weapon, hoarding medications, tearing and hiding bedsheets, or barricading the cell with furniture.
6. **Linked to poor judgment**—e.g., an inmate believing suicidal threats will gain favors from officers.
7. **Made by inmates with major mental illness**—particularly those experiencing depression or psychosis.

8. **Expressed in the context of acute psychosocial stressors**—such as sentencing, family conflict, or loss.
9. **Occurring during alcohol or drug withdrawal**—withdrawal heightens risk and may intensify suicidal thoughts.
10. **History of suicidal thoughts or behaviors**—recurrence of ideation with any of the above factors elevates concern for imminent risk.

Key Points on Ideation, Behaviors, and Attempts

1. **Specific intent and seriousness**

Suicidal thoughts expressed with specific intent to harm oneself are strongly correlated with serious suicide attempts or completed suicides. For this reason, **staff training in recognizing the characteristics of suicidal ideation and behaviors is paramount** from a prevention standpoint.

2. **Challenges of interpretation**

Determining whether an inmate who expresses suicidal ideation truly intends to kill themselves is a **complex and daily challenge** for correctional staff. Officers and health professionals alike must be trained to recognize the **characteristics of suicidal ideation** that help distinguish inmates at acute risk from those at lower risk.

3. **Weight of current versus past thoughts**

While all suicidal thoughts expressed by inmates must be taken seriously, not all carry the same level of immediate danger. **Active suicidal thoughts** must be given greater weight than past or historical suicidal thoughts, even though both remain important in assessing cumulative risk.

4. **Transience of ideation**

Suicidal thoughts are often **transient**, making them difficult to identify and intervene upon. Research has shown that less than 50% of those who express suicidal ideation will go on to attempt suicide (Daniel and Fleming). Nevertheless, ideation remains a **predictive marker** for future suicide attempts and must always be taken seriously—even when it does not guarantee progression to a completed suicide.

5. **Combination of ideation, plan, and means**

The **acute suicide risk scenario** occurs when an inmate expresses suicidal ideation, develops a specific plan, and has access to the means to carry it out. For instance, a detainee who states a desire to die, plans to hang himself, and has a bedsheet available to tie to a ventilation grate represents an immediate and serious risk.

6. **Behavioral clues**

Many inmates who consider suicide leave **behavioral warning signs of intent**. These may include giving away possessions, isolating themselves, refusing meals, avoiding recreation, or withdrawing from contact with officers and peers. Recognizing and acting on these telltale clues is vital.

7. **Sentinel events**

Suicide and suicide attempts are **sentinel events** in the correctional system. Every attempt requires immediate emergency response, clinical intervention, administrative review, and structured follow-up.

8. **Lethality of attempts**

Any suicide attempt, whatever its motivation, carries the risk of death—even when the inmate's original intent may not have been to die (Konrad, Daniel, Daigle, *et al.*). In correctional environments where methods are limited, inmates may resort to the most lethal available method, such as hanging, without fully appreciating its lethality. Thus, even so-called manipulative attempts can result in death.

CASE VIGNETTE 4.1—DENIAL OF IDEATION: MALE OF HIGH SOCIOECONOMIC STATUS

A middle-aged male of upper socioeconomic status, with strong family and community ties, was detained following an arrest. During intake, he was screened for suicide risk and denied any suicidal thoughts or intent. Because of his stable background and confident demeanor, staff accepted his denial without further probing or collateral inquiry.

Three days later, he was found dead in his cell, having hanged himself with a bedsheet. Review of the case revealed that the denial of suicidal ideation masked acute distress, and no follow-up questions were asked to explore risk factors such as prior mental health history or stressors related to the arrest. His case illustrates how denial of ideation can mislead staff and result in tragic consequences.

Cross References

- **Chapter 3 (Problems Identified in Lawsuits):** intake failures and superficial screening often hinge on unchallenged denials of risk.
- **Chapter 5 (Vulnerable Inmate):** individuals of higher socioeconomic or educational background may deny ideation to avoid stigma or perceived weakness.
- **Chapter 6 (Screening and Evaluation):** emphasizes the importance of probing denials and considering contextual stressors.

- **Chapter 11 (Training):** staff must be trained not to accept denials at face value but to recognize circumstances where risk remains high.

Denial of suicidal ideation does not equate to absence of risk. Correctional staff must probe beyond initial responses, especially when situational, psychiatric, or behavioral risk factors suggest otherwise.

"Denial at the door does not erase risk inside."

ASSESSING THE SERIOUSNESS OF SUICIDAL THOUGHTS AND BEHAVIORS

Officials, including correctional officers and mental health professionals, face significant challenges in determining the **seriousness of suicidal ideation and behaviors.** These challenges often fall into five major scenarios:

1. **Non-suicidal self-injury (NSSI)**
2. **Denial of suicidal ideation**
3. **Manner of communication of suicidal ideation**
4. **Method of choice**
5. **Staff attitude**

1. NON-SUICIDAL SELF-INJURY (NSSI)

Not all self-harming behaviors in custody are suicidal in nature. Frequently, inmates engage in **non-suicidal self-injury (NSSI)**, defined as the *intentional destruction of one's own body tissue without suicidal intent.* Common examples include cutting, burning, scratching, banging the head against surfaces, or hitting oneself. The **hallmark of NSSI** is the absence of an intent to die (Klonsky, 2014).

In correctional settings, inmates may use such behaviors for **secondary gain**, such as seeking attention, requesting a different cell assignment, securing transfer to a mental health or crisis-stabilization unit, or leaving restrictive housing such as disciplinary segregation. In these contexts, NSSI may not be associated with suicidal ideation. Many inmates also use NSSI to **relieve frustration, anger, or emotional pain.**

Although NSSI and suicide attempts are both forms of self-injurious behavior, they are not mutually exclusive. The same individual may engage in both at different times. Research indicates that NSSI can be a **predictor of future suicide attempts** and, thus, carries the same weight as prior suicide attempts in assessing suicide risk.

One captain in a large urban jail testified: *"Several suicide attempts that we would classify as attempts are, in reality, inmates acting out—sometimes for attention. If someone wraps something around their neck but does not secure it to a tie-off point, it will still be labeled as a suicide attempt."*

In practice, it is often **difficult to distinguish a manipulative act from genuine suicidal behavior** due to the inherent challenge of assessing intent. For this reason, officers may appropriately err on the side of caution and place such individuals under suicide watch as a preventive measure.

Some inmates who make repetitive suicidal statements and engage in frequent self-harm are described as **chronically suicidal**. Their behaviors may include multiple overdoses, wrapping ligatures around the neck, or repeated hanging attempts. Many exhibit these actions in the presence of staff or within earshot, while simultaneously denying an intent to die. However, impulsive or agitated inmates may unintentionally cause death during a so-called manipulative act. Clinically, many of these individuals meet criteria for **antisocial or borderline**

personality disorder, characterized by impulsivity, with little evidence of major depression or anxiety.

CASE VIGNETTE 4.2—CHRONIC SELF-INJURY AND AMBIGUOUS SUICIDALITY: TWENTY-FOUR-YEAR-OLD MALE

A twenty-four-year-old White male was incarcerated in a state prison after pleading guilty but mentally ill to charges of murder, armed robbery, and firearm possession. With only an eighth-grade education, no work history, and no family ties, he presented with multiple vulnerabilities. His history included juvenile detention beginning at age fourteen, chronic drug use since childhood, and a longstanding pattern of self-injurious behavior.

Over the years, he engaged in frequent self-harm, including self-cutting, flooding his cell, swallowing razors and batteries, and going on hunger strikes. After cutting episodes, he often removed surgical dressings, reopened wounds, and picked at scabs. He was repeatedly placed on constant observation and admitted to the prison crisis-intervention unit, where he received intensive therapy and medication adjustments.

When questioned, he consistently denied intent to kill himself, though he often expressed **passive death wishes**, such as *"I wish I were dead."* On one occasion, after overdosing on hoarded medication, he told a counselor, *"I need to do a better job trying to kill myself next time."* His diagnoses included borderline personality disorder, substance-use disorder, PTSD, anxiety disorder, and an unspecified mood disorder. He required eight years of ongoing psychiatric care.

Most of his self-harm incidents occurred in the presence of staff, allowing for rapid intervention and prevention of fatality. However, one evening, following perceived mistreatment by officers, he hanged himself in his cell and died. There were no immediate precipitants for his final act, underscoring the difficulty of predicting suicide in chronically self-injurious individuals.

Chronic self-injury often blurs the line between **manipulation and genuine suicidality**. Even when inmates deny intent, repeated self-harm combined with passive death wishes places them at high risk for eventual suicide. Correctional staff must approach such cases with vigilance, recognizing that a final fatal act may occur suddenly and without warning.

"Even cries for attention can end in silence."

Key Points: Non-Suicidal Self-Injury (NSSI)

1. **NSSI and manipulative suicide attempts are both forms of self-injurious behavior.** Although the underlying intent may differ, both place inmates at risk for serious harm.
2. **Inmates may die during manipulative self-injurious behaviors.** Even when the original intent is not to die, the lethality of methods used in custody—such as hanging or overdose—can result in unintended death.
3. **Suicide is not always foreseeable among those who engage in chronic manipulative suicidal behaviors.** The repetitive and ambiguous nature of such acts makes prediction difficult, and facilities often struggle to differentiate between manipulation and genuine intent.
4. **Chronic manipulative behaviors are less amenable to treatment interventions.** Individuals who engage in repeated self-harm for secondary gains often respond poorly to conventional

suicide prevention strategies, requiring specialized and sustained management approaches.

2. DENIAL OF SUICIDAL IDEATION

In correctional settings, many detainees and inmates are reluctant to disclose thoughts of self-harm. Correctional officers are often the least likely group to whom individuals will confide suicidal ideation. Instead, inmates may disclose to peers or keep their thoughts entirely to themselves.

A major reason for nondisclosure is the **stigma and discomfort associated with suicide-watch placement.** Inmates know that acknowledging suicidal ideation often results in being stripped of personal clothing, placed in a restrictive "Ferguson gown," and confined to a suicide-watch cell—often described as cold, wet, and dehumanizing. To avoid this experience, many will deny suicidal thoughts even when directly asked. For many, remaining in their assigned cell feels preferable to the degrading conditions of suicide-watch housing.

Denial of suicidal ideation is thus a **unique and challenging characteristic** of suicidal inmates. False denial of suicidal thoughts and intent, even when an individual is genuinely suicidal, is common. Studies indicate that fewer than half of inmates who die by suicide disclose ideation to staff immediately before taking their lives (Daniel and Fleming). Denial, therefore, cannot be considered a reliable indicator of safety. Furthermore, research has shown that **denial of ideation alone is an inadequate predictor of suicide risk** (Obegi).

Despite this, staff frequently accept inmate denials at face value, sometimes using them as the **sole basis for discontinuing suicide watch**. Such practice represents a deviation from the standard of care and is inconsistent with correctional health and safety standards. Decisions to remove an inmate from suicide precautions should be made only after a **comprehensive, well-documented suicide risk assessment**, particularly when other risk factors are present.

Careful observation of inmate behaviors and emotional states may yield **important clues to suicidal intent.** In some cases, suicide notes are discovered during cell searches only after a fatal act, revealing that risk was present but not disclosed.

Key Points: Denial of Suicidal Ideation

1. Denial of suicidal ideation must not be taken at **face value.**
2. Denial alone is an **inadequate indicator** of suicide risk.
3. Exclusive reliance on denial to discontinue suicide watch is **a deviation from the standard** of care.
4. **Suicide risk assessment** must be **conducted and documented** in the presence of obvious or substantial risk factors.

3. MANNER OF COMMUNICATION OF SUICIDAL IDEATION

The way an inmate communicates suicidal ideation often influences how seriously staff perceive and respond to it. Some detainees make **direct and explicit statements**, such as *"I want to kill myself"* or *"I can't go on."* Others may communicate indirectly, through ambiguous phrases like *"I wish I were dead"* or *"Things would be better without me."* In some cases, suicidal thoughts are expressed only through **behaviors**—such as giving away possessions, withdrawing from activities, or engaging in self-injury—without any verbal disclosure.

Communication may also occur **through third parties**. Inmates may tell peers about their suicidal thoughts, who, in turn, may or may not alert staff. Family members sometimes call facilities to warn of risk, but, as seen in several cases, such warnings are not always acted upon. Conversely, inmates may intentionally **conceal their ideation,** choosing not to disclose for fear of stigma, punishment, or restrictive suicide-watch placement.

The **tone, context, and consistency** of communication are critical factors in assessing risk. Repeated, specific statements of intent, especially when paired with observable changes in behavior, should always be treated as indicators of serious danger. Dismissing indirect or ambiguous expressions may result in missed opportunities for intervention.

Key Points: Manner of Communication

1. Suicidal ideation may be communicated **directly, indirectly, behaviorally, or through third parties.**
2. **Ambiguous or indirect statements** must be taken seriously, especially when consistent with other risk factors.
3. Inmates may **withhold or conceal ideation** due to stigma, fear, or aversion to suicide-watch conditions.
4. Staff must be trained to assess the **tone, context, and consistency** of communication as part of suicide risk evaluation.

4. METHOD OF CHOICE

The method chosen by an inmate to attempt suicide provides valuable insight into both **intent and lethality**. Some methods, such as superficial cutting or ingesting small, non-lethal quantities of substances, may reflect ambivalence or serve as a cry for help. Others—such as hanging, strangulation, or overdose with lethal medication—are highly lethal and leave little margin for survival.

In correctional settings, the **availability of means** strongly influences method of choice. Because firearms and other obvious tools are absent, inmates often resort to what is at hand: sheets, clothing, shoelaces, razors, or medications. Hanging is the most common method, owing to the presence of ligatures and tie-off points in cells, and its lethality contributes to the high proportion of correctional suicides completed by this method.

It is essential for staff to understand that, even when an act is perceived as manipulative, the **lethality of the method may result in death**—regardless of intent. For example, an inmate wrapping a ligature around the neck to seek attention may misjudge how quickly unconsciousness and death can occur. Similarly, an overdose intended to frighten staff may become fatal due to the potency of the ingested medication.

The **method of choice must therefore be considered an important marker of risk.** High-lethality methods demand immediate intervention and intensive observation, while even low-lethality behaviors should trigger careful evaluation and follow-up.

Hanging is by far the most common method—**more than 90 percent of suicides in jails and prisons are accomplished by hanging,** compared with the community, where nearly 70 percent of suicides are completed with a firearm.

This reality frequently emerges in legal complaints, where families allege that facilities essentially **"supplied the materials"** for suicide. Lawsuits often point to items such as jail-issued sheets, clothing, or razors as instruments of death. Additionally, officers may be challenged in court for failing to prevent hoarding of medications or other contraband later used in attempts. Such claims underscore the importance of **environmental controls, safe-issue policies, and consistent monitoring.**

Key Points: Method of Choice

1. The method chosen reflects both **intent and lethality**, and must be factored into risk assessment.

2. In correctional facilities, the **availability of means** (e.g., sheets, clothing, medication) shapes method of choice.
3. **Hanging is the most common and most lethal method** in correctional suicides.
4. Even manipulative behaviors using lethal methods can **result in unintended death.**
5. **All self-harming behaviors**, regardless of method, require evaluation and follow-up.

5. STAFF ATTITUDES

Another complicating factor is staff perception of intent. Correctional officials may view inmates who engage in repetitive self-harm as **manipulative.** Some staff assume that these inmates are merely antisocial, undeserving of professional attention, or dismiss them entirely as *"scum of society—if they did the crime, they must serve the time."* These attitudes can lead to missed opportunities for intervention and prevention.

In reality, manipulative and suicidal motives may coexist. An act that begins as attention-seeking can escalate into a fatal outcome, especially when the chosen method is highly lethal. Thus, even apparently manipulative behaviors must be treated as genuine suicide risks.

Many clinicians and correctional officers are naturally perceptive and empathetic, able to discern when an inmate is in crisis. However, when frontline providers operate under a **blanket assumption that all inmates are manipulative, attention-seeking, or antisocial**, they risk overlooking serious suicidal behaviors and losing the opportunity to intervene. As I have observed, the **decision-making of frontline service providers is heavily influenced by their attitudes and context**, which, in turn, shapes outcomes in suicide prevention. (Daniel, 2004)

Key Points: Staff Attitudes

1. **Staff perceptions matter**—dismissing inmates as manipulative or antisocial undermines prevention.
2. **Attitudes of frontline providers** directly influence whether crises are recognized and addressed (Daniel, 2004)

CONCLUSION

Assessing the seriousness of suicidal thoughts and behaviors in correctional settings is never straightforward. Inmates may engage in self-harm without intent to die, deny ideation outright, communicate risk in vague or indirect ways, or blur the line between manipulation and genuine crisis. Their chosen methods—especially hanging, which accounts for more than 90 percent of suicides in custody—leave little room for error.

These complexities place a heavy responsibility on correctional officers, mental health professionals, and administrators. Staff attitudes, in particular, can determine whether warning signs are recognized or dismissed. Viewing all suicidal behaviors as manipulative may provide a sense of control, but it risks overlooking the very signals that precede preventable deaths.

The lesson is clear: **every act of self-harm, every denial of ideation, and every ambiguous statement must be taken seriously.** Suicide risk assessment cannot be reduced to a checklist or a single question. It demands vigilance, empathy, and an understanding that manipulative acts can end in death, denials can mask true intent, and staff perceptions shape outcomes. In the courtroom, these nuances are exposed; in the facility, they can mean the difference between life and death.

REFERENCES

1. Bostwick, J. Michael, Robert A. Pabbati, John R. Geske, and J. Michael McKean. "Suicide Attempt as a Risk Factor for Completed Suicide: Even More Lethal Than We Knew." *American Journal of Psychiatry* 173, no. 11 (2016): 1094–1100. https://doi.org/10.1176/appi.ajp.2016.1507085
2. Centers for Disease Control and Prevention (CDC). *Suicidal Ideation.* National Center for Injury Prevention and Control, Division of Violence Prevention, 2022. https://www.cdc.gov/suicide/facts
3. Centers for Disease Control and Prevention (CDC). *Self-Directed Violence Surveillance: Uniform Definitions and Recommended Data Elements.* Version 1.0. Atlanta, GA: CDC, National Center for Injury Prevention and Control, 2011. https://www.cdc.gov/violenceprevention/pdf/self-directed-violence-a.pdf
4. Daniel, Anasseril E., and Jennifer R. Fleming. "Suicide in a State Correctional System, 1992–2002: A Review." *Journal of Correctional Health Care* 12, no. 1 (2006): 24–35. https://doi.org/10.1177/1078345806287541
5. Daniel, Anasseril E. "Decision-Making by Frontline Service Providers: Attitude or Context?" *Journal of the American Academy of Psychiatry and the Law* 32, no. 3 (2004): 386–389.
6. Klonsky, E. David. "Non-Suicidal Self-Injury: What We Know and What We Need to Know." *Canadian Journal of Psychiatry* 59, no. 11 (2014): 565–568. https://doi.org/10.1177/070674371405901101
7. Konrad, Norbert, Anasseril E. Daniel, Marc Daigle, *et al.* "Preventing Suicide in Prisons, Part I: Recommendations from the International Association for Suicide Prevention Task Force on Suicide in Prisons." *Crisis: The Journal of Crisis Intervention*

and Suicide Prevention 28, no. 3 (2007): 113–121. https://doi.org/10.1027/0227-5910.28.3.113

8. National Institutes of Health. *Suicide and Suicidal Behavior.* MedlinePlus, updated September 1, 2024. https://medlineplus.gov/ency/article/001554.htm
9. Obegi, Joseph H. "Recent Denial of Suicidal Ideation among Ideators, Attempters, and Suicide Decedents: A Literature Review." *Suicide and Life-Threatening Behavior* 51, no. 3 (2021): 515–525. https://doi.org/10.1111/sltb.12740

CHAPTER 5

THE VULNERABLE DETAINEE/INMATE—PREDICTABLE RISK, PREVENTABLE TRAGEDY

INTRODUCTION

Suicide in custody is not a random occurrence. It is the outcome of **identifiable and recurring vulnerabilities**, which, if recognized, can be mitigated. Drawing from more than 110 consultation cases over the last 25 years, this chapter examines inmates most at risk. The analysis is grounded in my professional experience as a forensic psychiatrist, supplemented by published research on inmate suicide dating back to the late 1970s, when scholarly attention to correctional suicides began to accelerate.

In addition to clinical and institutional lessons, numerous landmark court cases during the last five decades have clarified how judges and juries view vulnerability and foreseeability. These legal precedents highlight data points considered critical not only for prevention but also for determining liability. From a correctional risk management perspective, **understanding vulnerability means anticipating crisis, intervening effectively, and preventing tragedies that too often end in litigation.**

WHO ARE THE MOST VULNERABLE?

Based on accumulated research, case law, and direct consultation experience, the following groups are consistently identified as high-risk for suicide in custody:

1. **Young males (18–34)** of all races
2. **White males** over the age of 55
3. **Pre-trial detainees**, particularly in the first days and weeks of incarceration
4. **First-time arrestees of high social status**, facing sudden loss of reputation, career, and family support
5. **Inmates or detainees with diagnosed mental illness**
6. **Individuals with substance-use disorders**, including those in acute intoxication or withdrawal
7. **Veterans and soldiers** with a history of trauma, mental illness, or substance abuse
8. **Detainees with a past history of suicide attempts**, whether inside or outside custody
9. **Inmates in restrictive housing**, including solitary confinement and disciplinary segregation

Each of these categories will be illustrated through real consultation cases and analyzed through the combined lens of clinical risk and legal liability.

RISK FACTORS OF SUICIDAL BEHAVIOR AND SUICIDE

Demographic Factors

Age

A bimodal distribution has been observed in custodial suicides, with disproportionate representation among **younger detainees**

(ages 18–34) and those **older than 55**. Younger suicidal males often belong to socially disenfranchised and isolated groups, with limited family or community support. They also tend to be more impulsive, use substances heavily, and act quickly on suicidal urges.

Sex

Men die by suicide far more frequently than women, though women attempt suicide approximately three times more often. In my cohort of 110 individuals who died by suicide in custody, only 10 were women. Mentally ill women are at greater risk of completing suicide compared with their non-mentally ill counterparts. An exceptional risk exists among **middle-aged women accused of killing abusive husbands**; in my consulting experience, guilt and shame in these cases precipitated acute suicidal crises. In one such case, a woman hanged herself with a bedsheet soon after incarceration.

Race

Among younger cohorts, there is no significant difference in suicide rates by race. However, **older White males** are consistently overrepresented in custodial suicides. While Black inmates are incarcerated at disproportionately high rates in U.S. jails and prisons, their suicide rates are not proportionately higher—suggesting that **race itself is less predictive than other factors** such as age, psychiatric illness, or social support.

Marital Status

Many inmates who complete suicide are **single, never married, or divorced**, lacking significant family or community support. By contrast, **married inmates with children commit suicide less frequently**, indicating that marriage and family ties may provide a protective buffer against suicide risk.

Family History of Suicide

A **first-degree relative's suicide** is a significant risk factor for inmate suicide. By contrast, suicide among second-degree or distant relatives has not been shown to carry a direct link. Familial and genetic vulnerabilities, coupled with learned behaviors, are key predictive factors.

Adverse Childhood Experiences (ACEs)

History of **adverse childhood experiences (ACEs)**—including physical abuse, sexual abuse, and neglect—are strongly correlated with suicide vulnerability. These experiences predispose individuals to maladaptive behaviors, psychiatric illness, and self-harm later in life. While ACEs are **non-modifiable** by the time of incarceration, they remain **critical indicators for initiating early preventive interventions** once an individual enters custody. The long-lasting impact of trauma often resurfaces in correctional environments, amplifying stress, isolation, and despair.

Criminal Justice Process

Arrest

The immediate period following arrest is a time of **exceptionally high vulnerability**. Individuals who react disproportionately to incarceration, particularly **first-time arrestees with no criminal history**, face elevated suicide risk during the **first twenty-four to seventy-two hours of confinement**. High-profile individuals, whose arrests attract public attention, also experience acute distress during this window, making self-harm more likely.

Type of Offense

While violent crimes often lead to lengthy sentences, the **type of offense itself is not usually a strong predictor of suicide risk**. Two notable exceptions stand out:

1. **Sex offenses**, which carry profound stigma, shame, and fear of victimization
2. **Crimes of passion**, particularly **homicide by a battered spouse or partner**, where guilt and remorse may drive acute suicidality

Pre-Trial Status

Suicide risk is significantly higher among **pre-trial detainees.** According to the Bureau of Justice Statistics, between 2000 and 2019, **more than 75 percent of suicides in local jails involved individuals in pre-trial status.** Nearly half (46 percent) of these suicides occurred within the **first week of detention.**

In my consulting experience, approximately **90 percent of detainees who died by suicide were awaiting court proceedings**, including arraignment or trial. The **waiting period itself is not always the decisive factor**; rather, the heightened risk often stems from the **prospect of receiving a harsh or lengthy sentence.** This is especially true for **young adults, first-time offenders, or individuals of otherwise high social standing.** Suicide notes left by pre-trial detainees frequently describe anguish, shame, and fear at the prospect of spending many years behind bars.

CASE VIGNETTE 5.1—SERIOUS/STIGMATIZED CRIMINAL CHARGE: SEX OFFENSE

A middle-aged male of upper socioeconomic status, with strong family and community ties, was arrested on a serious sex-offense charge. The arrest carried significant stigma, and he quickly became acutely depressed and suicidal. However, when questioned directly, he denied suicidal ideation. Staff relied on his denial and did not initiate suicide precautions.

On the third day of detention, he was found dead in his cell, having used his bedsheet to hang himself. Despite multiple warning signs—including the nature of the charge, his pre-trial status, acute depressive symptoms, and the dramatic loss of social standing—no preventive measures had been taken.

Risk and Contributory Factors

- **Primary factors:** stigmatized criminal charge (sex offense), pre-trial detention, acute depressive presentation.
- **Secondary/contributing factors:** upper socioeconomic status, high community integration, shame from loss of status.

Stigmatized charges—particularly sex offenses—combined with pre-trial detention and acute depression, represent a **high-risk constellation for suicide.** Denial of suicidal ideation must not be accepted at face value in such circumstances.

> *"A sex-offense charge in pre-trial detention is a high-risk trigger for suicide, regardless of denial."*

Sentencing

Unanticipated or harsh sentences, as well as additional charges incurred during incarceration, are significant suicide risk factors. The period immediately following a **sentencing hearing** is especially critical. Inmates may return from court hearings in despair, experiencing hopelessness and shame at the prospect of long years ahead.

Although some courts recognize this heightened risk, they may not issue orders for immediate referral to mental health programs or placement on suicide precautions. Similarly, defense attorneys may fail to request such consideration on behalf of their clients. This gap between recognition of risk and action to mitigate it can have tragic consequences.

Institutional Factors

Type of Jails and Prisons

Suicides occur across correctional settings, but **rural jails demonstrate disproportionately higher rates.** Contributing factors include:

- Chronic **understaffing**
- Absence of or poorly designed **suicide prevention policies and procedures**
- **Inadequate staff training**, leaving frontline officers unprepared to recognize risk

Short-term lockups also present risks, as some lack formal suicide-screening procedures or have **limited access to mental health care.** In these environments, detainees may pass through intake without adequate assessment, heightening the danger during the earliest and most-vulnerable days of confinement.

Solitary Confinement

Solitary confinement—including administrative or disciplinary segregation and maximum-security isolation—is a major **institutional risk factor** for suicide. Inmates in these units are typically isolated **~23 hours per day**, with minimal human contact and sensory input. Many describe feeling trapped, with no way out.

A joint report by **Solitary Watch** and the **Unlock the Box Campaign** (2023) estimated that more than **122,000 people were held in isolated confinement in U.S. prisons and jails on a given day in 2019**, defined as 22 or more hours per day alone. Despite increasing pressure from lawmakers and advocates, U.S. correctional systems continue to use solitary confinement for **days, weeks, months, and even years.**

Data from the **U.S. Department of Justice Office of Inspector General (2024)** show that, of **187 federal prisoners who died by suicide in 2018, 86 (46 percent) were in restrictive housing** at the time, although only a fraction of the total population was housed there. In my own consultation caseload of **110 suicides**, 25 occurred in solitary confinement, underscoring the disproportionate risk.

Research has consistently documented the psychiatric harms of solitary. **Swartz and McDonald (2024)**, writing in the *American Journal of Public Health*, found that solitary confinement is strongly associated with increased suicide risk in U.S. prisons, both through the onset of new mental disorders and the exacerbation of preexisting ones. Disorders such as depression, anxiety, and psychosis are frequently intensified, producing hopelessness, insomnia, and agitation.

Earlier scholarship highlights the same dangers. In *Condemned to Die* (1981), **Robert Johnson** documented the devastating effects of death-row isolation, including despair and suicidality among prisoners. In *Perceptual and Motor Skills* (1990), **David Lester** (1990), in *Perceptual and Motor Skills*, linked prison overcrowding and poor conditions, including segregation, with elevated rates of suicide and homicide.

Collectively, these studies and reports demonstrate that solitary confinement is not simply an administrative tool but an **environment that precipitates or aggravates psychiatric symptoms and substantially increases suicide risk**. From a legal perspective, the foreseeability of these harms imposes a duty on correctional institutions to limit the use of solitary, provide timely mental health care, and implement alternatives for vulnerable populations.

CASE VIGNETTE 5.2—SOLITARY CONFINEMENT AND PAROLE DENIAL

A man in his twenties, originally incarcerated for a minor offense, was transferred to a maximum-security prison after escalating rule violations and violent behavior. His disciplinary record led to extended placement in **solitary confinement**, where he began engaging in repeated suicidal behaviors.

During this period, his family informed him that they would not accept him back if released on parole. Soon afterward, his parole application was denied, forcing him to confront the reality that he would have to serve 85 percent of his sentence. Within days of receiving this devastating news, he was found dead by hanging in his segregation cell.

Risk and Contributory Factors

- **Primary factors:** extended solitary confinement; parole denial; rejection by family; young-adult age group
- **Secondary/contributory factors:** escalation from minor offense to maximum-security placement; behavioral deterioration in custody; sense of hopelessness regarding future release.

Solitary confinement amplifies vulnerability, especially when combined with devastating personal losses such as family rejection and parole denial. The convergence of institutional isolation and shattered personal support can create a **predictable preventable-suicide crisis**.

"In solitary confinement, rejection and parole denial can turn despair into a death sentence."

Sexual victimization during incarceration

Forced or non-consensual sexual interactions—whether by other inmates or staff—represent one of the most devastating experiences in custody and a well-documented precipitant of suicidal behavior. Sexual victimization destroys a person's sense of safety, autonomy, and dignity. In correctional settings, victims may feel doubly trapped: unable to escape the environment and fearful of retaliation if they report the abuse.

Research consistently shows that incarcerated individuals who experience sexual assault are significantly more likely to attempt or complete suicide. Shame, stigma, and fear of disbelief often silence victims, while institutional barriers delay or prevent timely intervention. Even when policies exist under the **Prison Rape Elimination Act (PREA)**, implementation is often inconsistent, leaving vulnerable inmates without adequate protection or support.

Clinically, sexual victimization in custody may trigger acute crises, including severe depression, anxiety, post-traumatic stress disorder, and intense suicidal ideation. For some, the trauma compounds preexisting vulnerabilities such as prior abuse, mental illness, or lack of social support, dramatically increasing the risk of self-harm. From both a **prevention and a liability standpoint**, sexual assault within facilities represents a foreseeable risk, requiring proactive detection, protective housing, trauma-informed care, and vigilant monitoring.

CASE VIGNETTE 5.3—SEXUAL ASSAULT, SEGREGATION, MENTAL ILLNESS, AND PRIOR ATTEMPTS

A twenty-seven-year-old White male with a documented history of mental illness and prior suicidal behaviors was housed in **administrative segregation** with another inmate known for violence and sexual assault. He reported being repeatedly forced to perform oral sex under threat from his cellmate, who identified himself as a senior member of a violent gang.

The victim reported the assaults, and staff referred him for a **sexual-assault nurse examination (SANE)** in compliance with the **Prison Rape Elimination Act (PREA)**. However, he did not receive immediate **mental health counseling or supportive services** as required by policy. For several days, he was left without follow-up care, despite being in obvious psychological distress. During this time, he hanged himself in his jail cell.

Risk and Contributory Factors

- **Primary factors:** sexual assault during incarceration; administrative segregation housing; history of mental illness; history of prior suicide attempts.
- **Secondary factors:** gang intimidation and threat of further violence; failure to provide timely mental health intervention after the assault.
- **Contributory factors:** institutional neglect of PREA standards for post-assault care; isolation within segregation, compounding trauma.

Cross References

- **Chapter 3:** communication and documentation failures when reported risk is not acted upon
- **Chapter 4:** suicidal intent often escalates in the context of acute psychosocial stressors
- **Chapter 8:** housing environments and institutional failures that create or worsen risk
- **Chapter 11:** importance of staff training on PREA compliance and trauma-informed suicide prevention

Sexual victimization in custody, particularly when compounded by preexisting mental illness and segregation, creates an **acute and foreseeable suicide risk.** Institutional failure to provide timely mental health support following a PREA-mandated medical exam transformed this case into a preventable tragedy.

> *"After sexual assault in segregation, neglecting mental health care turned trauma into tragedy."*

Interfacility Transfers

Transfers between correctional institutions—whether from jail to prison or between prisons—are well-recognized **suicide risk factors**. Adjustment to a new institution can be stressful, especially when familiar supports are disrupted. One of the most critical concerns is the **continuity of mental health care**: psychiatric histories, diagnoses, and prescribed medications may not always follow the inmate promptly, creating dangerous lapses. While the wider adoption of **electronic medical records** has reduced such risks in recent years, breakdowns in communication and systemic failures continue to occur, with potentially tragic results.

CASE VIGNETTE 5.4—SYSTEMIC DISCONTINUITY OF CARE: TRANSFER, MEDICATION DISRUPTION, ASSAULT, AND SINGLE-CELL PLACEMENT

A forty-two-year-old African-American male entered state prison in 2009 to serve a twenty-year sentence. At intake, he was classified as seriously mentally ill, with a longstanding diagnosis of **bipolar disorder**, managed with a mood stabilizer and antidepressant. For more than a decade, he remained relatively stable, with regular psychiatric follow-up and only minor disciplinary infractions. He also maintained close contact with his mother and children through frequent visits and phone calls.

After fourteen years, he was transferred to another state prison. Anxious about the move, he expressed concern to his mother about whether his medications would be continued at the new facility. His fears proved justified: upon transfer, his psychiatric history and prescriptions were not forwarded. For several days, he received no treatment and grew increasingly anxious, depressed, and frustrated. During this period, he attempted to hang himself.

Two weeks later, he finally received a **telehealth psychiatric evaluation**, where he described severe anxiety, depression, irritability, and medication withdrawal. Three weeks later, he reported being assaulted by other inmates. Staff dismissed his claim and denied his request for protective custody. Following medical clearance, he was placed in a **single cell** while awaiting another transfer—still without access to his prescribed medications. Shortly thereafter, he hanged himself, using a shirt anchored to a cell bar.

Risk and Contributory Factors

- **Primary factors:** interruption of psychiatric medications; failure of continuity of care during transfer; untreated serious mental illness.
- **Secondary factors:** loss of family reassurance and stability due to transfer; assault by peers and lack of protective response; placement in single-cell housing.
- **Contributory factors:** systemic communication breakdown between facilities; reliance on delayed telehealth evaluation; institutional disbelief of reported victimization.

Interfacility transfers represent critical junctures where **continuity of care can collapse**. Medication disruptions, combined with institutional indifference and placement in high-risk housing, transformed a stable long-term inmate into a preventable-suicide death.

"When care collapses during transfer, stability unravels into tragedy."

Prior Suicide Attempts

A **prior suicide attempt** is often the most significant single predictor of suicide, both in clinical risk assessment and in legal liability. The **National Institutes of Mental Health (NIMH)** identifies past suicide attempts as a critical factor in determining vulnerability to future suicide, including among incarcerated populations. Failure to give due consideration to such history is frequently cited in litigation as evidence that correctional officials disregarded a detainee's **serious medical need.**

Legal Liability Considerations

Three characteristics shape how prior attempts are weighed in liability cases:

1. **Method of Attempt**—Near-lethal methods, such as hanging or overdose, are strongly correlated with future suicide. Daniel (2006) emphasizes the predictive weight of such serious behaviors.
2. **Temporal Relationship**—Clinically, attempts within the **preceding six to twelve months** are considered especially significant, although courts have not consistently treated recency as a liability factor.
3. **Medical Consequences**—Attempts requiring hospitalization, intensive care, or emergency medical attention carry greater weight.

In ***Kempf v. Northumberland County Prison*** (W.D. Pa., 2018), the court denied summary judgment because there was sufficient evidence of deliberate indifference to an inmate's suicide vulnerability. The decision underscored that recent suicide attempts—even in the context of substance-related incidents—can be considered legally significant risk factors.

Some Departments of Correction attempt to mitigate risk by maintaining registries of inmates with serious suicide attempts, designating them as **special-needs populations**, who require heightened monitoring. Yet such practices are inconsistent, and many institutions still fail to integrate past suicide history into risk assessments.

A common but flawed practice is to equate the seriousness of a past attempt with whether the inmate was placed on **suicide watch**. This approach is unreliable, as watch placement is often subjective, inconsistent, and not necessarily tied to the seriousness of the behavior or intent.

A history of prior suicide attempts—particularly **recent, near-lethal events**—is a **foreseeable, clinically urgent, and legally significant risk factor**. Ignoring this history undermines prevention and exposes facilities to substantial liability.

CASE VIGNETTE 5.5—PAST SUICIDE ATTEMPT IGNORED DESPITE MULTIPLE RISK FACTORS

In August 2022, a fifty-year-old female was arrested and booked into a county jail. At intake, the nurse noted she was depressed, withdrawing from heroin and alcohol, and stated: *"I don't want to be here anymore."* She was placed on **level-two suicide precautions** in a safety cell but was not referred to mental health services.

Over the next two days, she repeatedly expressed suicidal ideation, including a specific plan to jump from the second tier. Evaluations confirmed ongoing suicidal thoughts, auditory hallucinations, and active withdrawal. Despite these findings, her observation level was

downgraded—against policy—and, eventually, discontinued, clearing her for general-population housing.

Three days after booking, she ran to the railing of the upper tier in her unit and dove headfirst, sustaining catastrophic head trauma. She was transported to a hospital, where she died of blunt-force injuries.

Her past medical records revealed a history of **multiple prior suicide attempts**, including an earlier attempt to jump from a jail tier. She carried diagnoses of **schizophrenia, substance-use disorder, and recurrent psychiatric hospitalizations.**

The case was settled for **several million dollars**, reflecting the facility's policy violations and failure to protect an obviously high-risk inmate.

Risk and Contributory Factors

- **Primary factors:** multiple prior suicide attempts; diagnosis of schizophrenia; active heroin and alcohol withdrawal; specific suicidal plan and ideation
- **Secondary factors:** failure to refer to mental health services despite red flags; downgrade of precautions against policy; housing in a unit with lethal means
- **Contributory factors:** reliance on subjective judgments to discontinue watch; disregard of prior records and psychiatric history.

This case highlights how **ignoring prior suicide attempts** and disregarding clear clinical indicators can result in a foreseeable and preventable tragedy, ultimately exposing institutions to multimillion-dollar liability.

"Ignoring past attempts while downgrading precautions turned a predictable crisis into a multimillion-dollar tragedy."

Veteran and Soldier Status

Suicide among **U.S. military veterans** has become a growing public-health concern, linked to combat exposure, military service-related stressors, and post-traumatic stress disorder (PTSD). According to the **National Death Index (CDC, 2017)**, an average of **17 veterans die by suicide each day**, compared with 124 non-veteran Americans. In addition, **2–3 National Guard members or reservists**—who were never activated for combat—die by suicide daily. Rates vary by gender: female veterans die by suicide **1.8 times more often** than adult non-veteran females, while male veterans die by suicide **1.4 times more often** than adult non-veteran males. Similar to incarcerated populations, a **bimodal distribution** has been observed among veterans, with higher suicide rates in **young adults (18–34 years old)** and in **men older than 55.**

Involvement with the criminal-justice system compounds this risk. A nationally representative survey found that nearly **one-third of veterans (31.1 percent)** who had ever been arrested or booked reported a significantly higher rate of suicide than civilians (18 percent). **Finlay, *et al.* (2019)** reported that the prevalence of criminal-justice involvement was **61 percent higher among veterans with PTSD** compared with those without mental disorders.

Systematic reviews consistently show that military veterans involved in the justice system experience disproportionately high rates of mental health conditions, substance-use disorders, and personality disorders. Post-traumatic stress disorder (PTSD), in particular, has been repeatedly linked to increased morbidity, mortality, and suicidal behavior. A literature review by **Pompili, Serafini, and colleagues (2013)** in the *Journal of Nervous and Mental Disease* documented how PTSD amplifies suicide risk among veterans, particularly when compounded by co-occurring depression or substance misuse.

In my consulting caseload of 110 inmate suicides, **3 involved combat veterans**. While the overall risk factors for suicide among veterans resemble those of non-veterans, **PTSD is disproportionately present** in the veteran population. Arrest and incarceration may represent an **additional destabilizing risk factor**, particularly for those already burdened by combat trauma.

Symptoms of PTSD closely associated with suicidal ideation and behaviors include:

- Intrusive recollections of traumatic events
- Nightmares and sleep disruption
- Severe anxiety, agitation, and hyperarousal
- Depressed mood, emotional detachment, and numbness
- Profound guilt and shame, particularly among combat veterans

These symptoms, combined with the stress of incarceration and lack of adequate treatment, place veterans in custody at **substantial risk for suicide**.

CASE VIGNETTE 5.6—VETERAN WITH PTSD: IGNORED WARNING SIGNS AND IMPULSIVE BEHAVIOR

A 21-year-old Marine veteran with combat service in Afghanistan was incarcerated on **attempted murder charges** following a series of violent and impulsive incidents. His **VA psychiatric records** documented PTSD, depression, nightmares, intrusive thoughts, and impaired sleep. Two weeks prior to his arrest, a VA psychiatrist assessed him at **moderate-to-high acute suicide risk**, even though he denied active suicidal ideation. He had previously required **one-on-one suicide watch** during a VA inpatient admission.

While jailed pre-trial, he continued to display **impulsive behaviors.** The night before his death, a correctional officer observed a **makeshift noose** hanging from his light fixture. Instead of intervening, the officer dismissively remarked: *"What are you doing? Kill yourself? Take that down,"* and walked away. The following morning, the veteran was found motionless between the toilet and the bunk, a torn bedsheet wrapped around his neck. He was pronounced dead.

Risk and Contributory Factors

- **Primary factors:** documented PTSD; prior one-on-one suicide watch; VA psychiatrist's recent high-risk assessment; pre-trial detention
- **Secondary factors:** impulsive behavior; dismissive response by correctional staff; denial of ideation despite clear warning signs
- **Contributory factors:** failure to integrate VA psychiatric records into jail risk management; lack of intervention despite direct observation of a noose

Combat veterans with PTSD present **unique suicide vulnerabilities** due to impulsivity, intrusive symptoms, and trauma-related despair. When correctional staff ignore warning signs or dismiss imminent risk, preventable deaths occur, and liability is almost certain.

> *"When a noose is dismissed as a joke, a veteran's warning becomes a death sentence."*

Mental Disorders

Among the most significant and well-documented vulnerabilities to suicide in custody are **serious mental disorders.** Conditions such as **post-traumatic stress disorder (PTSD), schizophrenia, and major depressive disorder** profoundly disrupt mood, perception, judgment, and impulse control. Inmates with these illnesses often cycle between denial, impulsivity, hopelessness, and despair. Their symptoms—whether hallucinations, intrusive thoughts, or serious depression—place them at elevated risk for self-harm.

Correctional staff play a decisive role. Failure to recognize psychotic or depressive symptoms, or to act on visible signs of distress, often becomes the foundation for litigation. The cases addressed in this section illustrate how **unaddressed mental illness, compounded by systemic breakdowns, transforms predictable clinical risks into preventable tragedies**.

People with serious mental disorders are incarcerated at rates far higher than the general population. Estimates suggest they are **10 times more likely to be incarcerated**. Approximately **16–20 percent of incarcerated people** have a serious psychiatric disorder, such as schizophrenia, bipolar disorder, major depressive disorder, anxiety disorder, or PTSD. Among these, about **70 percent also have a co-occurring substance-use disorder**.

Retrospective studies consistently show that between **60 and 90 percent of those who die by suicide** have an identifiable mental disorder. Conversely, only about **20 percent of individuals who attempt suicide** do so without a preexisting psychiatric condition. In a recent study, **Oquendo, Wang, and colleagues (2024)** found that lifetime suicide attempts among otherwise psychiatrically healthy individuals were rare, underscoring the strong link between psychiatric illness and suicidal behavior.

Mood disorders, in particular, are the most consistently reported risk factors for suicidal behavior in incarcerated populations. NIH researchers have found that **mood disorders, impulse-control**

disorders, alcohol and substance-use disorders, psychotic disorders, and personality disorders convey the highest risk for suicide in the general public—and these patterns hold true in custody. The **presence of multiple co-occurring disorders** further elevates risk.

In my consulting caseload of **110 suicides**, every individual had one or more diagnosed psychiatric disorders. The majority (**n = 70**) had a **primary diagnosis of mood disorder**, followed by **anxiety disorder (n = 20)**, **psychotic disorder by history (n = 11)**, and **post-traumatic stress disorder (n = 9)**. About **22 individuals (20 percent)** had a substance-use disorder, almost always co-occurring with a mood or anxiety disorder. Many of those with substance-use disorders died during **intoxication or withdrawal.**

Among those with psychotic disorders, symptoms were often in remission at the time of death. Roughly **50 percent of psychotic individuals also had a co-occurring substance-use disorder**. Importantly, in my caseload, **no suicides were linked directly to command hallucinations or delusions.** One inmate with a diagnosis of schizophrenia, however, acted out impulsively and died by suicide—this case is detailed below.

Mood Disorders

Mood disorders, including **major depressive disorder, bipolar disorder, and unspecified mood disorders**, are among the most significant psychiatric vulnerabilities to suicide in custody. Depressive disorders are characterized by **persistent sadness, resignation, hopelessness, withdrawal from social contact, and changes in sleep and appetite.**

For many, the **first episode of depression** may emerge during incarceration, triggered by the inherent stress of adapting to a highly controlled environment. In these settings, **mental health professionals may sometimes underestimate depressive presentations**, viewing them as situational-adjustment reactions rather than clinical disorders requiring urgent attention.

Associated symptoms—including **nervousness, anxiety, agitation, and insomnia**—often provide important clues to the **severity and intentionality** of suicidal behavior. Careful attention to these signs is essential, as dismissal of early warnings has been repeatedly linked to preventable tragedies and subsequent litigation.

CASE VIGNETTE 5.7—MAJOR DEPRESSIVE DISORDER, DENIED MENTAL HEALTH ACCESS, SINGLE-CELL SUICIDE IN RURAL JAIL

A forty-nine-year-old male was arrested in 2019 for a probation violation and booked into a small rural jail. Unable to post a $50,000 bond, his probation was revoked due to unauthorized use of a controlled substance. A carpenter by trade with a high-school education, he had a documented history of **three to four psychiatric hospitalizations** for anxiety disorder and major depressive disorder.

Just prior to his arrest, he had been **evicted from his apartment**, further destabilizing him. Despite his psychiatric history, at intake screening, he denied suicidal ideation.

While in custody, he requested reassignment to a different housing unit, citing medical problems. His request was denied, with the explanation that he was classified as high custody due to a prior felony assault. This rejection deepened his depression, which he himself described as "deep depression."

His distress was documented. He wrote a **letter to his ex-wife** declaring his intention to kill himself. The day before his suicide, he used the **intercom** to request mental health assistance, saying, *"I don't know what's happening to me."* Staff responded dismissively, telling him the mental health professional was at lunch. No evaluation followed.

The next day, he was found **hanging in his single cell.** Witnesses described him in the hours before his death as **anxious, agitated, pacing the floor, refusing meals, and showing obvious signs of crisis.** The case was eventually settled out of court for a substantial amount.

Risk and Contributory Factors

- **Primary factor:** major depressive disorder with repeated hospitalizations
- **Secondary factors:** eviction and recent destabilization; denied housing-reassignment request; single-cell placement
- **Contributory factors:** failure to respond to explicit requests for help; dismissive staff response; denial of access to mental health services

Failure to recognize and respond to **documented depression and expressed suicidal intent** represents a clear breach of duty in correctional care. Ignoring direct pleas for help, particularly when combined with risk-enhancing conditions like **single-cell housing**, transforms clinical vulnerability into institutional liability.

"When depression meets dismissal, a rural jail cell becomes a death sentence."

Psychotic Disorders

Psychotic disorders, including **schizophrenia, schizoaffective disorder, and brief psychotic disorder**, represent some of the **highest-risk mental illnesses** for suicide in custody. Symptoms of psychosis may include **disorganized thought processes, delusions, perceptual disturbances (such as hallucinations), and bizarre behaviors**. Common behavioral manifestations in custody include **yelling, screaming, mumbling, talking to oneself, smearing feces, or defecating in open spaces.**

Some inmates with psychotic disorders express **persistent suicidal thoughts** with or without engaging in attempts, while others may engage in self-harm behaviors perceived by staff as manipulative. Importantly, **psychotic inmates who are suicidal often act with profound impulsivity**, increasing the unpredictability and lethality of their actions.

Psychotic symptoms such as **persecutory delusions** or **command hallucinations** can compound this risk. While not all suicides among psychotic inmates are driven directly by hallucinations or delusions, the **association of psychosis with impulsivity** creates an especially dangerous profile.

CASE VIGNETTE 5.8—SCHIZOPHRENIA, IGNORED PSYCHOTIC SYMPTOMS, BIZARRE BEHAVIOR, AND DELAYED RESPONSE

A twenty-four-year-old African-American male diagnosed with **schizophrenia** was booked into a large urban jail and died by suicide two days later. His family subsequently filed a lawsuit in state court alleging **negligence and wrongful death**.

The inmate was **well known to the jail** from prior admissions, during which he had been assigned to the psychiatric unit due to serious mental illness and a history of self-harm behaviors. Several correctional officers had supervised him before and were familiar with his psychiatric needs.

At intake, he exhibited **florid psychotic symptoms**: he defecated on himself, ate feces, and urinated on himself. Despite these bizarre and alarming behaviors, the booking officers failed to document his condition, make a mental health referral, or communicate his status to housing staff. Although he was given a special-needs classification of "*in house, alone, outhouse, alone*"—intended to alert staff that he required enhanced supervision—this designation was never acted on.

Instead of being placed in the psychiatric unit, he was sent to **general-population housing**. Over the next two days, his psychotic symptoms and bizarre behaviors continued. Fellow inmates became so alarmed by his deterioration and isolation that they discussed filing grievances, but their concerns were dismissed by staff.

On the day of his death, the correctional officer assigned to monitor the unit **left the floor for an extended period**, leaving him unsupervised. During this time, he hanged himself in his cell. Officers eventually discovered him, but there was a **delay in initiating life-saving measures**.

The lawsuit emphasized that officers ignored a clear record of serious mental illness and prior self-harm, failed to act on obvious psychotic symptoms at booking, denied knowledge of his special-needs classification despite documentation, and neglected to monitor him as policy required. **The case was ultimately settled, reflecting the weight of these failures and the foreseeability of his suicide.**

Risk and Contributory Factors

- **Primary factors:** known diagnosis of schizophrenia; prior psychiatric-unit placement; documented history of self-harm
- **Secondary factors:** bizarre psychotic behaviors at intake (defecating, eating feces, urinating on self); special-needs classification not acted upon
- **Contributory factors:** failure to document intake symptoms; failure to refer to mental health; inappropriate placement in general population; officer absence and delayed response.

This case underscores how **ignoring clear psychotic symptoms** and neglecting to enforce existing classifications or policies transforms an identifiable clinical crisis into a preventable death. Incarcerated individuals with schizophrenia require immediate referral and consistent monitoring; lapses in documentation, communication, and supervision directly drive liability.

"When bizarre behavior is ignored,
psychosis becomes a death sentence."

Psychological States

Certain psychological states are strongly associated with suicidal behavior in custody. Individuals who have made a final decision to end their lives often exhibit **sudden and dramatic changes in mood and behavior**. These changes are typically congruent with their underlying thoughts and intentions: withdrawal from other inmates and staff, refusal to participate in recreational activities, giving away possessions, and expressing resignation or acceptance.

By contrast, manipulative self-harm attempts often lack this congruence. In those cases, the individual's mood, behavior, and words may not align in a way that signals genuine intent, making differentiation difficult—but still critical.

Depression, anxiety, agitation, feelings of hopelessness, and a sense of being trapped are especially dangerous when they occur together, particularly in impulsive individuals. Statements such as *"I am done"* or *"I don't see a way out"* may precede serious suicidal acts. Even when inmates conceal their true intent, **emotional and behavioral cues** should alert staff to the possibility of imminent suicide.

Substance Abuse

Substance-use disorders are pervasive in correctional populations, with **up to 70 percent of incarcerated individuals** having a history of substance abuse. For many, substance use is directly tied to criminal activity. Research by **Lindsay Hayes** found that approximately **20 percent of jail suicides involved individuals who were intoxicated at the time of death** (Hayes, 2010).

While a history of substance abuse alone does not necessarily create acute suicide risk, **intoxication and withdrawal states are critical periods of vulnerability**. These conditions lower inhibitions, increase impulsivity, and amplify anxiety, agitation, and insomnia—all of which can push an individual toward self-harm.

From a litigation standpoint, liability often arises when **healthcare professionals fail to treat or monitor intoxication and withdrawal adequately**. A detainee diagnosed with alcohol or drug intoxication and withdrawal must be placed on an appropriate **withdrawal protocol**. The use of structured tools—such as the **Clinical Institute Withdrawal Assessment of Alcohol, revised (CIWA-Ar)** and the **Clinical Opiate Withdrawal Scale (COWS)**—is considered standard practice. Failure to follow such protocols has repeatedly been the basis of lawsuits.

Alcohol

Alcohol intoxication and withdrawal represent some of the **highest suicide risks**, particularly within the first **twenty-four to forty-eight hours** of detention. These crises are most often seen in **lockups and jails**, rather than prisons, since most incarcerated individuals have already gone through detoxification before transfer.

Special concern applies to **first-time arrestees or those of high social status**, who may be overwhelmed by the sudden loss of freedom and by stigma. By contrast, frequent detainees ("frequent flyers") may appear more accustomed to the environment but remain vulnerable.

Intoxicated detainees should **never be left alone** or placed in cells with access to ligature materials such as **telephone cords, electrical wiring, or rope-like structures**. Line-of-sight supervision is strongly recommended during the first days of custody.

Opiates (including Fentanyl)

Opiate withdrawal often begins within the **first twenty-four hours of detention** and may last up to **ten days**. Withdrawal produces a state of **agitation, restlessness, intense cravings, fatigue, and severe discomfort**, creating conditions conducive to suicidal behavior.

Many individuals relapse into opiate use after release, only to be rearrested soon after, perpetuating a cycle of **detoxification in jail, relapse in the community, and re-arrest**. Each iteration increases risk, particularly for those with histories of impulsivity, prior suicide attempts, or concurrent mental illness.

CASE VIGNETTE 5.9—SUBSTANCE INTOXICATION AND WITHDRAWAL: FENTANYL, FAILURE TO INITIATE PROTOCOL, SETTLEMENT IN RURAL JAIL

The estate of a thirty-three-year-old White male, known to abuse fentanyl, filed a lawsuit after he died by suicide in a small rural jail approximately seventy hours after booking. The complaint alleged civil-rights violations and medical negligence.

During the first three days of custody, the detainee displayed **clear signs of substance withdrawal**. He repeatedly pounded on his cell wall and pressed the call button, apparently to summon staff for help. A sergeant who visited his cell ordered him to quiet down but provided no medical assistance. Later, staff transferred him to a padded cell, presumably for behavioral control.

Inside the padded cell, his distress escalated. He continued pounding on the floor, refused meals, and complained of detox symptoms. Nursing notes documented **chills, nausea, and agitation**, but staff failed to initiate a withdrawal protocol or consult a physician. Despite his agitation, he was provided with a mattress, sheet, and blanket. The padded cell also contained a **visible anchor point at the door hinge**. Shortly thereafter, he hanged himself, using the sheet.

His **withdrawal symptoms**—chills, agitation, nausea, refusal to eat, and explicit complaints of detoxing—had been repeatedly observed but ignored.

Risk and Contributory Factors

- **Primary factors:** fentanyl intoxication and acute withdrawal, severe physical distress, agitation
- **Secondary factors:** failure to initiate withdrawal protocol, failure to consult medical provider, placement in padded cell with ligature point
- **Contributory factors:** provision of bedding despite high risk, lack of supervision

The estate's lawsuit emphasized **deliberate indifference** to obvious withdrawal symptoms and failure to implement detox protocols. The case was **settled**, reflecting the facility's liability for ignoring well-documented risk.

Untreated opioid withdrawal creates a **mental and physical crisis state** that can rapidly escalate to suicide if not managed with established protocols.

"He was detoxing before their eyes, but no one acted."

CASE VIGNETTE 5.10—SUBSTANCE WITHDRAWAL, METHAMPHETAMINE, PSYCHIATRIC ILLNESS, ABUSIVE RELATIONSHIP, SETTLEMENT IN URBAN JAIL

A twenty-six-year-old Caucasian female was arrested after being pulled over for speeding while driving with emergency lights activated. During the attempted arrest, she stabbed a highway patrol officer in the shoulder with a knife. Toxicology confirmed **amphetamine and methamphetamine intoxication** at the time. She was charged with attempted murder of a police officer and driving under the influence of drugs, and booked into a maximum-security urban jail.

At intake, her medical screening documented a history of **suicide attempts**, prior use of psychiatric medications (last taken three days earlier), and methamphetamine abuse (last use the day of arrest). Despite this, **no withdrawal protocol was initiated**, in direct violation of jail policy and accepted correctional standards.

Two months later, while housed in maximum security, she attempted suicide by hanging in her cell. She survived but suffered **severe anoxic brain injury**, leaving her permanently impaired.

Additional vulnerabilities compounded her risk: a diagnosis of **major depressive disorder**, paranoia, auditory hallucinations, and a controlling abusive relationship. She reported that her boyfriend monitored her constantly through cameras, controlled her communications, and threatened her family. In her own words, she felt the world was "so cruel" that she "wanted to die."

Risk and Contributory Factors

- **Primary factors:** methamphetamine intoxication and withdrawal, untreated psychiatric illness, history of suicide attempts

- **Secondary factors:** failure to initiate withdrawal protocol, lack of psychiatric intervention, maximum-security placement
- **Contributory factors:** abusive and coercive relationship, delusional beliefs, auditory hallucinations, feelings of entrapment

Her estate filed a lawsuit alleging **medical negligence and civil-rights violations**. The case was **settled**, acknowledging the facility's failure to manage withdrawal appropriately and provide timely psychiatric care. Withdrawal syndromes, when combined with psychiatric illness and psychosocial stressors, create a **perfect storm of vulnerability**—requiring urgent medical and psychiatric intervention.

"Her cries for help were silenced by withdrawal, psychosis, and neglect."

PROTECTIVE FACTORS

Protective factors are conditions that **reduce the probability of suicidal behavior** even when risk is elevated (Centers for Disease Control, 2024). Individuals who hold strong religious beliefs or faith in a higher power tend to show lower rates of suicidal ideation, especially when suicide is viewed as morally wrong. Religious or spiritual practices, as well as moral objections to suicide, may act as deterrents.

Social support is another protective factor. Marriage frequently serves as a buffer against suicide, unless the relationship is highly conflictual. Similarly, having **young children** or a strong relationship with a parent—particularly with one's mother—can reduce risk.

More broadly, **social connectedness** protects against loneliness and isolation. **Future orientation**, such as expressing specific, concrete plans for life after release, may also serve as a protective factor.

However, protective factors are not guarantees. Even those with strong supports or religious commitments may still engage in suicidal behavior under extreme situational or psychological strain.

CRITICAL RISK FACTORS

Drawing from more than 110 consultation cases, a set of **critical risk factors** emerges that correctional staff and clinicians must assess. While not every individual with risk factors will attempt suicide, failure to evaluate and address them often leads to preventable tragedies and is frequently cited in liability claims.

Risk factors fall into two categories: **static** and **dynamic.**

Static Risk Factors

1. Recent near-lethal suicide attempt (within one year)
2. History of suicide watch in the same institution
3. Actively symptomatic mental disorder (e.g., depression, psychosis)
4. First-time arrest, especially among those of high social status
5. Pre-trial detention status
6. Active substance abuse involving alcohol, fentanyl, or methamphetamine
7. Solitary confinement or restrictive housing
8. Veteran status with post-traumatic stress disorder
9. Family history of suicide in a first-degree relative

Dynamic Risk Factors

1. Active suicidal ideation with intent or plan
2. Active or recent suicidal behaviors, including making a ligature or hoarding medications/drugs

3. Acute mental-status changes (e.g., depression, anxiety, agitation)
4. Recent significant behavioral changes, including isolation or withdrawal
5. Alcohol, fentanyl, or methamphetamine intoxication and withdrawal
6. Recent changes in legal status, including new charges, unexpected sentencing, or parole denial
7. Sexual victimization while incarcerated
8. Acute loss of social- or family-support system
9. Denial or delay in psychiatric treatment or follow-up

CONCLUSION

Suicide in custody is not random. It arises from a web of **identifiable vulnerabilities**—demographics, legal and institutional factors, psychiatric illness, substance intoxication and withdrawal, and unique psychosocial stressors, such as combat trauma or victimization. Each of the ten cases in this chapter illustrates how **predictable risks became preventable tragedies** when warning signs were missed, risk and protective factors were ignored, or interventions were delayed.

The evidence from more than 110 consultations reinforces that **risk is multidimensional**, shaped by both **static factors** (such as past attempts, mental illness, or solitary confinement) and **dynamic factors** (such as acute withdrawal, recent sentencing, or sudden loss of support). Failure to recognize and respond to these factors is not simply a clinical oversight—it forms the foundation for liability when courts conclude that officials acted with **deliberate indifference** to an obvious and serious medical need.

At the same time, protective factors—religious beliefs, family ties, social connectedness, and future orientation—underscore that not all inmates at risk will succumb. Identifying these buffers and integrating them into treatment and supervision plans can make the difference between life and death.

Ultimately, the central lesson of this chapter is that suicide in custody is best understood as a **predictable outcome of identifiable vulnerabilities**. When staff are trained to assess both risk and protection, to act swiftly on withdrawal symptoms, to address psychiatric illness, and to intervene when legal or personal crises arise, correctional facilities can prevent avoidable deaths. The recurring patterns documented here are not only clinical realities but also **legal warning signs**: if ignored, they invite preventable tragedy and costly litigation.

REFERENCES

1. Carson, E. Ann, and Mary Cowhig. *Suicide in Local Jails and State and Federal Prisons, 2000–2019—Statistical Tables.* Washington, DC: Bureau of Justice Statistics, October 2021. https://bjs.ojp.gov/press-release/suicide-local-jails-and-state-and-federal-prisons-2000-2019-statistical-tables
2. Centers for Disease Control and Prevention. 2024. "Risk and Protective Factors for Suicide." Atlanta, GA: CDC. Accessed September 17, 2025. https://www.cdc.gov/suicide/risk-factors/index.html
3. Daniel, Anasseril E. 2006. "Preventing Suicide in Prison: A Collaborative Responsibility of Administrative, Custodial, and Clinical Staff." *Journal of the American Academy of Psychiatry and the Law* 34 (2): 165–175.
4. Daniel, Anasseril E. 2009. "Suicide-Related Litigation in Jails and Prisons: Risk Management Strategies." *Journal of Correctional Health Care* 15 (1): 19–27.
5. Finlay, Alexander J., Maurizio Pompili, and Maria A. Oquendo. 2019. "Suicide Risk Assessment in Correctional Settings."

International Journal of Environmental Research and Public Health 16 (11): 2018–2025.

6. Hayes, Lindsay M. 2010. *National Study of Jail Suicide: 20 Years Later.* Washington, DC: U.S. Department of Justice, National Institute of Corrections.
7. Johnson, Robert. 1981. *Condemned to Die: Life under Sentence of Death.* New York: Routledge.
8. *Kempf v. Northumberland County Prison*, No. 2:15-cv-01125-WD (W.D. Pa. Sept. 12, 2018).
9. Lester, David. 1990. *Suicide in Jails and Prisons: An International Comparison. Perceptual and Motor Skills, 71((3) 1042*
10. National Institute of Mental Health (NIMH). 2008. "Suicide Risk Factors and Prevention Strategies: Review of Epidemiologic Evidence." *Epidemiologic Reviews* 30 (1): 133–154. https://doi.org/10.1093/epirev/mxn002
11. Oquendo, Maria A., Melanie M. Wall, Shuai Wang, Mayank Mattoo, Carlos Blanco, *et al.* 2024. "Lifetime Suicide Attempts in Otherwise Psychiatrically Healthy Individuals." *JAMA Psychiatry* 81 (3): 276–286. https://doi.org/10.1001/jamapsychiatry.2023.5022
12. Pompili, Maurizio, Alexander J. Finlay, and Maria A. Oquendo. 2020. "Suicide among Incarcerated Individuals: Epidemiology, Risk Factors, and Interventions." *Lancet Psychiatry* 7 (6): 487–497.
13. Swartz, Lisa H. and McDonald, Robert, 2024. "Solitary Confinement and Suicide Risk: Implications for Correctional Policy." *American Journal of Public Health* 114 (3): 345–352.
14. "Suicide Watch and Unlock the Box Campaign." 2022. Campaign Briefing Paper. Washington, DC: Unlock the Box/ACLU.

CHAPTER 6

SCREENING AND SUICIDE RISK ASSESSMENT: GATEWAYS AND PITFALLS

INTRODUCTION

S*uicide prevention in correctional settings* begins at the door. **Screening** is the first step: it identifies who needs urgent attention. **Suicide risk assessment** (SRA) follows: it determines how to protect them. These two processes are the foundation of safe custody and legally defensible practice.

Attorneys and courts focus on them closely. They ask: Was screening performed? Was it adequate? Did the risk assessment occur? Were results documented, communicated, and acted upon? Failures in any step—superficial screening, missed records, overreliance on denial, poor communication, or premature release from precautions—are central to suicide litigation.

SCREENING—THE FIRST STEP

Screening is the gateway to suicide prevention in correctional facilities, yet it is also one of the most commonly mishandled processes I have observed in my consultations. The expectation is simple: every individual entering custody must be assessed for suicide risk in a structured, individualized, and clinically meaningful way. The reality, however, is that screening is often reduced to a mechanical exercise—a form completed quickly, questions asked superficially, and warning signs overlooked. When screening is perfunctory, preventable suicides follow, and liability soon follows with them.

All incoming detainees must undergo screening for **health and mental health problems, including suicide risk**, because entry into custody itself represents a period of **high vulnerability for self-harm.** The **National Commission on Correctional Health Care** (NCCHC) **standard** states that "receiving screening is performed on all inmates on arrival at the intake facility to ensure that all emergent and urgent mental health needs are met." Suicide vulnerability is one of the most urgent screening-component needs at the time of intake. The **American College of Physicians (ACP) position paper (item 11)** likewise recommends that policymakers and administrators adopt adequately funded procedures to ensure screening of all persons entering U.S. jails for behavioral-health conditions, including suicide risk, history of serious mental illness, need for prescribed psychotropic medications, exposure to trauma, and co-occurring substance-use disorders. These organizations emphasize that **screening must be tied to evidence-based policies** for treatment, housing, and support of persons with behavioral-health conditions. There is near-universal acceptance that **screening is a critical element of suicide prevention** in jails and prisons.

The **intake mental health screening is designed to prevent inmates who are mentally unstable, suicidal, or urgently in need of**

clinical care from being admitted to the general population without referral for further evaluation. Yet some lockups and even the U.S. Marshals Service have at times minimized screening, reasoning those detainees are held only briefly or assuming that screening was conducted at a transferring facility. These practices create dangerous blind spots and have been repeatedly cited in litigation.

Screening is usually completed at the time of booking by a nurse or trained correctional officer using a standardized questionnaire, recorded in paper or electronic form. A typical screening instrument consists of twenty to twenty-five questions and is intended to gather information on **static risk factors (such as past attempts, psychiatric history) and dynamic risk factors (such as recent stressors, intoxication, withdrawal, or acute mental health symptoms), as well as protective factors.** Ideally, screening should capture both long-standing vulnerabilities and **recent precipitants** that may trigger self-harm. As shown in **Chapter 5**, these precipitants—loss of family support, stigmatizing charges, solitary confinement, or untreated withdrawal—are frequently the tipping points in custodial suicides.

The outcome of the screening should guide next steps. Depending on responses and presentation, the detainee may be referred immediately to a mental health professional, placed on suicide precautions, or housed in a more-protective environment. Any failure in this process—whether by incomplete questioning, failure to review records, or inadequate follow-up—can jeopardize the ultimate goal of keeping the detainee safe. **Halfhearted or cursory questioning must be avoided.** The screener must ensure that **follow-up procedures are carefully and systematically performed**, because a screening form, no matter how well designed, is only as effective as the diligence and judgment of the staff who administer it.

Purpose of Screening

The intake screening thus has multiple purposes:

1. **Identification of at-risk individuals.** Capture prior suicide attempts, serious mental illness, current ideation, recent stressors, and substance use/withdrawal among the strongest predictors of near-term risk (Large, *et al.* 2017; Carter, *et al.* 2017).
2. **Housing assignment.** Assign detainees appropriately—general population, observation cell, or constant watch—depending on assessed risk.
3. **Communication with staff.** Generate alerts to ensure custody and clinical staff share risk awareness.
4. **Tailored intervention.** Trigger referral to mental health professionals, crisis counseling, medication continuation or adjustment, and withdrawal protocols when needed.
5. **Preventing crisis escalation.** Interrupt the rapid progression from ideation to attempt in a regimented and stressful environment.
6. **Continuity of care.** Ensure ongoing psychotropic-medication treatment and regular follow-up for those with chronic conditions.
7. **Meeting the standard of care.** Screening is universally recognized as a required procedure; failure to perform it is often cited in negligence and deliberate-indifference claims (NCCHC, 2018; Daniel, 2022).

PROBLEMS IDENTIFIED IN LAWSUITS (SCREENING)

Based on consultation in 110 cases, recurring failures include:

- **Inadequate questionnaires** (too few items, no prompts, no weighted red flags)

- **Group screening,** which suppresses disclosure
- **Failure to review prior records,** including from the same jail
- **Failure to act on withdrawal or acute distress,** leading to preventable deterioration
- **Poor communication** (e.g., no alerts created)
- **Falsified or incomplete documentation**

Attorneys consistently focus on screening practices when filing suicide-related lawsuits. The key questions raised are:

1. **Was screening ever conducted?**
2. **How was screening performed?**
3. **Were appropriate protective actions taken?**
4. **How were screening decisions communicated to other staff?**

The legal argument is that any flaw in screening—whether omission, inadequate procedure, or poor follow-through—translates directly into a lack of protection for the inmate and ultimately to the suicide itself. Failure to conduct adequate screening and referral often arises from **insufficient training**, **staffing shortages**, or **misunderstanding of documentation and communication procedures**. Whatever the cause, the result is the same: preventable deaths, costly litigation, and findings of negligence or deliberate indifference.

Inadequate Questionnaire

A recurring theme in litigation is the use of poorly designed or poorly executed screening questionnaires. Some facilities rely on instruments with only a few superficial questions, such as "Are you suicidal today?" or "Have you ever attempted suicide?" Such narrow approaches fail to address the complexity of suicide risk and provide no actionable guidance for referrals. In one **Chapter 3 case**, a sixty-year-old detainee denied suicidal ideation and past attempts at intake. The intake worker, satisfied with a "no," asked no follow-up questions and failed to review the detainee's prior psychiatric history. After the man's suicide, the lack of probing and the limited scope of the questionnaire became central issues in litigation. Similarly, in **Chapter 4**, a middle-aged man arrested on a sex offense denied ideation; staff accepted his denial at face value and placed him in general population. He hanged himself within 3 days. Both cases illustrate how superficial screening tools, compounded by lack of probing, fail to protect detainees at obvious risk.

Lack of communication

Even when screenings are conducted, their findings often fail to reach those who need to know. In many jails, mental health alerts must be entered into electronic jail information-management systems (JIMS) to flag high-risk detainees for both custody and clinical staff. When alerts are not entered, ignored, or inconsistently used, dangerous lapses occur. A **Chapter 5 case** involved a 24-year-old with schizophrenia whose florid psychotic behaviors at booking (defecating on himself, eating feces) were neither documented nor communicated to mental health staff. He was treated as a routine intake and placed in general population, where he died by suicide 2 days later. In this case, the failure of communication at screening was the decisive factor in establishing liability.

Failure to refer to mental health professionals

Screening is only the first step; it must lead to immediate referral when risk is identified. Many lawsuits highlight cases where detainees screened positive for risk but were not referred for timely mental health evaluation. In **Chapter 3**, a 23-year-old withdrawing from opioids was recognized as distressed but not placed on a withdrawal protocol or referred for urgent psychiatric assessment. He hanged himself 2 days later. Similarly, in **Chapter 5**, a 50-year-old female with a history of multiple suicide attempts repeatedly expressed suicidal thoughts, yet her screening results were downgraded, and she was returned to general population, contrary to policy. She later jumped to her death, and the case was settled for millions. These examples highlight that identifying risk without referral is legally and clinically meaningless.

Inadequate training of screeners

Another recurrent allegation in lawsuits is that those tasked with screening are not adequately trained. Intake staff often receive minimal instruction on how to conduct a meaningful suicide risk screening, probe responses, or document findings. As a result, questioning becomes cursory, important details are missed, and opportunities for intervention are lost. In the **group-screening case from Chapter 3**, 10 detainees were asked together, "Are you suicidal today or any time in the past?" Predictably, all denied. A properly trained screener would have recognized the futility of such a practice. Instead, one of the detainees—who had a known history of suicidal ideation—was placed in general population, where he later died by suicide. Training deficiencies not only undermine the purpose of screening but also provide plaintiffs with compelling evidence of systemic negligence.

In summary, the screening failures fall into predictable categories: inadequate questionnaires, failure to probe denials, breakdowns in communication, lack of referral, and poor training. Each represents not just a procedural lapse but a critical missed opportunity to protect life. In litigation, these failures are linked directly to the duty of care owed to detainees. In practice, they demonstrate that **screening is**

not a box to check—it is the front line of suicide prevention and the foundation for legal defense.

When done well, screening identifies those at imminent or near-term risk, informs housing and monitoring decisions, initiates psychiatric referral, and creates alerts for staff. When bypassed or performed superficially, it represents a missed chance to prevent suicide and becomes a liability centerpiece.

DO'S AND DON'TS OF SUICIDE SCREENING

Do's

- Ask about past suicide attempts, psychiatric hospitalizations, current ideation, recent stressors, and psychotropic medications.
- Review prior records, both in the facility and community.
- Create alerts in the jail information system, and communicate directly with custody staff.
- Refer immediately to a qualified mental health professional when indicated.
- Place detainees on suicide precautions when risk is evident.

Don'ts

- Don't rely on group screening.
- Don't accept denial of ideation at face value.
- Don't use overly short or incomplete questionnaires.
- Don't ignore withdrawal, agitation, or bizarre behavior.
- Don't falsify or skip documentation.

SUICIDE RISK ASSESSMENT (SRA)

While screening identifies detainees who may be at risk for suicide, **suicide risk assessment (SRA)** is the process by which qualified mental health professionals—psychiatrists, psychologists, or other clinicians—determine the *level and immediacy* of that risk. Unlike the standardized checklist of intake screening, SRA involves **clinical judgment informed by static and dynamic factors**, contextual circumstances, and protective elements such as future-oriented thinking or a supportive network.

The central question for the evaluator is direct and urgent: *Would this detainee take their life now or in the near future?* For individuals already placed on suicide watch, the parallel question is: *How likely are they to refrain from further suicidal thoughts or behaviors if removed from precautions?* These decisions are necessarily **probabilistic** and **subjective**, though grounded in identifiable, objective risk factors.

From a legal perspective, attorneys understand the inherent subjectivity of clinical decisions. However, in litigation, they consistently examine the following:

1. What was the likelihood of self-harm at the time of assessment?
2. Was the detainee **acutely suicidal**?
3. If acutely suicidal, were they appropriately placed on suicide watch?
4. Were they **prematurely discharged** from precautions?
5. Did the provider comply with the **standard of care**?
6. Did the assessment follow the facility's **suicide prevention and -intervention policies**?

From a forensic standpoint, problems arise when evaluators **minimize or ignore clear risk factors** and fail to use their best professional judgment. When risk is trivialized, and protective measures are not taken, such oversights become the foundation of negligence and deliberate-indifference claims.

Where screening is broad, SRA is deep. It is performed by a qualified mental health professional and requires **probabilistic clinical judgment**: weighing static risk factors (e.g., prior attempts, serious mental illness), dynamic factors (e.g., acute stressors, hopelessness), and protective elements (e.g., family support, future orientation).

Courts ask: Was the inmate acutely suicidal? Were precautions in place and maintained? Were they discharged prematurely? Did the provider comply with policy and standard of care?

CORE ELEMENTS OF SUICIDE RISK ASSESSMENT (SRA)

Suicide risk assessment in corrections is not about prediction, but prevention. Its goal is to identify those at acute risk and implement safeguards to protect life. While the process is necessarily probabilistic and subjective, courts and professional standards demand that it be **thorough, well-reasoned, and documented**. The following elements are essential:

1. **Clinical Judgment and Legal Standard**

   At the heart of SRA is the clinician's **best professional judgment**. From a legal standpoint, liability often turns on whether the provider acted with *reckless indifference*—that is, whether they consciously disregarded obvious signs of risk. Too often, clinicians accept denial of suicidal ideation at face value and conclude that an inmate is not suicidal, despite multiple red flags. Courts have repeatedly ruled that a single "no" is not enough. What protects both the inmate and the provider is a comprehensive evaluation, good-faith decision-making, and accurate documentation.

2. **Structured Clinical Interview**

   The assessment should include direct questioning about suicidal ideation, intent, plan, and past behaviors, as well as indirect expressions of hopelessness ("I don't care if I live"). A full **mental-status examination** provides essential data on thought processes, mood, affect, and judgment. Particular attention should be given to **vulnerable mental states**—acute depression, anxiety, agitation, hopelessness, and insomnia—which frequently precede suicidal acts in custody.

3. **Review of Records and History**

An assessment that ignores available records is incomplete. Facility files often reveal prior suicide attempts, previous placements on watch, psychiatric hospitalizations, medication history, and responses to treatment. Reviewing these records distinguishes chronic self-injurious behavior from acute suicide risk and prevents clinicians from overlooking obvious patterns.

4. **Collateral Information from Staff and Family**

Custody officers and family members often provide critical insight. Behavioral changes such as withdrawal from peers, sudden requests for single-cell housing, refusal of food or medication, or oblique statements of despair may be more revealing than a detainee's denial in a clinical interview. Gathering and documenting these reports is an essential safeguard and a common point of failure in lawsuits.

5. **Behavioral Observation**

The evaluator's direct observations are indispensable. Warning signs include extreme agitation, rapid mood swings, sudden calmness following agitation, or complete withdrawal from interaction. These changes may signal that the inmate has made a "final decision." Ignoring observable behavior, especially when combined with risk history, is a recurring failure in litigation.

6. **Structured Assessment Tools (Adjuncts, Not Substitutes)**

   Tools such as the **Columbia Suicide Severity Rating Scale (C-SSRS)** and **SAD PERSONS** provide structure but are not correction-specific.

   - **C-SSRS** offers detailed scoring of ideation and attempts but relies heavily on self-disclosure, which inmates often withhold.
   - **SAD PERSONS** is simple but omits corrections-specific risk factors and overemphasizes substance abuse.

   Courts have recognized that reliance on such tools alone is inadequate. They can supplement judgment, but they cannot replace a thorough assessment.

7. **Risk Stratification and Documentation**

   The ultimate task is to stratify risk into practical levels—low, moderate, high, or acute—and match interventions accordingly: housing, observation frequency, suicide watch, or referral to specialized mental health units. **Documentation is crucial**: the record must show that risk factors were weighed, judgment applied, and protective measures implemented. Courts do not require perfection, but they do require evidence that the clinician did not deliberately ignore risk.

8. **Interaction of Static and Dynamic Factors**

   Finally, effective assessment requires recognition of the interplay between **static factors** (diagnosis, history of attempts) and **dynamic factors** (current mental state, acute stressors, institutional environment). For example, a detainee with chronic depression may escalate to acute risk after a parole denial or a transfer that disrupts medication continuity. Assessment must consider how these elements converge in the moment of crisis.

PROBLEMS IDENTIFIED IN LITIGATION IN SUICIDE RISK ASSESSMENT (SRA)

Problems in suicide risk assessment (SRA) are frequently raised in suicide-related litigation. Attorneys scrutinize whether an assessment was completed, whether it was adequate, and whether its findings were acted upon. The key legal question is whether the evaluator acted with **reckless indifference** to an inmate's serious medical need—disregarding obvious risks, neglecting protective steps, or ignoring established policy standards (*Estelle v. Gamble*, 1976; *Farmer v. Brennan*, 1994).

1. **Absence of Suicide Risk Assessment**

   In many cases, the records lack any documented SRA prior to a suicide. These omissions are often decisive, making defense difficult. Courts have found that brief mental-status exams or crisis interviews without a comprehensive SRA do not meet the standard of care. The **absence of documentation** itself is viewed as a critical liability.

CASE VIGNETTE 6.1: ABSENCE OF SUICIDE RISK ASSESSMENT, PREA FOLLOW-UP FAILURE, AND DELAYED EMERGENCY RESPONSE

A male in his late twenties, convicted of burglary and kidnapping, and serving a lengthy sentence, had a documented history of major depressive disorder with anxious distress, polysubstance-use disorder, multiple prior suicide attempts, psychiatric hospitalizations, and childhood trauma. Soon after his detention, he engaged in self-harm by ingesting Tylenol and razor blades, leading to his placement on suicide watch and subsequent medical treatment.

Within a month, he attempted again, striking his neck with a razor, and was again briefly placed on suicide watch. The following month, he was transferred to segregation. During a screening, he minimized or denied his extensive psychiatric history, recording "no" for most risk factors, despite well-documented prior attempts and treatment.

Later that month, he reported being sexually assaulted by a cellmate and was referred under PREA protocol. However, no follow-up counseling was provided, and records after his death showed falsified entries documenting services that never occurred. Days later, he was found hanging in his segregation cell, using his bed linen as a ligature. Officers failed to check on him for approximately two hours, and, once he was discovered, staff critically delayed entering the cell and initiating life-saving intervention.

Despite his multiple suicide attempts and placement on suicide watch, no comprehensive suicide risk assessment was ever performed.

Risk and Contributory Factors

- **Documented history** of major depressive disorder, polysubstance use, suicide attempts, psychiatric hospitalizations, and trauma
- **Denial/minimization** of risk factors during screening accepted at face value
- **Failure to perform** a structured suicide risk assessment (SRA)
- **Lack of PREA-mandated** follow-up counseling after reported sexual assault

- **Falsification** of records
- Extended gaps in segregation monitoring (two hours without discovery)
- Critical delay in emergency response once discovered

Cross References

- **Chapter 4 (Suicidal Behaviors):** Denial of suicidal ideation does not equal absence of risk
- **Chapter 5 (Vulnerable Inmates):** Impact of childhood trauma, psychiatric disorders, and sexual victimization
- **Chapter 7 (Monitoring and Supervision):** Failures in rounds and falsified observation logs
- **Chapter 9 (First Two Weeks):** Heightened risk during initial adjustment and segregation placement
- **Chapter 12 (Risk Management):** Legal liability from failure to follow PREA and deliberate indifference in delayed response.

The absence of structured risk assessment, combined with failures in PREA follow-up and falsified records, allowed a high-risk inmate to die by suicide. Operational lapses—not lack of policy—directly contributed to his death.

> *"Policies without follow-through become empty paperwork; the absence of real risk assessment and timely intervention can turn a foreseeable crisis into a preventable death."*

2. **Inadequate Assessment**

   Even when documented, SRAs often fall short due to:

- **Superficial questioning**, such as asking only, "Are you suicidal?" without probing underlying risk factors or psychosocial context.
- **Overreliance on denial.** Nearly half of individuals who died by suicide denied suicidal ideation in the week or month before their death, demonstrating that denial is a poor marker of safety (Obegi, *et al.* 2021).
- **Cursory encounters.** Although no fixed duration is required, a meaningful assessment typically requires at least twenty minutes to explore history, risk and protective factors, and current mental state, followed by documentation.
- **Failure to review records.** In **case vignette 6.2** (twenty-eight-year-old male with three recent attempts) and in **case vignette 3.3** (fifty-eight-year-old male stepped down after denial), clinicians ignored critical past history. Prior attempts are among the most powerful predictors of suicide (Large, *et al.* 2017; Carter, *et al.* 2017).
- **Failure to document or communicate findings** to custody staff, which leaves front-line officers unaware of risk and unable to act.
- **Falsified documentation.** Courts have viewed fabricated or backdated notes as clear evidence of deliberate disregard.

Both clinical and legal standards emphasize that **thoroughness, not minimal questioning or a checklist**, is the foundation of a defensible risk assessment.

CASE VIGNETTE 6.2—CURSORY EVALUATION DESPITE MULTIPLE RECENT SUICIDE ATTEMPTS

A 28-year-old White male was admitted to state prison after making three suicide attempts in the ninety days prior to his admission, including overdose, wrist cutting, and an attempted hanging. Despite this critical recent history, the evaluating clinician performed only a cursory assessment. The recent suicide attempts were not meaningfully considered in the formulation of risk, and the detainee was cleared for housing in the general population without referral for ongoing psychiatric care or placement on heightened monitoring.

Risk and Contributory Factors

- **Multiple suicide attempts** within ninety days prior to incarceration
- **Use of varied and escalating methods**: overdose, cutting, hanging
- **Lack of comprehensive psychiatric assessment** at intake
- **Clinician's failure** to integrate history into risk formulation
- **Absence of referral** for ongoing psychiatric care
- **Placement** in general population without monitoring

Recent suicide attempts are among the strongest predictors of future suicidal behavior (Large, *et al.* 2017; Carter, *et al.* 2017).

"A history of suicide attempts is the single-most-reliable predictor of future risk. Ignoring it is not clinical judgment—it is negligence."

3. **Failure to Obtain Collateral Information**

   Correctional officers interact with inmates daily and are often the first to observe changes in behavior—withdrawal, agitation, isolation, or verbal hints. Families may also alert staff about acute risk. Failing to gather or act upon these observations is a recurring error and one that has repeatedly figured in litigation.

4. **Premature Discontinuation of Suicide Watch**

   Prematurely removing inmates from suicide precautions, without step-down monitoring or a clear safety plan, is another critical failure. **Case 6.2** illustrates this problem: despite expressing adamant suicidal intent only days earlier, the inmate was stepped down from acute care after a vague denial and died within twenty-four hours. Guidelines emphasize that discontinuation of precautions must be justified by a **thorough reassessment and protective measures** (National Commission on Correctional Health Care, 2018).

CASE VIGNETTE 6.3—INADEQUATE RISK ASSESSMENT, PREMATURE REMOVAL FROM WATCH, AND TRANSFER TO LOWER CARE

A White male in his late fifties was admitted to jail in early winter. Intake screening flagged multiple suicide risk factors: prior suicide attempts, psychiatric hospitalizations, ongoing depression, and psychotic symptoms. He told staff plainly that, if left alone in his cell, he would attempt hanging.

Staff initially placed him on high suicide precautions. A psychiatrist evaluated him, diagnosed a psychotic disorder and a substance-use disorder, began medication, and ordered fifteen-minute observation checks. Over the next several days, the detainee repeatedly expressed hopelessness, helplessness, and a continuing intent to kill himself. Staff described him as impulsive, unstable, and not readily redirectable.

Despite these ongoing and escalating indicators, the psychiatrist documented, during a cold midwinter period, that the patient "denied current ideation," concluded he was no longer at acute risk, discontinued suicide watch, and transferred him to a lower level of custodial care.

Risk and Contributory Factors

- **Multiple historical risk factors**: prior attempts and psychiatric hospitalizations
- **Current presenting symptoms**: depression, psychotic symptoms, and explicit statement of intent
- **Substance-use disorder**, comorbidity
- **Impulsivity** and poor impulse control
- **Seasonal/contextual risk** (early-winter isolation, which can exacerbate despair)
- **Clinical reversal** based on a brief "denial" despite persistent behavioral indicators.
- **Removal from heightened observation** and transfer to lower supervision while risk markers persisted

Cross References

- **Chapter 4 (Suicidal Behaviors):** Importance of method and expressed intent as predictors
- **Chapter 5 (Vulnerable Inmates):** Effect of comorbid psychotic and substance-use disorders on suicide risk.
- **Chapter 6 (Screening and SRA):** How dynamic risk requires repeated assessments and cautious clinical judgment
- **Chapter 7 (Observation Practices):** Risks of prematurely discontinuing suicide precautions and downgrading monitoring
- **Chapter 12 (Liability and Oversight):** Courts scrutinize clinical decisions that contradict observable behavior.

A single, brief denial during evaluation should never override repeated behavioral indicators of imminent risk. Clinical decisions to discontinue precautions and reduce supervision must be based on

consistent, observable improvement—not a single statement—and should be documented with corroborating behavioral evidence.

"Clinical reversals based on a single 'I'm fine' can be lethal—sustained behavior, not lone denials, must drive safety decisions."

From a legal standpoint, this was a textbook example of **deliberate indifference**: a qualified professional, aware of substantial risk factors, consciously disregarded them and prematurely discharged the patient from protective status. The settlement underscores the central lesson: **thoroughness, comprehensiveness, and caution are the pillars of a defensible SRA.**

5. **Evaluator Qualifications and Training**

   The adequacy of an SRA depends heavily on the evaluator. Ideally, psychiatrists, psychologists, or licensed clinicians trained in correctional-suicide prevention should conduct these assessments. In some facilities, however, contracted crisis workers with limited familiarity with correctional norms and risk factors perform evaluations. Attorneys frequently probe clinician **credentials, training records, and knowledge of facility policy.** Inadequately trained evaluators pose both clinical dangers and significant legal liability.

   In summary, the problems identified in SRAs reveal systemic weaknesses that go beyond individual clinical lapses. They include **absent or inadequate assessments, superficial questioning, poor documentation, failures in communication, premature discontinuation of precautions, and use of underqualified evaluators.** Together, these failures demonstrate that SRA is not merely a clinical formality but a **core standard of care** in correctional settings. Every aspect of the process—thoroughness, duration, information gathering, documentation, communication, and evaluator competence—becomes critical when examined under the lens of litigation.

CONCLUSION

Effective suicide prevention in correctional settings begins with screening and suicide risk assessment. Intake evaluations must be thorough, dynamic, and supported by structured tools that consider history, behavior, and context. Repeated assessments are essential during periods of heightened vulnerability, such as segregation, psychiatric crisis, or after traumatic events. Denial of suicidal intent should never outweigh corroborating risk factors. When facilities fail to assess and respond adequately, preventable deaths and legal liability follow. Conversely, consistent, evidence-based screening not only protects vulnerable inmates but also demonstrates due diligence, reducing exposure to costly litigation and judicial scrutiny.

REFERENCES

1. Carter, Gregory, Alison Milner, Kathryn McGill, Jane Pirkis, Nav Kapur, and Matthew J. Spittal, 2017. "Predicting Suicidal Behaviors Using Clinical Instruments: Systematic Review and Meta-analysis of Positive Predictive Values for Risk Scales." *BMJ Open* 7 (3): e014979. https://doi.org/10.1136/bmjopen-2016-014979
2. Daniel, Anasseril E. *Suicide in Jails and Prisons: Preventive and Legal Perspectives.* 1106 Design, Inc., Phoenix, AZ, 2022
3. *Estelle v. Gamble*, 1976. 429 U.S. 97.
4. *Farmer v. Brennan*, 1994. 511 U.S. 825.
5. Large, Matthew M., Christopher J. Ryan, Gregory Carter, and Navneet Kapur. "Can We Usefully Stratify Patients According

to Suicide Risk?" *BMJ* 359 (2017): j4627. https://doi.org/10.1136/bmj.j4627

6. National Commission on Correctional Health Care (NCCHC), 2018. *Standards for Mental Health Services in Correctional Facilities.* Chicago: NCCHC.
7. Obegi, Joseph H. 2021. "How Common Is Recent Denial of Suicidal Ideation among Ideators, Attempters, and Suicide Decedents? A Literature Review." *General Hospital Psychiatry* 72: 92–95. https://doi.org/10.1016/j.genhosppsych.2021.07.009

CHAPTER 7

STAYING AHEAD OF CRISIS—MONITORING, TREATMENT, AND EMERGENCY MANAGEMENT

INTRODUCTION

Suicide prevention in correctional facilities requires more than policies on paper—it requires constant vigilance in daily practice. Once an individual enters custody, the risk of self-harm increases substantially, particularly in the first days of detention. Critical steps such as **screening** and **suicide risk assessment** identify vulnerabilities, but these efforts are effective only if followed by **consistent, careful monitoring and intervention.**

Correctional officers (COs) and mental health (MH) professionals share responsibility in this domain. Monitoring is not a passive act; it is an **active, ongoing process** that requires observation, communication, judgment, and rapid response when signs of risk emerge. When lapses occur—whether through inattentive checks, reliance on malfunctioning equipment, or disregard of policies—they often become the focal point of litigation. Courts have repeatedly interpreted failures in monitoring as evidence of **deliberate indifference** to an inmate's serious medical need (Daniel, 2022; Hayes, 2010).

This chapter examines how monitoring functions at three critical levels:

1. **Correctional officers' monitoring** through rounds and direct observation
2. **Mental health professionals' monitoring and follow-up** through assessments, MSRs ("kites"), and continuing clinical care
3. **Special settings** such as solitary confinement and video surveillance, where monitoring presents unique challenges

ARREST AND BOOKING

The **arrest-and-booking process** is the first point of formal contact between an at-risk individual and correctional staff. At this stage, arrestees often present with acute intoxication, withdrawal, or emotional crises, all of which elevate suicide risk. Arrest reports typically include observable factors such as intoxication, bizarre behavior, or suicidal statements.

Examples of suicidal behaviors at arrest include:

- Walking into traffic
- Attempting to jump from a moving patrol car
- Threatening suicide with a firearm
- Taking a hostage while threatening to kill both self and others
- Dousing oneself with gasoline and attempting self-immolation

In some facilities, suicide-screening questionnaires explicitly ask the arresting officer whether the individual appeared suicidal at the time of arrest. **Failure to convey this impression has been the basis of litigation**, as in *Gordon v. Kidd* (11th Cir. 1992), where the court recognized that ignoring obvious suicidal behavior at booking could support a deliberate-indifference claim.

CASE VIGNETTE 7.1—HOLDING-CELL NEGLECT

A twenty-four-year-old African-American male, intoxicated with fentanyl, expressed suicidal thoughts at booking. He displayed early signs of withdrawal but was left unmonitored in a holding cell for several hours before planned transfer to the infirmary. Although policy required fifteen-minute checks, no officer was assigned. The detainee was under only video surveillance, but no one actively monitored the feed. He waved repeatedly at the camera before removing his shirt, fashioning a ligature, and hanging himself from the light fixture.

Risk and Contributory Factors

- **Acute intoxication with fentanyl** and early-withdrawal signs (physiologic and psychological destabilization)
- **Failure to perform a suicide risk assessment** at intake despite clear indicators
- **Passive, unattended video surveillance** (monitoring without active personnel), producing a false sense of security
- **Extended time in holding cell pending transfer** (delay to infirmary), when closer clinical supervision was required
- **Removal of clothing (created ligature from shirt)**—access to means facilitated by unsupervised holding
- **Systemic staffing/triage failure:** policy existed (fifteen-minute checks) but no operational assignment/enforcement

"Video watched from a desk is not the same as eyes at the cell—unattended surveillance and unassigned checks turn a solvable crisis into a preventable death."

CASE VIGNETTE 7.2—PLASTIC-BAG ASPHYXIATION

A 47-year-old White female was arrested for stealing a police van and placed in a holding cell at a detention center. She was left unattended for hours with a plastic lunch bag. Surveillance footage later revealed she made several attempts to ingest the bag. She was eventually found unresponsive on the floor, cyanotic, and pulseless. Emergency responders initiated resuscitation, and she was transported to a university hospital, where she died days later.

Risk and Contributory Factors

- **Unusual arrest circumstances** (stealing a police van) indicating possible acute psychiatric disturbance or impulsivity
- **No timely medical or psychiatric assessment**, despite unusual behavior at arrest
- **Placement in holding cell without continuous supervision**, leaving her unmonitored for hours
- **Provision of unsafe item** (plastic lunch bag) in a restricted environment, creating a clear opportunity for self-harm.
- **Repeated ingestion attempts visible on video** but unnoticed or ignored until collapse.

"Even the most ordinary object—a lunch bag—can become a lethal instrument when supervision is absent and risk is ignored."

Both cases illustrate how **inadequate monitoring at intake and holding**—even in the presence of surveillance equipment—can result in preventable deaths and subsequent litigation.

MONITORING

The **National Commission on Correctional Health Care (NCCHC)** standards underscore the importance of direct observation: "Inmates on suicide precautions are observed at staggered intervals not to exceed fifteen minutes for those at moderate risk, and continuously for those at acute risk. Documentation of such observation must be accurate, contemporaneous, and subject to supervisory review" (NCCHC 2018).

This standard reflects the principle that monitoring must be **active, unpredictable, and well-documented.**

Despite clear policies, failures in monitoring remain a recurring theme in suicides and subsequent lawsuits. Common failures include:

- **Rote welfare checks** conducted mechanically, without meaningful observation
- **Failure to confirm life and breathing**, leading to inmates being overlooked when unresponsive
- **Blocked or covered cell windows** not addressed by officers
- **Overreliance on video surveillance** without real-time monitoring
- **Inadequate supervision in booking/holding areas**, where detainees are acutely vulnerable

Litigation Implications

Courts consistently view failures in monitoring as evidence of **deliberate indifference** when policies exist but are ignored in practice. Litigation often highlights:

- Missed fifteen-minute or hourly checks
- False documentation of rounds never performed
- Ignoring visible distress signals (e.g., waving at cameras, verbal threats)
- Failing to intervene when policies required escalation

These failures allow plaintiffs to argue that staff **knew of and disregarded a serious risk**, satisfying the high bar for constitutional liability.

Correctional Officers: Practical Guidance

For correctional officers, monitoring must be concrete, actionable, and consistent. The following practices reduce suicide risk and provide legal protection:

- **Observe at staggered intervals** (not predictable routines).
- **Confirm life and breathing** during each check.
- **Address blocked windows immediately**—require removal of towels, papers, or clothing.
- **Use both sight and sound**—watch posture and movement, and listen for distress.
- **Engage briefly with the inmate** when feasible ("Are you okay?").
- **Document precisely**—note time, behavior, and any changes.
- **Convey concerns promptly** to supervisors and MH staff.
- **Never falsify logs**—false entries have been pivotal in lawsuits.
- **Check the environment** for hazards (anchor points, contraband, makeshift nooses).
- **Respond to family warnings** seriously, and escalate as policy requires.

These steps operationalize NCCHC standards and protect officers and facilities from negligence claims.

Monitoring by Mental Health Professionals

Mental health staff play a different but equally critical role in ongoing monitoring. Their duties include:

- Reviewing **Medical Service Requests (MSRs or "kites")**, which often contain early warning signs. Failure to review or act on MSRs has been cited in litigation (Daniel, 2022)
- Conducting **follow-up assessments** after suicide-watch placement or discharge. Premature release without adequate review has been linked to preventable deaths.
- Collaborating with COs to ensure **two-way communication** about behavior changes.

Common pitfalls for MH staff include:

- Overreliance on denial of suicidal ideation
- Inadequate documentation of risk assessments
- Failing to review prior psychiatric and incarceration records
- Ignoring staff or family concerns
- **Ignoring Medical Services Requests (kites)**: Inmates often request help in writing when verbal access is limited; disregarding these kites has been central to litigation.
- **Premature release from suicide watch**: Taking denial of suicidal ideation at face value, without weighing past attempts and risk factors
- **Inadequate communication with officers**: Clinicians failing to document and share findings, leaving custody unaware of the inmate's status.

- **Insufficient reassessment**: Failing to perform timely follow-ups after acute episodes or environmental stressors such as transfers, parole denials, or assaults.
- **Failure to review history**: Not considering prior suicide attempts, psychiatric admissions, or medication use when evaluating current risk.

Cross References

Monitoring and Follow-Up Failures by Mental Health Professionals
Earlier chapters also reveal a recurring pattern of mental health staff missing critical opportunities for monitoring, follow-up, and timely intervention. These lapses often become central allegations in litigation:

- **Chapter 5 (Case Vignette 5.1)** Twenty-one-year-old Marine with PTSD: VA records documented recent high-risk behavior, and psychiatrists had previously assessed him as at moderate-to-high acute risk. Despite these indicators, when a jail officer noted a makeshift noose in his cell, mental health staff were not notified, and no reassessment occurred. The lack of coordinated follow-up and clinical monitoring was a key point in the lawsuit.
- **Chapter 5 (Case Vignette 5.2)**—Inmate with schizophrenia in a large urban jail: Mental health alerts were not properly entered, and psychiatric staff never reviewed bizarre behaviors documented at booking. Clinicians missed opportunities to transfer him to a psychiatric unit and, instead, left him in general population, where he ultimately hanged himself. The case highlighted the consequences of failure to monitor a known severely mentally ill inmate.

- **Chapter 6 (Case Vignette 6.2)**—Fifty-eight-year-old male with multiple past suicide attempts: Despite five prior attempts, repeated psychiatric hospitalizations, and ongoing hopelessness, a psychiatrist prematurely discontinued suicide watch after accepting the inmate's denial of ideation at face value. The absence of thorough reassessment and continued monitoring was cited as reckless disregard in the lawsuit.
- **Chapter 6 (Case Vignette 6.3)**—Twenty-seven-year-old male in segregation, recent sexual assault: A therapist falsified records, marking "no mental health complaints" despite the inmate's documented trauma and recent PREA incident. No suicide risk assessment was performed, and he was left unmonitored until he hanged himself. In litigation, falsified monitoring records became pivotal evidence against the provider.
- **Chapter 8 (Case Vignette 8.4)**—Angela White, keep-on-person [KOP] medication overdose: Intake screening documented a prior suicide attempt, yet no suicide risk assessment was conducted. Mental health staff failed to reassess after her placement on KOP medication, a policy error that allowed her to accumulate lethal doses of verapamil. This lack of follow-up was central to the Sixth Circuit's analysis of deliberate-indifference claims.

In these cases, failures by mental health professionals involved premature discharge from suicide watch, ignoring obvious risk factors, failing to reassess after new stressors (e.g., sexual assault, withdrawal), and even falsifying documentation. From a litigation standpoint, courts viewed these lapses as evidence that clinicians either failed to use their best professional judgment or consciously disregarded an inmate's serious medical need.

MEDICAL SERVICES REQUESTS ("KITES"): MISSED WARNINGS AND LITIGATION RISKS

Medical Services Requests (MSRs), often called "kites," are one of the most common ways incarcerated individuals communicate health and mental health concerns to staff. Inmates who are reluctant to speak directly with officers or clinicians may use kites to express distress, request medication, or report suicidal thoughts. Because of their accessibility and documentation value, kites are a front-line tool in suicide prevention—but also a frequent source of liability when mishandled.

From a preventive standpoint, kites serve as an early-warning system. Inmates may reveal suicidal ideation, worsening depression, withdrawal symptoms, or medication problems in writing before these concerns become visible to staff. NCCHC standards emphasize that requests relating to mental health or suicide risk must be triaged and addressed without delay.

From a legal standpoint, kites are powerful evidence. In litigation, plaintiffs' attorneys frequently point to ignored or delayed kites as proof of deliberate indifference. The argument is simple but persuasive: the inmate reached out for help, and the system failed to respond. Courts have repeatedly found that a pattern of disregarding written requests for care—particularly those mentioning self-harm—may rise above negligence to constitutional violation (Cohen, 2020).

Common Pitfalls in Handling Kites

1. Dismissal as routine—Suicide-related content is misclassified as "non-urgent."

2. Delays in response—Staff may take days or weeks to act, even when urgent issues are raised.
3. Improper screening—Correctional staff or non-clinical personnel may decide the request does not require mental health review
4. Lost or missing kites—Paper slips may be misplaced or destroyed, leaving no record of the inmate's request
5. Lack of follow-up—Responses may be logged, but no actual clinical evaluation occurs.

Best Practices for Prevention and Legal Protection

1. **Written policy:** Establish clear guidelines requiring same-day triage of all kites raising mental health or suicide concern
2. **Training:** Ensure officers and nurses recognize suicide-related language and understand the importance of escalation.
3. **Tracking:** Use electronic systems to log and monitor kites, reducing the risk of loss.
4. **Clinical oversight:** Require that mental health professionals, not custody staff, review all suicide-related kites
5. **Documentation:** Record not only the receipt of the kite but also the clinical outcome (e.g., evaluation, suicide-watch placement, medication adjustment).

By treating kites as urgent clinical signals rather than routine paperwork, facilities can protect vulnerable inmates while strengthening their legal defense. Properly handled, kites can demonstrate responsiveness and diligence; mishandled, they become Exhibit A in deliberate-indifference litigation.

SOLITARY CONFINEMENT

Solitary confinement or administrative segregation is one of the most challenging environments for suicide prevention. Inmates isolated for twenty-two to twenty-three hours daily experience elevated risks of depression, anxiety, psychosis, and suicide.

The **American Psychiatric Association (APA)** adopted a position statement in 2011, reaffirmed in 2017, opposing prolonged segregation of individuals with serious mental illness, due to the risk of decompensation and suicide (APA 2017).

Monitoring Standards

Best practice discourages placing suicidal inmates in solitary confinement. If segregation is unavoidable, monitoring must be intensified:

- **Daily evaluations** for high-risk inmates
- **Weekly checks** for others
- Incorporation of **Suicide Risk Assessments (SRA)** into monitoring

CASE VIGNETTE 7.3—SOLITARY-CONFINEMENT SUICIDE

A fifty-seven-year-old male serving a long sentence for a violent crime was found hanging in his segregation cell in 2017. He used an electrical cord anchored overhead. He had asthma, COPD, and prior head injury but no history of psychiatric treatment or suicide attempts. Two days earlier, he reportedly used synthetic cannabinoids ("Spice"). Investigations revealed that segregation rounds were not properly performed.

The lawsuit alleged that correctional officers failed to conduct required rounds, allowed him access to hazardous materials, and placed him in solitary confinement in violation of his rights under the Eighth Amendment.

Risk and Contributory Factors

- **Age and medical fragility:** Fifty-seven-year-old male with asthma, COPD, and prior head injury
- **Long sentence for violent crime:** possible hopelessness and institutional despair
- **Recent use of synthetic cannabinoids ("Spice"):** associated with agitation, impulsivity, and psychiatric instability
- **Housing in segregation:** isolation and reduced observation increased vulnerability
- **Failure of staff supervision:** segregation rounds were not properly performed or documented
- **Environmental hazard:** presence of an electrical cord overhead that could serve as an anchor point.

"In segregation, lapses in rounds turn isolation into abandonment—and unattended hazards into lethal opportunities."

VIDEO SURVEILLANCE: MERITS AND PITFALLS

Video surveillance has become a common feature in correctional facilities, often promoted as an additional safeguard against suicide. While cameras can enhance oversight, they also present serious limitations if used as a substitute for direct human monitoring.

Merits

- **Continuous coverage:** Cameras provide constant visibility of cells and common areas, particularly useful where staffing levels are low.

- **Rapid detection (when actively monitored):** Live monitoring can allow for quick recognition of suicide attempts or medical emergencies.
- **Documentation and accountability:** Recordings provide an objective record of events, showing whether required monitoring was performed and assisting in litigation defense.

Pitfalls

- **False reliance:** Cameras cannot replace in-person supervision. In several cases (see Chapter 7, Case 7.1; Chapter 5, Case 9), inmates died by suicide while on video observation because no staff actively watched the feed.
- **Blind spots:** Just as poor sightlines in cell design create dangerous gaps (see Chapter 8), cameras may miss critical angles or be intentionally obstructed by inmates.
- **Delayed response:** In Chapter 7's holding-area cases, video existed, yet staff failed to notice behaviors in real time. This reflects a dangerous reliance on technology without sufficient human attention.
- **Legal liability:** Courts and plaintiff attorneys often argue that reliance on cameras without active monitoring constitutes *deliberate indifference*. Video feeds prove that staff had the ability to observe risk but neglected to act.

Best Practices

- Treat cameras as **supplemental tools**, not primary monitoring systems.
- Require **real-time monitoring** whenever video observation is part of suicide prevention protocols.

- Conduct **daily functionality checks** to ensure cameras are working properly, similar to best practices for intercoms (see Chapter 8).
- Mandate **documentation and logging** of live monitoring, and preserve recordings for accountability.
- Always integrate cameras with **direct observation and suicide risk assessments**. If an inmate is high-risk, video coverage must support—but never replace—fifteen-minute or constant watch per NCCHC standards.

Video surveillance, when implemented correctly, strengthens suicide prevention and provides evidentiary protection for staff and facilities. However, when staff rely solely on cameras, without active observation, the system itself becomes a liability.

INTERVENTION AND TREATMENT

Effective suicide prevention in correctional settings does not end with screening or monitoring. It requires active, sustained intervention and treatment aimed at reducing risk, stabilizing the inmate, and providing the medical and mental health support necessary to prevent self-harm. The intervention process is multidisciplinary, involving psychiatrists, psychologists, nurses, correctional officers, and administrators, each with distinct but complementary roles. When carried out with diligence and empathy, interventions can mitigate acute crises, reduce long-term vulnerability, and protect both inmates and facilities from preventable tragedies and legal liability.

Crisis Intervention

Crisis intervention represents the **immediate response to an inmate expressing suicidal ideation or engaging in suicidal behavior**. It requires rapid assessment, supportive counseling, and temporary safety measures such as placement in a safe cell. In many facilities, correctional staff initiate referrals when they observe acute distress, bizarre behavior, or self-harming acts.

Key elements of crisis intervention include:

- **Rapid stabilization** through one-on-one interaction, reassurance, and active listening
- **Environmental safety**, ensuring removal of dangerous objects and ligature points
- **Referral to qualified mental health professionals**, who determine whether suicide watch, psychiatric evaluation, or crisis-stabilization unit (CSU) placement is warranted.

Legal implications are significant. When crisis signs are ignored, or when referrals are delayed, facilities may face liability for deliberate indifference. Courts have emphasized that **failing to take suicidal statements seriously or delaying psychiatric evaluation** constitutes a deviation from the standard of care.

Crisis Stabilization Units (CSUs)

Many larger jails and prisons have developed **Crisis Stabilization Units** designed to house inmates in acute psychiatric or suicidal crises. These units offer constant observation, structured therapeutic interventions, and immediate access to psychiatric services. Placement in a CSU reflects best practice when suicide risk cannot be managed in general-population housing.

From a legal standpoint, **failure to provide access to crisis stabilization** has been highlighted in litigation as a breach of constitutional duty. Facilities that lack specialized units must rely on transfer agreements with external psychiatric hospitals, and failure to initiate such transfers when clinically indicated can form the basis of negligence or deliberate-indifference claims.

Medication Management

Medication is often central to suicide prevention, whether treating depression, anxiety, psychosis, or withdrawal syndromes. Key considerations include:

- **Accuracy of Medication Administration Records (MAR):** Errors in recording or administering medication can compromise safety and serve as evidence in lawsuits.
- **Directly Observed Therapy (DOT):** Essential for inmates at risk of hoarding or diverting medication.
- **Hoarding and Bartering:** Correctional facilities must maintain strict protocols, as hoarded pills have been implicated in overdose suicides.
- **Involuntary Medication:** In rare cases, refusal of essential psychiatric medication may require involuntary treatment. In *Washington v. Harper* (1990), the Supreme Court held that inmates may be involuntarily medicated if they pose a danger to themselves or others, provided procedural safeguards are in place. This ruling remains directly relevant to suicide prevention when refusal of treatment places the inmate at imminent risk.

Legal implications: *Steele v. Shah* (1996) highlighted liability when abrupt discontinuation of medication contributed to an inmate's suicide. Courts examine whether prescribing practices, continuation of treatment, and monitoring adhered to accepted standards.

Medication-Assisted Treatment (MAT) for Substance Withdrawal

Substance withdrawal—especially opioids and alcohol—represents one of the most dangerous precipitating factors for suicide in custody. **MAT protocols**, using medications such as buprenorphine or methadone, reduce withdrawal symptoms and lower suicide risk.

The Substance Abuse and Mental Health Services Administration (SAMHSA) strongly endorses MAT as best practice in correctional settings. Yet, many jails remain reluctant to provide MAT, citing diversion risks or resource limitations. Courts increasingly view this reluctance as a deviation from the standard of care, particularly when withdrawal leads to self-harm or suicide attempts.

EMPATHY AND UNDERSTANDING

Beyond protocols, risk assessments, and treatment algorithms lies the **human encounter** between the inmate in crisis and the professionals charged with their care. Inmates entering a suicidal crisis often experience **overwhelming fear, shame, anxiety, and despair**, compounded by the loss of autonomy that incarceration brings. For some, the cell itself intensifies feelings of hopelessness, while interactions with staff may be perceived as judgmental, indifferent, or even hostile.

Mental health professionals and correctional nurses play a unique role in countering these perceptions. A calm, empathic presence can de-escalate agitation, restore dignity, and communicate that the individual's suffering is seen and taken seriously. Even small acts—sitting at eye level, using the inmate's name, listening without interruption—can create a bridge to trust. Research consistently shows that **perceived empathy and respect from staff** reduces suicidal ideation and increases treatment engagement in correctional settings (Liebling, 2011; Daniel, 2022).

Correctional officers, often first responders in crisis, also influence outcomes. When officers acknowledge concerns respectfully, follow through on requests for help, and avoid dismissive remarks, they contribute to a culture of safety rather than one of neglect.

From a legal perspective, courts rarely evaluate the tone of interactions. Instead, they focus on observable actions or omissions. Yet, in practice, empathy enhances clinical judgment and prevention. An inmate who feels heard is more likely to disclose suicidal thoughts honestly, giving staff the information necessary for safety and treatment planning.

Ultimately, suicide prevention in correctional settings requires more than compliance with standards. It demands a **blend of clinical skill, operational diligence, and human compassion**. Recognizing inmates not just as case files or risk profiles but as people in pain, is both a moral obligation and a practical necessity in reducing suicide risk.

EMERGENCY MEDICAL MANAGEMENT

Timely life-saving measures are critical once a suicide attempt is underway. Correctional staff are often the first responders, and courts scrutinize their training and actions.

Core Practices

- **"Man down" response:** Immediate recognition and response to emergencies.
- **Cardiopulmonary resuscitation (CPR):** All staff should be certified and recertified regularly.
- **Automated external defibrillators (AEDs):** Readily available in housing units; designed for use by laypersons.

- **Cut-down tools:** Located in housing areas, enabling rapid release of hanging inmates.
- **Tourniquets and bleeding-control kits:** To address self-inflicted lacerations.

Case Law

- ***Estate of Clark v. Walker* (2017):** Liability when officers failed to respond promptly to an inmate in medical distress.
- ***Mata v. Saiz* (2005):** Failure to provide timely medical care constituted deliberate indifference.

CASE VIGNETTE 7.4—DELAY IN LIFESAVING MEASURES

A forty-year-old African-American male pretrial detainee was found hanging in his cell five days after arrest. Staff stood by without administering CPR until EMS arrived. Despite a pulse being present, the delay contributed to his death. The facility had no suicide prevention policies, and officers were not trained in CPR. The case was settled for millions of dollars.

Risk and Contributory Factors

- **Pre-trial status:** Recent arrest (five days in custody) is associated with heightened suicide risk.
- **Lack of suicide prevention policy:** No structured procedures were in place for identifying or responding to risk.
- **Untrained staff:** Correctional officers had not been trained in CPR or emergency response.
- **Failure of immediate intervention:** Staff stood by, waiting for EMS, despite a detectable pulse.

- **Critical delay in life-saving measures:** Failure to provide basic resuscitation until EMS arrival contributed directly to death.
- **Institutional liability:** Multimillion-dollar settlement reflects systemic negligence.

"When officers are untrained and policies absent, hesitation replaces action—and preventable deaths become inevitable."

CASE VIGNETTE 7.5—DELAY IN LIFESAVING MEASURES

A twenty-seven-year-old Native-American male in a state prison sustained a fatal vascular injury after cutting his forearm with a sharpened weapon. Although the inmate was bleeding heavily, the responding officer delayed calling for help for five minutes. Another officer applied a tourniquet only after an additional delay. He died despite later medical intervention. Allegations focused on inadequate emergency training and delayed response.

Risk and Contributory Factors

- **Young adult (twenty-seven years old)** with increased impulsivity and vulnerability
- **Native-American ethnicity:** overrepresented in correctional-suicide statistics, reflecting broader systemic inequities
- **Use of weaponized contraband:** access to a sharpened object in custody highlights lapses in security and searches
- **Severe vascular injury** from forearm laceration leading to rapid blood loss
- **Delay in calling for help (≈5 minutes):** critical time lost in initiating emergency response

- **Additional delay before tourniquet applied:** officers hesitated in delivering immediate life-saving intervention
- **Inadequate emergency training:** staff were ill-prepared for catastrophic-bleeding scenarios
- **Institutional liability:** allegations centered on deficient training and preventable delays

"In emergencies, minutes matter—delays in calling for help or applying aid transform survivable injuries into fatal outcomes."

CONCLUSION

Monitoring, intervention, and emergency medical management are the linchpins of suicide prevention in correctional facilities. Failures in these domains transform recognized risks into fatal outcomes and open the door to litigation. Correctional officers and mental health professionals must work in concert, guided by established standards, reliable policies, and empathy for those in crisis. The case vignettes in this chapter illustrate that **preventable suicides are rarely the product of a single lapse but rather a convergence of systemic failures**—failures that facilities must confront to protect lives and defend against liability.

REFERENCES

1. American Psychiatric Association. 2017. *Position Statement on Segregation of Prisoners with Mental Illness.* Washington, DC: American Psychiatric Association.
2. Daniel, Anasseril E. 2022. *Suicide in Jails and Prisons: Preventive and Legal Perspectives*, Phoenix, AZ: 1106 Design Inc.
3. *Estate of Clark v. Walker*, 865 F.3d 544 (7th Cir. 2017).
4. *Estelle v. Gamble*, 429 U.S. 97 (1976).

5. *Farmer v. Brennan*, 511 U.S. 825 (1994).
6. *Gordon v. Kidd*, 971 F.2d 1087 (4th Cir. 1992).
7. Hayes, Lindsay M. 2010. *National Study of Jail Suicide: 20 Years Later.* Washington, DC: U.S. Department of Justice, National Institute of Corrections.
8. Liebling, Alison, and Helen Arnold. 2004. *Prisons and Their Moral Performance: A Study of Values, Quality, and Prison Life.* Oxford: Oxford University Press.
9. *Mata v. Saiz*, 427 F.3d 745 (10th Cir. 2005).
10. National Commission on Correctional Health Care (NCCHC). 2018. *Standards for Mental Health Services in Correctional Facilities.* Chicago: NCCHC.
11. Substance Abuse and Mental Health Services Administration (SAMHSA). *Medications for Opioid Use Disorder Treatment Improvement Protocol* (TIP 63). Rockville, MD: SAMHSA, 2018
12. *Steele v. Shah*, 87 F.3d 1266 (11th Cir. 1996).
13. *Washington v. Harper*, 494 U.S. 210 (1990).

CHAPTER 8

HOUSING, CELL FIXTURES, CONTENTS, AND SUPPLIES—OFTEN-OVERLOOKED FACTORS

"Courts have made clear: when hazards are visible and policies ignored, a cell becomes not just a place of confinement but the scene of liability."

—Anasseril E. Daniel

INTRODUCTION

M*ore than 90 percent of suicides* in correctional facilities occur inside a cell (Hayes, 2010). This stark reality obligates administrators to provide a safe environment—one devoid of obvious means of self-harm and simultaneously responsive to inmates in acute distress. A safe environment does not mean only the absence of hazards; it must also include protective mechanisms, such as functioning intercoms and emergency-communication devices that allow inmates in crisis to reach staff promptly.

When facilities ignore obvious environmental risks, or when staff fail to conduct regular, competent safety audits, courts frequently interpret such lapses as deliberate indifference. Litigation in this area is often fueled not by subtle oversights, but by persistent, well-documented hazards that are preventable and repeatedly identified in both research and case law (Dye, 2010; Fruehwald, *et al.* 2017; Gold 2017; Daniel, 2022).

The most effective prevention strategies integrate **suicide-resistant housing design** (fixtures, furnishings, supplies, and clothing) with **operational diligence**, including unpredictable yet thorough cell checks and regular safety audits. Even the best-designed cell cannot guarantee safety without staff vigilance. In fact, in more than 93 percent of the cases I have consulted, hanging was the method of suicide—most often accomplished with ligatures secured to available tie-off points inside the cell.

Another overlooked factor is **cell visibility**. Poor sightlines, blind spots created by architectural design, or intentional obstruction of cell-door windows (e.g., by hanging towels or papers) are common in litigation following suicide. Research has shown that structural changes—such as suicide-resistant fixtures, improved sightlines, and housing units designed for continuous monitoring—are strongly correlated with reductions in suicide rates (Liebling, 2004; Liebling, *et al.* 2017).

CASE VIGNETTE 8.1—SPRINKLER-HEAD ANCHOR POINT

A thirty-five-year-old woman with a history of psychiatric care, including two hospitalizations and a prior suicide attempt by overdose, was detained in a municipal lockup. She also had a strong family history of suicide. In the days preceding her death, she experienced an acute psychotic break.

On the day of her suicide, she displayed manic behavior, and, because of statements indicating self-harm potential, she was placed in a "suicide observation" cell. Hours before her death, an officer observed her standing on the toilet for an extended period but assumed she was adjusting her hair or makeup and failed to intervene.

She was later discovered hanging from a knotted bedsheet anchored to a defective sprinkler head. A suicide note was also found. Post-investigation revealed that officers had failed to inspect the cell for obvious anchor points and that the sprinkler head had been in disrepair for years. Administrators admitted they knew of the problem and had repaired sprinkler heads in adjacent hallways but not in this cell; nevertheless, this cell was not removed from suicide-observation designation. The case was settled for a substantial sum.

Risk and Contributory Factors

- **Individual vulnerabilities**: prior psychiatric hospitalizations, history of suicide attempt by overdose, and strong family history of suicide
- **Acute psychotic break**: heightened risk due to loss of reality testing and impaired judgment
- **Recent warning signs**: manic behavior and explicit statements of self-harm potential
- **Observation failures**: officer saw her standing on the toilet for extended periods but misinterpreted the behavior and failed to intervene
- **Environmental hazard**: defective sprinkler head left unrepaired for years, providing a tie-off point
- **Failure to audit environment**: staff neglected to inspect and remediate obvious hazards in designated suicide-observation cells
- **Administrative negligence**: leadership admitted knowledge of defective fixtures and failed to remove the cell from observation use

- **Institutional liability**: settlement for substantial sum reflected the preventable nature of the death.

"An observation cell is only as safe as its weakest fixture—leaving a defective sprinkler head in place made tragedy inevitable."

LIGATURE MATERIALS AND TIE-OFF POINTS

Ligature materials commonly include **facility-issued sheets and towels**, which can be torn or used whole to fashion nooses. Other documented ligatures include:

- Electrical cords
- Telephone cords
- Sports bras
- Velcro straps from suicide smocks
- Standard clothing (shirts, T-shirts, jumpsuits)
- In rare cases, toilet paper twisted and stiffened with paste

TABLE 1

Suicide Risk for Cell Components

CELL COMPONENT	TYPICAL SUICIDE RISK	COMMON PROBLEM
Bed Frame	High	Horizontal bars, gaps, or exposed edges allow ligature attachment
Shelves and Desks	Moderate-High	Sharp edges and protrusions; structural gaps for tying
Windows	High	Bars or grilles used for hanging; broken glass as a cutting tool

CELL COMPONENT	TYPICAL SUICIDE RISK	COMMON PROBLEM
Doors	High	Gaps in door frames, handles; meal slots used for hanging
Ventilation Grilles	High	Holes and edges provide anchor points
Plumbing Fixtures	High	Pipes, taps, and exposed fittings used for ligature
Lighting Units	Moderate	Bulbs or covers removed to access wiring or sharp edges
Hooks/Hangers	High	Fixed hooks used for hanging
Mirror	Moderate	Broken glass for cutting
Toilet	Low-Moderate	Rare ligature point

FACILITY-ISSUED RAZORS

Besides sheets and mattresses, **disposable razors** present a critical risk. Inmates have used jail-issued razors to inflict lethal injuries to the neck and arms. Courts have found that providing unrestricted access to razors, without adequate supervision, may constitute **deliberate indifference**—especially when:

- The inmate had a known history of self-harm.
- Staff failed to comply with issuance/return policies.
- Alternatives (such as supervised barber services or electric razors) were not used.

Two cases highlight this:

- *Lord v. Beahm*, 7th Cir. (2020)—Court found negligence where razors were distributed without adequate supervision.

- *Strickler v. McCord*, D. Del. (2009)—Similar allegations when razors were improperly managed.

Following the 2022 suicide of **Michael Nieves** at Rikers Island, news coverage revealed that the **New York City Department of Corrections** allowed razors under a "minimum standards" policy issued by the Board of Corrections. After Nieves' death, this practice was heavily criticized.

Mishara and Martin (2019) found that strict **issue-return systems** significantly reduce self-harm. Even minimal access to sharp instruments increases risk of serious injury or death.

CASE VIGNETTE 8.2—RAZOR SUICIDE

A high-profile sixty-year-old detainee, facing a sexual assault charge, committed suicide by slitting his jugular vein with a **jail-issued disposable razor** on his third day of detention.

Despite being under close observation, officers did not discover him for several hours because he had concealed himself under a blanket. He died from exsanguination due to massive blood loss.

Background review revealed:

- He had previously attempted suicide at home by overdose immediately before detention.
- He was admitted to a hospital for suicidal ideation the day prior to booking.
- At intake, he screened positive for psychiatric instability but was nevertheless allowed access to a razor.

Risk and Contributory Factors

- **Recent and escalating suicidal behavior:** prior suicide attempts by overdose and recent hospitalization for suicidal ideation the day before booking
- **Positive intake screen for psychiatric vulnerability** that was not honored in decisions about access to sharp objects
- **Access to a jail-issued disposable razor** despite documented recent ideation and hospitalization—failure of contraband, control-and-issuance protocols
- **Concealment under bedding:** detainee hid under a blanket, exploiting predictable observation patterns and visual blind spots
- **Rapid, catastrophic method (jugular laceration):** chosen method produced fatal exsanguination in a short time frame, reducing chance of rescue
- **Breakdown in clinical-to-custody communication:** treatment/hospitalization the day prior apparently did not result in heightened precautions or temporary restriction of sharp implements

"Access to a tiny blade turned hours of unnoticed concealment into irreversible loss—control of means and erring on the side of restriction must follow recent ideation."

CELL DESIGN, VISIBILITY, AND SIGHTLINES

Poor sightlines and obstructed visibility remain recurrent factors in custodial suicides. In numerous cases I have consulted, inmates intentionally **covered their cell-door windows** with towels, papers, or clothing, effectively preventing officers from observing their condition.

In many of these cases, officers either failed to insist on removal of coverings or ignored institutional policies requiring unobstructed observation. Courts have repeatedly found that failure to enforce such policies may constitute deliberate indifference.

Research supports that **improved architectural design** and **strict enforcement of unobstructed sightlines** reduce suicide risk. Liebling (2004) and Liebling, *et al.* (2017) documented correlations between suicide-resistant design, reduced blind spots, and improved monitoring practices.

INTERCOMS AND SUICIDE PREVENTION

Intercom systems serve as a **critical safety net** in correctional environments. Their functions include:

1. **Direct line to staff**—allowing inmates to signal distress or call for help.
2. **Emergency alerts**—enabling staff to summon immediate medical or mental health response.
3. **Continuous access**—ensuring inmates have 24/7 means of contacting staff between rounds.
4. **Psychological reassurance**—reducing feelings of isolation when help feels immediately available.

CASE VIGNETTE 8.3—INTERCOM FAILURE

A fifty-nine-year-old man, detained on alcohol-related charges, was placed on withdrawal protocol. His long-term partner called the jail, warning staff that he had threatened suicide. The officer receiving the call ignored the message.

Three days later, he was found by his cellmate with a ligature fashioned from clothing. The cellmate pressed the **intercom**, but it did not work—it had been **intentionally muted by staff** to avoid being disturbed. He banged on the door for help; officers arrived too late.

Although paramedics briefly restored a pulse, the man died in the hospital two days later.

Risk and Contributory Factors

- **Known risk history:** detainee's partner called to warn staff he had threatened suicide, but the message was ignored
- **Alcohol-withdrawal protocol:** a period of heightened vulnerability with increased risk for impulsivity, depression, and self-harm
- **Failure of staff communication:** no follow-up assessment or precautions after receiving the external warning call
- **Technology failure:** intercom muted by staff to avoid being disturbed, eliminating a critical lifeline for emergency alerts
- **Cellmate's delayed ability to summon help:** reliance on banging on the door wasted precious minutes
- **Delayed staff response:** officers did not intervene in time, and although paramedics restored a pulse, delayed care contributed to death days later
- **Institutional indifference:** intentional disabling of safety equipment demonstrates disregard for detainee safety

"An intercom is a lifeline—muting it for convenience turned a warning cry into silence and a preventable death."

Intercom Case Law

CASE	CIRCUIT	YEAR	CORE ISSUE	INTERCOM RELEVANCE
Boncher v. Brown County	7th	2001	Jail suicide	Alleged failure to respond to inmate's intercom calls
Lemire v. CDCR	9th	2013	Prison suicide	Known broken intercoms and unmonitored video systems
Estate of Hocker v. Walsh	10th	1994	Jail suicide	Inoperative intercom prevented staff response

Best Practices—Intercom

- Conduct **daily testing** of all intercom units.
- Require **immediate acknowledgment** of every call.
- Integrate intercom use into suicide prevention **training curricula**.
- Document and review all intercom-related incidents.

KOP (KEEP-ON-PERSON) MEDICATIONS

Allowing incarcerated persons to retain and self-administer selected medications can improve adherence and reduce operational burden during med-pass. However, KOP programs also elevate risk of overdose, hoarding, trading, and diversion—especially when psychotropics or cardiovascular agents with high lethality in overdose are kept in-cell. Research and practice reviews in correctional settings consistently link medication access/misuse to self-harm incidents and suicides, underscoring the need for tight eligibility criteria and exclusions for high-risk drugs (Marzano, *et al.*, 2016; Mishara and Martin, 2019; Daniel, 2021).

Why facilities adopt KOP:

- Improves adherence for stable, low-risk patients (e.g., inhalers, topical agents, select non-lethal meds).
- Reduces congestion and staffing load during med rounds.
- Increases patient autonomy for non-psychiatric, low-risk regimens.

Why KOP is risky:

- Overdose potential when lethal medications are stockpiled.
- Diversion/trading in units, undermining safety and clinical integrity.
- False sense of safety when no formal competency or suicide risk check precedes KOP enrollment.

Best-practice safeguards:

- Risk-stratified policy that clearly excludes high-lethality medications (certain calcium-channel blockers, TCAs, lithium, some antipsychotics/benzodiazepines, opioids) from KOP
- Competency-to-self-administer assessment (documented) before KOP approval and periodic re-checks
- KOP vs. DOT split: Reserve Directly Observed Therapy (DOT) for patients with serious mental illness, active suicidality, cognitive impairment, recent attempts, or suspected diversion
- Inventory controls: blister packs, pill counts, tamper-evident packaging, and immediate discontinuation of KOP upon risk elevation
- Clinical triggers to revoke KOP—acute mood destabilization, new SI, intoxication/withdrawal, disciplinary behavior tied to hoarding or trading

- CQI audits: regular chart and incident reviews to ensure policy adherence and prompt remediation

Practice note: In my experience and literature review, there are no cases where **KOP status alone**—without broader policy or clinical failures—was the sole basis of liability. Courts typically weigh facility-policy design, implementation, exclusions, and clinical decision-making, not KOP in isolation.

CASE VIGNETTE 8.4—ANGELA WHITE (*ANDREWS V. WAYNE COUNTY*)

Profile:

- Individual: Female, thirty-nine years old; no prior criminal history; Master's degree; respected community standing
- **Clinical background**: Major depressive disorder (recurrent), substance use (heroin/cocaine positive at booking), multiple medical comorbidities (e.g., seizure disorder, chronic pain)
- Medication regimen at issue: Included verapamil (a calcium-channel blocker with high lethality in overdose)

Custody course and KOP decision:

- At intake, she reported a prior suicide attempt but denied current SI.
- She was placed on self-administration (KOP) for some medications, including verapamil; psychiatric meds were watch-take
- Within the second night of detention, she ingested ~45 tablets of verapamil under KOP and was found unresponsive
- She was transported to the hospital and died shortly after; the medical examiner ruled suicide by overdose (toxicology: verapamil 1100 ng/mL)

Key failures (clinical and policy):

- No formal suicide risk assessment beyond intake screening, despite prior attempt and active depressive disorder
- No competency-to-self-administer determination documented prior to KOP approval
- Policy lacked explicit high-risk medication exclusions (e.g., verapamil) and did not require DOT for high-risk patients
- Missed opportunity to place all psychiatric/cardiovascular high-risk meds on DOT, given her risk profile

Litigation and appellate posture:

- Family filed 42 U.S.C. §1983 deliberate-indifference and *Monell* claims, plus state-law negligence/wrongful death, alleging constitutionally inadequate medical care and unsafe KOP policy.
- Policy change: Shortly after the case was filed, the county revised its KOP policy to exclude verapamil and other high-lethality agents from **self-administration.**
  - Sixth Circuit decision: (*Andrews v. Wayne County*, 2020). The Court affirmed in part and reversed in part:
  - *Monell* (municipal) liability: Insufficient evidence of a county-wide policy/custom causing the violation—no municipal liability
  - Individual-staff §1983 claims: The record, viewed favorably to plaintiffs, could support a jury finding of deliberate indifference against certain medical staff who knew of serious risk yet permitted KOP access to a lethal medication without adequate safeguards. Those claims were allowed to proceed.

- Teaching points:
  - Appellate courts may reject *Monell* without dismissing individual deliberate-indifference claims.
  - Post-incident policy change (e.g., removing verapamil from KOP) telegraphs what should have been in place beforehand.
  - KOP cannot be "one-size-fits-all"; high-risk meds = DOT; high-risk patients = DOT + enhanced monitoring

Table 2

Medications/ Risk/Lawsuits

HIGH-RISK MEDICATIONS	LITIGATION-RISK/POLICY GUIDANCE
Tricyclic antidepressants: e.g., Amitriptyline	High lethality in overdose Multiple lawsuits tied to suicide due to hoarding Generally contraindicated for KOP DOT recommended
SSRIs, e.g., Fluoxetine	Moderate overdose risk, a few lawsuits KOP may be allowed for low-risk inmate DOT for high-risk inmates
Benzodiazepines, e.g. Diazepam, Clonazepam	High abuse, diversion risk A few lawsuits alleging KOP Not recommended for KOP
Opioid Pain Medications, e.g., Oxycodone, Methadone	High lethality Lawsuits after they were permitted in KOP DOT recommended, with counts

HIGH-RISK MEDICATIONS	LITIGATION-RISK/POLICY GUIDANCE
Antipsychotics, e.g., Clozapine, Olanzapine	Toxic in overdose Lawsuits claiming negligence Failure in allowing stockpiling Not suitable for KOP Must be given DOT
Anti-Hypertensives, e.g., Verapamil, Propranolol	Documented causes of cardiac collapse Claims of deliberate indifference for allowing KOP
Anticonvulsant, e.g., Valproate, Carbamazepine	Hepatic and Neurotoxicity Claims of medical negligence DOT recommended for high-risk inmates
Over-the-counter medications, e.g., Acetaminophen	Overdose/Suicide from hoarding Claims of medical negligence KOP recommended, with monitoring

TELEPHONE CORDS AND SUICIDE

Telephone cords are a well-documented suicide hazard. Hayes (2010) identified them as one of the most common ligatures in U.S. jails. Modern best practice is to eliminate or shorten cords, or to use cordless wall-mounted handsets. International standards recommend suicide-resistant phones as part of environmental design (Konrad, Daigle, Daniel, *et al.*, 2006).

Facilities—not private contractors—hold primary authority over the **location** and **safety specifications** of telephones. Companies such as GTL and Securus install equipment under contract, but design and placement decisions rest with correctional authorities. Courts have consistently held that **correctional facilities bear primary duty of care.**

CASE VIGNETTE 8.5—*BRADLEY FARMER V. MISSOURI BOARD OF POLICE COMMISSIONERS AND SECURUS TECHNOLOGIES, INC.*

Procedural History

In *Farmer v. Missouri Board of Police Commissioners, et al.*, the estate of Bradley Farmer filed suit in the U.S. District Court, alleging violations of constitutional rights under 42 U.S.C. §1983, as well as negligence and wrongful death claims. Defendants included the Kansas City Board of Police Commissioners, correctional staff, and Securus Technologies, the private contractor that provided inmate telephone services. The plaintiff alleged that Farmer's suicide by hanging with a jail telephone cord was a foreseeable hazard that should have been prevented. Summary judgment was ultimately granted in favor of Securus, while certain claims against correctional officials and the Board proceeded.

Facts

Bradley Farmer, an adult-male detainee, was housed in a Kansas City detention facility where traditional wall-mounted telephones with standard cords were available for inmate use. He died by suicide, using one of these cords as a ligature. His estate brought claims asserting that the presence of telephone cords in cells and dayrooms constituted a known suicide hazard.

The lawsuit alleged that Securus, as the contracted telephone provider, bore liability for failing to provide "suicide-resistant" equipment and that the correctional facility acted with deliberate indifference by permitting the continued use of corded telephones, despite established correctional standards discouraging them.

As part of the litigation, expert testimony emphasized the role of correctional authorities—not private vendors—in determining the design, installation, and location of phones within secure environments. It was documented that the facility administration, not Securus, dictated placement, length, and physical specifications of cords under the service contract.

Issues

1. Did the presence of telephone cords in the facility constitute deliberate indifference to Farmer's known risk of suicide?
2. Could liability be extended to a private vendor (Securus) for installing and maintaining equipment according to the facility's specifications?
3. Was the duty of care to eliminate or modify suicide hazards in housing units primarily that of the correctional-facility administration?

Court's Analysis and Holding

The Court recognized that telephone cords are a well-documented suicide hazard in correctional facilities, with multiple national studies and best-practice guidelines recommending cord-free or shortened models (see Hayes, 2010; Konrad, Daigle, Daniel, *et al.*, 2006). However, the Court concluded that liability for environmental design and safety rested with the correctional facility—not the telephone vendor.

Summary judgment was granted for Securus Technologies. The Court found that Securus merely supplied and maintained equipment under the terms and specifications provided by the facility and bore no independent duty to redesign equipment beyond contract obligations.

Expert-Consultant Perspective

I served as an expert witness for the defense (Securus). I emphasized in my opinions:

- The well-established principle that facilities, not vendors, control environmental-design decisions, including the placement and safety of telephones.
- National correctional standards clearly identify telephone cords as suicide hazards, placing responsibility on correctional leadership to mitigate risks.
- From a risk management standpoint, vendors cannot unilaterally alter equipment without facility authorization, and liability for failing to implement suicide-resistant modifications rests with the facility administration.

Outcome

- **Securus Technologies:** Dismissed from the case on summary judgment.
- **Correctional Defendants:** Case allowed to proceed on claims of deliberate indifference and negligence.

Risk Management Takeaways

1. **Primary Responsibility Lies with Facilities**—Correctional agencies, not private vendors, determine equipment specifications, placement, and safety modifications.

2. **Telephone Cords Are Known Hazards**—Best practice is to install cordless or shortened-cord phones in secure housing areas or to limit access through controlled locations.
3. **Policy Enforcement Is Critical**—Even if safe design is implemented, failure to enforce monitoring policies can result in liability.
4. **Vendor Role Is Secondary**—Vendors operate under contract specifications; liability claims against them are difficult to sustain unless they deviate from agreed terms.
5. **Documentation of Safety Decisions**—Facilities should maintain clear records of environmental audits and suicide prevention decisions regarding telephones and similar equipment.

CONCLUSION

The environment of incarceration is often overlooked in suicide prevention, yet it is central to risk. **Sprinkler heads, ligature materials, razors, poor sightlines, malfunctioning intercoms, and telephone cords** have all been repeatedly implicated in suicides and lawsuits.

Many suicides are preventable with:

- **Suicide resistant cell design** (fixtures, furnishings, and supplies)
- **Strict policies** regarding razor distribution, medication control, and observation
- **Operational vigilance** in enforcing unobstructed visibility and functioning intercoms
- **Systemic accountability**, where facilities—not contractors—bear ultimate responsibility

Andrews v. Wayne County adds a crucial dimension: **KOP medication policies** can convert a "suicide-resistant" housing unit into a pharmacy of high-toxicity means if not tightly controlled. Post-booking and during early custody, facilities should presume restriction—not privilege—for KOP, especially for cardiovascular and psychoactive agents, and require clinician review, custody coordination, and documentation before any KOP is granted.

Proactive environmental audits, strict control of issued items and KOP medications, and reliable emergency systems save lives and **sharply reduce liability**. Courts view failures in these areas as evidence of **deliberate indifference**. Conversely, well-implemented policies and consistent staff diligence not only save lives but also protect facilities.

REFERENCES

1. *Andrews v. Wayne County*. 930 F.3d 404 (6th Cir. 2020)
2. *Boncher v. Brown County*. 272 F.3d 484 (7th Cir. 2001)
3. Daniel, Anasseril E, "A Multidimensional Approach to Suicide Prevention in Jails and Prisons: The Best Defense Against Liability Lawsuits," *Journal of Operational Psychiatry* 2021
4. Dye, M.H. "Deprivation, Importation, and Prison Suicide: Combined Effects of Institutional Conditions and Inmate Composition," *Journal of Criminal Justice* 38, no. 4 (2010): 796–806
5. *Estate of Hocker v. Walsh*. 22 F.3d 995 (10th Cir. 1994)
6. *Farmer v. Kansas City Board of Police Commissioners*, No. 4:20-cv-00801 (W.D. Mo. 2022)
7. Fruehwald, S., Frottier, P., Matschnig, T., and Eher, R. "The Relevance of Prison Environment for Prison Suicide." *Crisis* 28, no. 3 (2017): 122–130

8. Gold, G. H. R., "Jail Suicide Litigation and Facility Liability," *Journal of Law and Psychiatry* 35, no. 2 (2017): 155–174
9. Hayes, Lindsay M., *National Study of Jail Suicide: 20 Years Later* (2010), Washington, DC: U.S. Department of Justice, National Institute of Corrections
10. Konrad N., Daigle M. S., Daniel A. E., Dear, G., Frottier P., Hayes L. M., Kerkhof A., Liebling A., and Sarchiapone M., "Preventing suicide in prisons. Part II: International comparisons of suicide prevention services in correctional facilities." *Crisis: The Journal of Crisis Intervention and Suicide Prevention* 28, no. 3 (2007): 122–130. https://doi.org/10.1027/0227-5910.28.3.122
11. *Lemire v. California Department of Corrections and Rehabilitation.* 726 F.3d 1062 (9th Cir. 2013).
12. Liebling, Alison, *Prisons and Their Moral Performance: A Study of Values, Quality, and Prison Life* (2004). Oxford: Oxford University Press.
13. Liebling, A., Arnold, H., and Straub, C., *Suicide: Monitoring, Prevention, and Design*. Cambridge: Cambridge University Press, 2017
14. *Lord v. Beahm.* 952 F.3d 902 (7th Cir. 2020)
15. *Marquin de Portillo v. County of San Diego.* No. 3:21-cv-00065, S.D. Cal. (2021)
16. Marzano, L., Hawton, K., Rivlin, A., Smith, E. N., Piper, M., and Fazel, S., "Prevention of Suicidal Behavior in Prisons." *Crisis* 31, no. 1 (2010): 21–31
17. Mishara, Brian L., and Martin N. "Suicidal and Self-Injurious Behaviors in Correctional Settings," *Journal of Correctional Health Care* 25, no. 2 (2019): 155–168.
18. *Russell v. City of Mount Vernon.* 708 F.2d 52 (2d Cir. 1983)
19. *Strickler v. McCord.* 611 F. Supp. 2d 559 (D. Del. 2009)

CHAPTER 9

THE CRITICAL FIRST TWO WEEKS OF INCARCERATION—RISKS, REALITIES, AND LESSONS

INTRODUCTION

The first two weeks of incarceration represent the most dangerous period for suicide in correctional facilities. Research consistently shows that the risk of suicide is disproportionately elevated during this early stage, especially in local jails and lockups, where individuals may be experiencing the immediate psychological shock of arrest, intoxication, withdrawal, or pretrial uncertainty. Hayes's national studies of jail suicide documented that nearly half of suicides in jails occur within the first week of confinement, with the highest concentration in the first twenty-four to seventy-two hours (Hayes 2010). A Bureau of Justice Statistics review found that nearly one-third of jail suicides occur within the first three days—and almost half within the first two weeks (Mumola, 2005). A systematic review by Fazel, Ramesh, and

Hawton (2017) confirmed that the immediate post-admission period represents the peak of vulnerability.

Key factors associated with suicides during this period include:

- **Recent arrest or new charges**, often perceived as devastating by the detainee
- **Withdrawal from alcohol, opioids, or stimulants**, producing agitation, anxiety, or psychosis
- **Disorientation and fear**, especially among first-time detainees
- **Isolation in holding or intake areas**, often with insufficient monitoring
- **Humiliation and shame**, particularly when offenses involve domestic violence or sexual allegations

Courts have held that correctional agencies must anticipate these risks and implement structured screening, monitoring, and intervention protocols. Facilities that lack policies, training, or consistent supervision for new admissions have repeatedly faced litigation following suicides in the earliest stages of incarceration.

PROFILE OF HIGH-RISK DETAINEES

Based on research and extensive consulting experience, several demographic and clinical characteristics repeatedly surface in suicides during early incarceration:

- **Age:** Young adults (younger than twenty-five) and elderly men (older than fifty-five) show disproportionate risk.
- **Gender:** Men comprise the majority of cases, though women in custody *attempt* suicide at higher rates.
- **Race/Ethnicity:** White detainees are overrepresented in jail-suicide statistics.

- **Socioeconomic Status:** Marginalized individuals with histories of poverty, unemployment, and unstable housing are particularly vulnerable.
- **First-Time Arrestees:** Those experiencing the criminal justice system for the first time may respond with fear, hopelessness, and impulsivity.
- **Substance-Use Disorders:** Alcohol and opioid abuse are especially dangerous, given the dual risks of intoxication and withdrawal.
- **Mental Illness:** Mood disorders, psychotic illnesses, and prior psychiatric hospitalizations are consistently linked to suicide risk.
- **Prior Suicide Attempts:** The single-most-predictive factor, particularly if recent or near-lethal.

From a clinical and legal perspective, detainees presenting with multiple overlapping vulnerabilities (e.g., first arrest + intoxication + history of prior suicide attempt) must be treated as high acuity cases requiring immediate and sustained monitoring.

PSYCHOLOGICAL REACTIONS TO ARREST AND DETENTION

Arrest and incarceration represent profound psychological stressors. Common reactions include acute anxiety, humiliation, hopelessness, and fear of the future. Detainees may experience "catastrophic thinking"—believing that their life is effectively over because of the arrest. Those falsely accused may feel especially distressed, perceiving their confinement as unjust and unbearable.

Immigration detainees under Immigration and Customs Enforcement (ICE) custody have also exhibited elevated suicide risk. Reports by advocacy organizations and government watchdogs document suicides linked to prolonged detention, language barriers, cultural isolation, and inadequate mental health care (Human Rights Watch 2018). While ICE detention is distinct from criminal incarceration, the same principles of screening, monitoring, and treatment apply.

LOCKUPS: HIGH-RISK SETTINGS FOR SUICIDE

Lockups are short-term detention facilities operated by municipal police departments or county-sheriff's offices, where individuals are held immediately following arrest and prior to arraignment, bail hearing, or transfer to a jail or prison. The Bureau of Justice Statistics defines lockups as facilities designed for stays of less than seventy-two hours, although, in practice, detainees may be held longer due to administrative or court delays (Mumola, 2005). Unlike jails, which are typically administered by counties and subject to state and national correctional standards, lockups often fall under the administrative control of local police departments with varying levels of oversight, staffing, and funding.

Administrative structure and funding

Because lockups are generally operated at the municipal level, budgetary support often depends on local tax revenues. This limited funding affects staffing levels, suicide prevention training, and the availability of mental health services. As a result, suicide prevention policies in lockups are frequently less developed and inconsistently applied compared to larger jail systems.

Common system problems in lockups

Drawing from both empirical research and my consulting caseload, I have observed recurrent systemic problems in lockups that contribute to suicides:

1. **Lack of stringent monitoring at booking**—detainees may be left unobserved for long periods.
2. **Poor or absent screening**—suicide risk questionnaires may be skipped or applied superficially.
3. **Lack of clear suicide prevention policies**—many lockups operate without structured guidelines.
4. **Budgetary constraints**—inadequate funding limits staffing and mental health resources.
5. **Poor staffing ratios**—officers may be tasked with multiple responsibilities, reducing vigilance.
6. **Insufficient staff training**—officers are often not adequately trained in suicide prevention.
7. **Easy accessibility to means**—poorly maintained cells with obvious ligature points or unsafe materials.

These systemic weaknesses amplify risk and create fertile ground for litigation when suicides occur.

CASE VIGNETTE 9.1—LOCKUP SUICIDE: IGNORED ACUTE CRISIS

A thirty-four-year-old female was arrested for destruction of property, assault, and domestic disturbance. At the time of her arrest, she was intoxicated and highly agitated; she displayed erratic behavior. She resisted arrest, fought during transport, and remained combative in the lockup. Officers forcibly removed her shirt after she attempted to use it dangerously and placed her in a holding cell.

While in the cell, she repeatedly yelled at officers to shoot her, fought with staff, and asked EMT personnel to send her to a psychiatric hospital. Surveillance footage showed her banging on the door, calling for help, and acting in visible distress. Officers did not respond. She then removed her sports bra, tied it around her neck and to the cell doorknob, and hanged herself. She was found unresponsive minutes later.

Her history included multiple psychiatric hospitalizations, bipolar disorder, conduct disorder, polysubstance abuse, ADHD, and a strong family history of abuse and suicide. Despite this background and her obvious acute crisis, she was left unmonitored.

This case settled for millions of dollars. The family filed both a **§1983 deliberate-indifference claim** and a state wrongful-death claim. The combination of her psychiatric history, acute crisis, and staff disregard of visible behaviors created overwhelming evidence of negligence and deliberate indifference.

Risk and Contributory Factors

- **Extensive psychiatric history:** multiple hospitalizations, bipolar disorder, conduct disorder, ADHD, polysubstance abuse, and strong family history of suicide
- **Acute intoxication and agitation:** presented in severe emotional and behavioral crisis at arrest and transport
- **Expressed suicidal intent:** repeatedly asked officers to shoot her and requested psychiatric hospitalization from EMTs
- **Observable behavioral red flags:** yelling, banging, visible distress caught on surveillance but ignored.
- **Improper observation:** placed in a holding cell without continuous monitoring despite known crisis and suicide risk

- **Environmental hazard:** access to a sports bra and doorknob created a lethal ligature opportunity
- **Failure to intervene:** staff disregarded overt pleas for help and suicidal statements
- **Institutional liability:** 42 U.S.C. §1983 deliberate-indifference and wrongful-death claims resulted in a multi-million-dollar settlement.

"Visible crisis demands action—ignoring pleas and suicidal threats in lockup can turn minutes of neglect into years of litigation."

COMPARATIVE COMMENTARY: ***Colburn v. Upper Darby Township***
The contrast between Case Vignette 9.1 and ***Colburn v. Upper Darby Township*** (1991) highlights the role of multiple risk factors in shaping liability.

In *Colburn*, the detainee's only apparent risk factor was **alcohol intoxication**. Despite her eventual suicide using a concealed firearm, the court concluded that officers could not reasonably have predicted her imminent suicide. The Third Circuit held that liability required proof that staff knew or should have known of a "particular vulnerability to suicide." The presence of intoxication alone, without additional observable signs, was insufficient.

By contrast, **Case Vignette 9.1 involved converging and obvious risk factors:** intoxication, agitation, repeated suicidal statements, prior psychiatric history, and observable erratic behaviors. Staff ignored clear cries for help, failed to enforce monitoring protocols, and disregarded evidence of acute distress. From a legal perspective, courts are far more likely to find *deliberate indifference* when staff fail to act in the face of multiple, obvious vulnerabilities rather than a single, ambiguous factor.

This comparison demonstrates how courts differentiate between **speculative risk** and **obvious risk**, with liability hinging on whether staff reasonably should have foreseen the suicide and acted to prevent it.

US MARSHALS SERVICE

The U.S. Marshals Service (USMS) plays a unique role in the correctional landscape. It is responsible for housing individuals in federal custody who are awaiting trial, sentencing, or transportation to designated Bureau of Prisons (BOP) facilities. Because the Marshals do not operate their own detention centers, they contract with local jails, private prisons, and state facilities to house detainees. These intergovernmental agreements often create gaps in accountability when it comes to suicide prevention, since policies and staffing practices vary widely across facilities.

Research has shown that **suicide is a leading cause of death in short-term federal detention**, particularly within the first twenty-four to forty-eight hours of confinement (Hayes, 2010). Detainees held under USMS authority are especially vulnerable, because they are often in transit, housed in unfamiliar jails, and may not receive continuity of mental health care during transfer. These factors, combined with the variability of local-jail practices, place detainees at heightened risk for self-harm.

CASE VIGNETTE 9.2—U.S. MARSHALS TRANSFER: IGNORED WARNINGS AND LACK OF SCREENING

A young man in his early twenties was transported by the U.S. Marshals Service to a local jail while awaiting transfer to his home state to complete a one-year sentence for possession of marijuana.

During his first night in custody, he was housed in a **single-man cell.** Surveillance later revealed that he made repeated suicidal statements, including: "*I will be a dead ma*n" and direct pleas for the officers to take his life. Despite these clear warning signs, he was left unmonitored for extended periods.

That evening, he attempted suicide by fashioning a noose from a towel and tying it to the door handle inside his cell. He was discovered unresponsive and transported to a local hospital, where his urine screen tested positive for amphetamines.

The estate of the deceased filed a **civil-rights lawsuit** alleging deliberate indifference to his serious medical needs. Deposition testimony from detention officers revealed that none of the staff were properly trained in suicide risk recognition or prevention protocols. Moreover, the young man had never been screened for suicide risk upon his arrival at the jail.

From a clinical standpoint, the detainee was in a state of **acute mental health crisis**, exhibiting agitation, fear, and disorganized behavior. Officers misinterpreted his cries for help as aggression rather than distress. This misinterpretation, compounded by the absence of proper screening, referral, and monitoring, contributed directly to his preventable death.

Risk and Contributory Factors

- **Acute mental health crisis**: agitation, fear, and disorganized behavior on arrival
- **Explicit suicidal statements**: the detainee repeatedly said, "I will be a dead man" and begged officers to take his life
- **No suicide screening at intake**: transferred detainee was never evaluated for mental health risk despite obvious distress
- **Improper housing**: placed alone in a single-man cell without heightened precautions

- **Extended unmonitored periods**: left alone despite active, verbalized suicidality
- **Environmental hazard**: access to towel and low door handle created an anchor point for ligature
- **Staff-training deficiencies**: deposition revealed officers had no suicide-recognition or -prevention training
- **Misinterpretation of behavior**: staff viewed agitation and pleas as aggression instead of crisis, delaying intervention
- **Legal liability**: civil-rights lawsuit alleged deliberate indifference to serious medical needs; lack of training and screening were central claims

"When clear cries for help are misread as aggression, risk assessment fails—and liability follows."

Best Practices for U.S. Marshals Service and Contract Jails

To reduce the risk of suicide among detainees in U.S. Marshals custody, facilities should adopt the following practices:

- **Universal Screening at Intake**

  Every detainee transferred under Marshals custody should undergo suicide screening immediately upon arrival at the local jail. Screening should include both standardized instruments and officer observations, with follow-up questions to clarify risk factors.

- **Close Monitoring During High-Risk Periods**

  Because suicide risk peaks within the **first twenty-four to forty-eight hours of detention**, enhanced observation should be required for all new arrivals, including staggered checks, video monitoring, and direct staff interaction.

- **Training of Staff**
  Local jail officers and USMS contract staff should be trained to recognize verbal and behavioral signs of distress. Training should emphasize that yelling, agitation, or bizarre behavior may indicate acute psychiatric crisis rather than mere aggression.

- **Prohibition of High-Risk Housing Assignments**
  Single-cell placement should be avoided for detainees presenting acute mental health symptoms or suicidal ideation. When segregation is necessary, staff must increase observation and document safety checks consistently.

- **Rapid Referral to Mental Health Staff**
  Any detainee expressing suicidal thoughts, engaging in self-harm behavior, or showing significant changes in mood or behavior must be referred to qualified mental health professionals without delay.

- **Clear Lines of Accountability**
  The Marshals Service must ensure that intergovernmental agreements with local jails include detailed suicide prevention policies, compliance monitoring, and consequences for failure to adhere to federal standards.

- **Emergency Preparedness**
  All staff must be trained and equipped to initiate life-saving measures (CPR, AED use, hemorrhage control) immediately upon discovery of a suicide attempt. Delays in response have been central in litigation and settlements.

These best practices not only align with **Performance-Based Detention Standards (PBDS)** but also address the recurring themes in litigation: failure to screen, failure to monitor, and failure to intervene. Implementing them consistently across local jails and contract facilities is essential to protect detainees and reduce institutional liability.

DRUG-INTOXICATION AND -WITHDRAWAL RELATED SUICIDE

Drug and alcohol intoxication, as well as acute withdrawal, are among the most dangerous periods for incarcerated individuals—particularly within the **first two weeks of confinement**. Research consistently highlights alcohol, opioids, and methamphetamine as the most common substances linked to suicide in custody, while benzodiazepine withdrawal is a rarer but still recognized risk factor (Hayes, 2010; Fazel, *et al.*, 2017).

Suicide Risk during Withdrawal

Withdrawal often presents with physical symptoms—tremor, sweating, nausea, diarrhea, insomnia, headache—as well as psychological symptoms, including agitation, anxiety, depression, and confusion. These symptoms may increase vulnerability to suicidal behavior, especially if untreated or poorly managed. Importantly, incarcerated people frequently **conceal substance-use histories**, and denial of suicidal ideation during intake screening cannot be taken at face value if obvious withdrawal symptoms are present (Daniel, 2022).

Warning signs for suicide during withdrawal include:

- Severe agitation, irritability, or desperation
- Verbal statements expressing hopelessness or fear of withdrawal
- Requests for stronger medication or complaints of inadequate care
- Deteriorating physical state without appropriate medical intervention

CASE VIGNETTE 9.3—DRUG WITHDRAWAL: MISSED CLINICAL WARNINGS AND ISOLATION

A man in his mid-thirties, well known to local deputies for his chronic alcohol and opiate abuse, was arrested and confined to jail. During intake screening, he was reluctant to provide a complete history of his substance use, though he was already showing **clear withdrawal symptoms**—including perspiration, tremor, agitation, and complaints of severe headache.

Nursing staff placed him on an opioid-withdrawal protocol, using the **Clinical Opiate Withdrawal Scale (COWS)**. The scoring indicated escalating withdrawal symptoms, but he was given only symptomatic treatment and no medication-assisted treatment (MAT). Crucially, the nurse failed to contact the jail physician or obtain appropriate-medication orders.

By the third day of confinement, his symptoms worsened. He pleaded for more-effective treatment, but his requests were ignored. Instead, he was moved to an **isolation cell** with assistance from officers—despite visible withdrawal distress and their knowledge of his long-standing addiction.

While he denied suicidal ideation at intake and during the following days, he deliberately **concealed his prior suicide history**, which included multiple overdoses and a previous hanging attempt. Left untreated and unsupervised in isolation, he used available cell materials to hang himself.

This tragedy illustrates systemic failures: nursing staff *mismanaged medical withdrawal care*, correctional staff **ignored clinical warning signs**, and both groups failed to recognize how substance withdrawal can directly precipitate suicide.

Risk and Contributory Factors

- **Severe substance-use disorder:** long-standing alcohol and opioid abuse, with history of overdoses and a previous hanging attempt (concealed at intake)
- **Active withdrawal:** early signs—sweating, tremor, agitation, severe headache—documented but not addressed with evidence-based medication-assisted treatment.
- **Inadequate medical response:** nursing staff provided only symptomatic care, failed to contact the jail physician, and did not escalate as withdrawal worsened
- **Escalating distress ignored:** despite visible deterioration and pleas for better treatment, requests were disregarded
- **Improper housing:** moved to isolation cell during acute withdrawal, increasing psychological despair and reducing monitoring
- **Incomplete screening:** denial of suicidal ideation and omission of past suicide attempts led to false reassurance; no follow-up reassessment despite clinical red flags
- **Staff misinterpretation:** correctional staff underestimated withdrawal's suicide risk and did not initiate closer observation
- **Institutional liability:** systemic failures in withdrawal management and suicide monitoring resulted in a substantial legal settlement

Cross References

- **Ch. 5 (Vulnerable Inmates):** substance-use disorders and concealed histories are major early-custody risk factors
- **Ch. 6 (Screening and SRA):** importance of dynamic reassessment beyond initial intake when clinical status changes

- **Ch. 7 (Monitoring and Supervision):** need for enhanced observation during acute withdrawal or escalating medical distress
- **Ch. 8 (Housing Environment):** isolation cells heighten risk when combined with untreated withdrawal.
- **Ch. 12 (Risk Management):** Failure to follow withdrawal protocols and provide medication-assisted treatment is a frequent litigation trigger

"Withdrawal is a medical emergency—untreated distress can turn silence into suicide and negligence into liability."

Legal and Clinical Implications

Courts have repeatedly recognized substance withdrawal as a serious medical need under the Eighth Amendment. Failure to provide adequate withdrawal treatment or to protect detainees from obvious withdrawal-related suicide risk may constitute deliberate indifference.

Negligence or deliberate-indifference claims in withdrawal-related suicides often hinge on:

- **Failure to recognize withdrawal as a suicide risk factor.**
- **Failure to provide MAT** (e.g., methadone, buprenorphine, naltrexone), despite well-established clinical standards (Substance Abuse and Mental Health Services Administration [SAMHSA], 2020).
- **Improper placement in isolation cells,** where monitoring is minimal and means of self-harm may be available
- **Ignoring family warnings** or inmates' indirect statements about desperation or fear of withdrawal

Best Practices for Prevention

- **Universal Screening:** Intake protocols must include detailed inquiry about substance use, prior withdrawal episodes, and suicide attempts.
- **Medication-Assisted Treatment:** Facilities should follow SAMHSA guidelines in initiating MAT for opioid and alcohol withdrawal, rather than relying solely on symptomatic treatment.
- **Close Monitoring:** Individuals undergoing withdrawal should never be placed in isolation cells. They require enhanced observation and, when indicated, placement in a medical or crisis-stabilization unit.
- **Training:** Both medical and correctional staff must be trained to recognize withdrawal-related behavioral changes as potential suicide warning signs.
- **Accurate Documentation:** Withdrawal protocols, COWS scoring, and staff responses must be fully documented for continuity of care and legal protection.

CONCLUSION

The **first two weeks of confinement** remain the most dangerous period for suicide in correctional settings. Whether in **lockups**, during **transport under the U.S. Marshals Service**, or amid the challenges of **drug withdrawal**, the same themes repeat: screening is missed or poorly done, monitoring is inconsistent, mental health warning signs are ignored, and critical interventions are delayed. Each of the case vignettes in this chapter underscores how predictable failures in these high-risk environments translate into preventable deaths.

The message for correctional administrators and staff is clear: **suicide prevention during the earliest phase of detention is both**

a clinical and operational priority. From intake screening to withdrawal management, from supervision in holding cells to policies on isolation, every decision in this period carries heightened legal and human consequences.

Courts have consistently recognized suicide risk in early confinement, intoxication, and withdrawal as a **serious medical need** under the Eighth and Fourteenth Amendments. When correctional facilities fail to act on obvious warning signs, they open themselves not only to tragic outcomes but also to substantial liability for negligence and deliberate indifference.

The cases reviewed in this chapter demonstrate that **prevention is not complicated**—it requires adherence to basic standards: competent screening, vigilant monitoring, timely medical and psychiatric care, safe-housing decisions, and access to effective treatment for substance withdrawal. Where these practices are absent, lawsuits follow; where they are implemented consistently, lives are saved and liability is reduced.

In short, the **high-risk early-confinement period** is where suicide prevention and risk management converge most powerfully. Correctional systems that fail to recognize this window of vulnerability will continue to face needless deaths and costly litigation. Those that embrace best practices—rooted in training, accountability, and humane treatment—will protect both the people in their custody and the integrity of their institutions.

REFERENCES

1. *Colburn v. Upper Darby Township* (1991). 946 F.2d 1017 (3d Cir.).
2. Daniel, Anasseril E., *Suicide in Jails and Prisons: Preventive and Legal Perspectives.* (2022) Phoenix, AZ: 1106 Design, Inc.

3. Fazel, Seena, T. Ramesh, and Keith Hawton, 2017. "Suicide in Prisons: An International Study of Prevalence and Contributory Factors." *The Lancet Psychiatry* 4 (12): 946–952
4. Hayes, Lindsay M., *National Study of Jail Suicide: 20 Years Later.* (2010) Washington, DC: U.S. Department of Justice, National Institute of Corrections
5. Human Rights Watch. *Code Red: The Fatal Consequences of Dangerously Substandard Medical Care in Immigration Detention.* New York: Human Rights Watch, 2018
6. Mumola, Christopher J., 2005. *Suicide and Homicide in State Prisons and Local Jails.* Washington, DC: U.S. Department of Justice, Bureau of Justice Statistics
7. U.S. Department of Justice, Office of the Inspector General. *Review of the United States Marshals Service's Prisoner Detention and Care Program.* Washington, D.C.: DOJ OIG, 2017
8. U.S. Marshals Service. *Prisoner Operations Fact Sheet.* Washington, D.C.: USMS, 2021

CHAPTER 10

POLICIES, PROCEDURES, AND PRACTICE

INTRODUCTION

Written policies are the backbone of suicide prevention in correctional facilities. Accreditation agencies, state statutes, and federal-court rulings all demand that jails and prisons adopt policies addressing suicide risk. Yet, history shows that policy alone is not enough. Facilities may maintain manuals that look comprehensive on paper but fail to translate into daily practice. Courts have repeatedly ruled that what matters is not simply the existence of policies but whether staff actually implement them in the housing units, intake areas, and medical clinics where vulnerable inmates are held.

This chapter examines the evolution of suicide prevention policies in corrections, the common problems in their development and enforcement, and the widening gap between written standards and operational reality. Drawing from case law, national standards, and my consultation experience, I show how inadequate documentation, inconsistent implementation, and cultural resistance undermine prevention efforts and expose facilities to liability.

Finally, I propose a legally defensible framework—rooted in the NCCHC standards and informed by litigation outcomes—that can help facilities not only meet professional guidelines but also withstand legal scrutiny. Suicide prevention policies must be more than words on paper—they must become lived practices that protect inmates, support staff, and safeguard institutions against preventable tragedies and costly lawsuits.

HISTORY OF SUICIDE PREVENTION DEVELOPMENT AND THE STANDARD OF CARE

Over the past five decades, suicide prevention in correctional facilities has evolved from a neglected responsibility to a recognized standard of care. In the 1970s and early 1980s, inmate suicides were often treated as isolated tragedies, with little systemic response. That changed as class-action lawsuits and federal oversight highlighted the constitutional duty of correctional institutions to protect those in their custody.

The landmark Supreme Court decision in *Estelle v. Gamble* (1976) established that incarcerated individuals have a constitutional right to adequate medical care under the Eighth Amendment, extending later to mental health care. Soon after, federal appellate courts reinforced the principle that suicide prevention falls within this duty. In *Bowring v. Godwin* (1977), the Fourth Circuit explicitly recognized that prisoners are entitled to psychiatric and psychological treatment when medically necessary. The Court later clarified in *Farmer v. Brennan* (1994) that officials may be held liable for "deliberate indifference" when they disregard known risks, a principle that has become central in suicide-related litigation.

Parallel to these legal developments, professional organizations such as the National Commission on Correctional Health Care (NCCHC) and the American Correctional Association (ACA) issued standards requiring suicide prevention policies. Over time, core elements of these standards—including intake screening, housing assessments, suicide-watch procedures, staff training, and program evaluation—became widely accepted benchmarks of adequate care.

Today, suicide prevention is not an optional program but a mandated responsibility. Policies addressing suicide risk are now required by accreditation agencies, state law, and consent decrees arising from Department of Justice (DOJ) investigations. This shift has transformed suicide prevention into a defining measure of whether a facility meets its constitutional obligations. Yet, as this chapter demonstrates, the gap between written policy and actual practice remains one of the greatest challenges—and one of the most common sources of liability.

Key Milestones in Suicide Prevention Standards

- **1976—*Estelle v. Gamble*:** Supreme Court recognizes prisoners' constitutional right to adequate medical care, including mental health care.
- **1977—*Bowring v. Godwin*:** Fourth Circuit affirms that psychiatric treatment must be provided when medically necessary.
- **1980—Civil Rights of Institutionalized Persons Act (CRIPA):** DOJ gains authority to investigate systemic abuses in correctional facilities, including suicide prevention failures.
- **1994—*Farmer v. Brennan*:** Supreme Court defines "deliberate indifference" as the threshold for liability when staff ignore known risks.

- **1990s—Early DOJ Consent Decrees**: Mandated reforms to intake screening, suicide watch, and monitoring procedures.
- **1990s–2000s—NCCHC and ACA Standards**: Suicide prevention incorporated into accreditation requirements, including screening, housing, staff training, and program evaluation.
- **2000s–Present—Institutional Practice**: Suicide prevention recognized as a standard component of correctional healthcare and a frequent focus of litigation.

POLICIES ON PAPER VS. PRACTICE ON THE GROUND

Large and medium-sized jails often operate with comprehensive suicide prevention policies designed to meet accreditation standards such as those of the NCCHC or ACA. These policies typically address all critical elements—screening, training, suicide-watch procedures, housing, communication, and post-incident review.

By contrast, small rural jails and police lockups face significant challenges. With limited budgets, understaffing, and high turnover, they frequently struggle to implement comprehensive suicide prevention programs. In some cases, they operate with only rudimentary policies—or none at all. While these constraints are real and deserve recognition, the absence of policy or training remains a critical liability risk. Courts have consistently held that facilities must take reasonable preventive steps, regardless of size or resources. Even modest measures—such as intake screening, staff orientation on suicide warning signs, or clear emergency response procedures—can make a meaningful difference in both prevention and legal defensibility.

CASE VIGNETTE 10.1—DEATH IN POLICE LOCKUP WITHOUT SUICIDE PREVENTION POLICY

A twenty-eight-year-old White male died by hanging while in the custody of a police lockup. Prior to his arrest, he had been intoxicated with drugs and possibly alcohol, and displayed erratic behavior during transport. Upon arrival, he was placed in a cell equipped with a video-monitoring system; however, no one was actively monitoring the feed.

The detainee was in acute mental health crisis and exhibited clear signs of intoxication, making him a heightened risk for suicide. Despite this, he was placed in a standard cell without active supervision. The lockup had no comprehensive suicide prevention program in place. Its rudimentary "policy" was limited to restrictions on personal garments and amenities inside the cell. Critical elements identified by NCCHC standards—such as intake screening, risk assessment, suicide-watch procedures, staff-communication protocols, and emergency-response training—were absent.

As a result, staff had not received training on recognizing mental health symptoms or suicide warning signs. When the detainee was discovered hanging, officers lowered his body and noted that he still had a pulse. Yet paramedics were never contacted, and he soon succumbed to the hanging.

This case underscores a recurring liability theme in small lockups: the absence of a comprehensive suicide prevention policy. Larger and medium-sized jails may face lawsuits for noncompliance with existing policies, but small facilities that operate without any policy at all are especially vulnerable. Courts and plaintiffs' attorneys highlight these gaps as evidence that the facility disregarded widely known and preventable risks. In this instance, lack of monitoring, absence of staff training, and failure to summon emergency medical assistance compounded the liability exposure.

Lessons Learned

- Suicide prevention policies must extend beyond basic rules about clothing or cell amenities. They must align with NCCHC standards and include intake screening, housing considerations, staff training, suicide-watch procedures, and emergency-response protocols.
- Facilities relying on technology such as video monitoring must ensure active supervision; otherwise, such systems are ineffective and damaging in litigation.
- Every staff member, even in small rural facilities, requires at least minimal suicide prevention training, particularly in recognizing acute intoxication, mental health crisis, and warning signs.
- Timely activation of emergency medical services when signs of life are present is essential to demonstrating due diligence.

"Resource constraints are real, but even the smallest facility cannot afford to have no policy at all. Modest, well-implemented steps can save both lives and liability."

PROBLEMS IN POLICY DEVELOPMENT ACROSS THE COUNTRY

Suicide prevention policies are now required in virtually all U.S. correctional facilities through state statutes, accreditation standards (e.g., NCCHC, ACA), and federal oversight. Yet in practice, the quality and comprehensiveness of these policies vary widely across the country.

Even when comprehensive policies exist, another common problem is the **gap between policy and practice**. Policies may be drafted to satisfy accreditation requirements or inspections but are not consistently implemented on the ground. In litigation, plaintiffs' attorneys often highlight this gap as evidence of deliberate indifference: staff failed to follow their own policies, or administrators failed to ensure compliance.

State-level variations also contribute to inconsistency. Some states mandate detailed suicide prevention requirements, while others leave standards largely to local discretion. As a result, two facilities of similar size and population in different states may operate under very different levels of guidance and oversight.

Despite these challenges, courts have made clear that **resource limitations do not excuse the absence of reasonable suicide prevention efforts**. Even in rural jails or lockups, minimal measures such as intake screening, staggered checks, and timely access to emergency medical services are expected. Facilities that cannot demonstrate these basic practices remain vulnerable to lawsuits.

"Policies written for the books but ignored in practice invite litigation; prevention requires both words on paper and actions on the ground."

The Litigation Lens: Why Policies Fail

Over the past twenty-five years, in my consulting and expert-witness work, I have reviewed policies from small police lockups, rural jails, and large state prisons. Time and again, I have observed that deficiencies in policy design or implementation are not merely technical flaws—they are central to how lawsuits are framed, litigated, and won.

Common Deficiencies

- **Minimal or Rudimentary Policies**—limited to clothing/property rules, absent essential NCCHC components
- **Policies That Look Good on Paper but Fail in Practice**—adopted for accreditation but ignored in daily operations
- **Ambiguous or Nonbinding Language**—reliance on "should" or "may" instead of "shall."
- **Outdated or Inconsistent Standards**—lagging behind NCCHC, DOJ consent decrees, or case law.
- **Lack of Training Mandates**—no requirement for documented, ongoing suicide prevention training.

SUICIDE PREVENTION POLICY FRAMEWORK

The **Suicide Prevention Policy Framework** noted here guides correctional administrators, legal counsel, and clinical leaders in creating **comprehensive, standards-based, and legally defensible suicide prevention policies**. The framework integrates guidance from the **National Commission on Correctional Health Care (NCCHC)**, the **American Correctional Association (ACA)**, and other recognized authorities. It is offered solely as a **structured blueprint—not a complete or ready-to-adopt policy**. Each facility must adapt the framework to its own mission, resources, staffing, and population, translating these principles into detailed procedures that meet professional best practices and can withstand judicial and regulatory scrutiny.

The author provides this material for educational purposes only and does not assume responsibility or liability for its direct adoption as an operational policy.

1. Purpose

Establish a comprehensive, auditable framework to prevent, detect, and respond to suicide risk—protecting life, supporting staff performance, and meeting constitutional and accreditation expectations.

A well-defined purpose shows the facility's recognition of risk and its intent to exercise reasonable professional judgment.

2. Scope and Applicability

Applies to all staff (custody, medical, QMHPs (Qualified Mental Health Professionals), psychiatrists, contractors, volunteers) and all locations (booking, housing, segregation, infirmary/medical, transport, court, clinics) 24/7.

Broad, explicit scope demonstrates that the facility intends universal compliance and avoids gaps that plaintiffs may argue left some detainees unprotected.

3. Key Definitions

- **Suicide:** Death from self-directed injurious behavior with intent to die
- **Suicide Attempt:** Non-fatal self-directed injurious behavior with any intent to die
- **Suicidal Ideation (SI):** Thoughts of taking one's life (passive or active), with or without plan
- **Non-suicidal Self-Injury (NSSI):** Self-harm without intent to die
- **Acute Risk:** Present indications of intent/plan/means; acute intoxication/withdrawal with high impulsivity

- **Suicide Risk Assessment (SRA):** Clinical evaluation integrating history, presentation, collateral data, and risk/protective factors
- **Constant Observation (CO):** Continuous line-of-sight by staff; in-person checks logged at least every five minutes; ligature-reduced housing
- **Close Observation (Q10–15):** Staggered, in-person checks every ten to fifteen minutes; unobstructed view.
- **Enhanced Routine (Q30):** Staggered checks every 30 minutes with purposeful engagement; step-down from higher levels.

Precise definitions reduce ambiguity, promote consistent application across disciplines, and strengthen the facility's defense by showing it anticipated potential areas of misinterpretation.

4. Roles and Collaborative Responsibility

- **Administrator/Chief:** Appoints Facility Suicide Prevention Coordinator (FSPC); ensures resources; mandates compliance; reviews audits; conducts drills; resolves barriers.
- **Facility Suicide Prevention Coordinator (FSPC):** Leads program; tracks placements/levels; verifies training; runs audits/CQI; convenes post-incident reviews; ensures cross-discipline information flow.
- **Custody Supervisors:** Enforce housing/observation orders; verify staggered checks; spot-audit logs each shift; correct noncompliance in real time.
- **Officers:** Identify warning signs; initiate interim precautions; perform/document checks; call emergencies; communicate changes immediately.

- **Nursing/Medical:** Screen for intoxication/withdrawal; initiate CIWA-Ar/COWS protocols; coordinate with QMHP/psychiatrist; ensure medication continuity.
- **Psychiatrist:** Provide evaluation, medication management, consultation on risk formulation, and oversight for complex/acute cases.
- **QMHPs:** Perform SRA; issue/adjust observation, housing, and property orders; develop safety plans; determine discontinuation of precautions; provide follow-up care.
- **All Staff:** Immediate duty to act and communicate safety-critical information; document promptly and accurately.

Clearly assigning duties and collaborative expectations demonstrates due diligence and prevents "finger-pointing" gaps that can be exploited in litigation.

5. Training and Drills

- **Initial and Annual (all staff):**
  - Recognition of **signs and symptoms of mental illness**
  - **Suicide risk and protective factors**
  - Distinguishing SI, attempts, NSSI, denial, and "manipulative" presentations.
  - Housing and observation levels; **staggered** rounds; ligature awareness
  - **Emergency management:** cut-down, CPR, AED, EMS activation, role assignments
  - Documentation essentials; falsification risks; litigation lessons
  - **Drills:** Multidisciplinary, **twice/year** (day/night), timed entry/cut-down/AED; corrective action logged.

Courts scrutinize training records; demonstrating proactive and recurrent training supports claims of reasonable care and organizational commitment.

6. Intake Screening (No Group Screenings)

- **Timing:** Private, one-to-one screening at booking **and** before housing
- **Interpreter:** Use certified interpreters as needed
- **Tool:** Evidence-informed instrument; *no shout-out/group* methods
- **Content:** Prior attempts (method/timing), current SI/plan/means/intent, mental health history/meds/hospitalizations, substance use/last use, withdrawal risk, recent stressors/legal events, protective factors, collateral (police report, transfer papers, prior EMR flags, family).
- **Positive/concerning: Immediate interim precautions** (see Number 8) + **same-shift** QMHP referral.

All individuals must receive a structured suicide risk screening at booking or admission, using an evidence-based tool and performed by trained personnel. Intake screening is frequently examined in litigation; a documented, standardized process shows proactive identification of risk and compliance with accepted correctional health standards.

7. Triggered Re-Screening and Escalation

Re-screen or refer to QMHP when: new charges/sentencing/parole denial; segregation placement; acute behavior change (isolation, giving away property, refusing meals, agitation/pacing/insomnia); intoxication/withdrawal; medical decompensation; **family warnings**; return from hospital/watch/transfer; ligature preparation or hoarding meds observed.

The policy should require prompt re-screening whenever warning signs appear—such as new charges, bad news from court, medical or psychiatric changes, or concerning staff or peer observations. Demonstrating a system for dynamic, event-driven screening counters claims that the facility ignored obvious, evolving risk.

8. Interim Precautions (Custody-Initiated)

If acute risk suspected and QMHP not present:

- Move to safest available housing (ligature-reduced room if possible).
- Remove ligature-forming items (belts/strings/sheets/cords).
- Issue safety smock/blanket as indicated.
- Start **CO or Close** based on risk.
- Notify QMHP/medical **immediately**, and **document** actions/times.

Line staff must be empowered and obligated to place a detainee on suicide precautions immediately when acute risk is suspected, pending clinical assessment. Giving custody staff this authority shows that the facility prioritizes safety over hierarchy and prevents delays that have been criticized in case law.

9. Clinical Evaluation and Orders (QMHP/Psychiatrist)

- **Timeframes:** Acute risk → **immediate**; positive screens → **same shift**.
- **SRA** includes: current/past SI/attempts; access to means; mental disorders; withdrawal; stressors; protective factors; risk formulation.

- **Orders must specify**:
  - Observation level (CO/Q10–15/Q30) and **step-down criteria**
  - Housing and allowed property (sheets/blankets, safety items)
  - Medication/KOP vs **DOT**; withdrawal monitoring if applicable
  - **Follow-up frequency**; triggers to **escalate**
- **Discontinuation/downgrade of precautions: QMHP** (Qualified Mental Health Professional) **only**

QMHPs—and psychiatrists when indicated—must assess risk, set observation levels, determine housing, and document rationale. Clear clinical authority supports defensibility by showing that expert judgment, not ad-hoc decisions, guided precaution changes.

10. Observation Levels (Minimums)

- **CO:** Continuous line-of-sight; **staggered** entries ≥Q5 minutes; ligature-reduced room; safety smock/blanket unless QMHP authorizes more. Relief in place **before** observer leaves
- **Close (Q10–15):** Staggered in-person checks; unobstructed view; cut-down tool immediately available
- **Enhanced (Q30):** Staggered checks with purposeful engagement (programs, calls, MH check-ins); clearly documented as step-down

Video never replaces in-person checks.

Policies should define distinct levels of observation (e.g., constant, fifteen-minute, routine), specify criteria for each, and require documentation of checks. Ambiguity in levels or inconsistent application is a frequent target in suicide litigation; clear standards and proof of compliance are essential.

11. Housing and Ligature Mitigation

- Maintain **inventory of ligature points** per unit; update after incidents.
- Designate preferred rooms for CO/Close; ensure working intercoms and clear windows.
- No upper bunks/upper tiers for at-risk inmates.
- Limit sheets/blankets on CO unless QMHP authorizes special items.
- **Cut-down tools:** accessible within sixty to ninety seconds of every cell; checked and logged each shift.

Housing assignments must account for suicide risk and the physical safety of the cell, including removal or remediation of ligature points and hazardous fixtures. Regular safety audits and documentation demonstrate proactive risk reduction—a key defense against claims of deliberate indifference.

12. Intoxication and Withdrawal (Alcohol/Opiates/Stimulants)

- Screen all intakes; apply **CIWA-Ar** (alcohol) and **COWS** (opioids); document scores and thresholds.
- Provide **MAT** where permitted; otherwise, apply symptomatic care per protocol.
- Elevate observation during acute withdrawal (often Close or CO).
- Transfer to **hospital/EMS** for severe symptoms, seizures, delirium, unstable vitals, or deterioration.

Policies must address screening and safe management of individuals experiencing alcohol or drug intoxication or withdrawal, including medical monitoring and timely referral for treatment. Courts often scrutinize deaths linked to unmanaged withdrawal; clear protocols and documentation show due diligence.

13. Medication Continuity and KOP Controls

- Reconcile psychotropics/MAT (community pharmacy/VA/ records).
- **No KOP** for high-risk inmates when hoarding/diversion risk exists; use **DOT**.
- Avoid gaps on transfer/return; monitor adherence.

Continuity of prescribed psychotropic and other high-risk medications must be ensured at intake and during custody, with careful review of "keep-on-person" (KOP) practices to prevent misuse or overdose. Cases have found liability where facilities failed to control access to lethal medication or abruptly stopped treatment.

14. Restrictive Housing and Special Settings

- Avoid segregation for acutely suicidal inmates; if unavoidable, maintain CO/Close with **daily QMHP rounds**, purposeful out-of-cell time, and written justification.
- During transport/court/medical trips, maintain observation/ property restrictions; send **Safety Alert** (see Number 16).

The policy should outline additional precautions for segregation, disciplinary housing, medical units, and other high-risk environments where isolation can intensify suicidal behavior. Specific safeguards for these areas show awareness of heightened risk and have been pivotal in defending against failure-to-protect claims.

15. Emergency Response (All Staff)

- **Immediate entry** when safe; support body; **cut ligature** at suspension point; begin **CPR/AED; call EMS** at once.
- Minimum roles:
  - **Responder 1:** Entry/cut-down/CPR
  - **Responder 2:** Radio code/EMS; retrieve AED/cut-down tools
  - **Supervisor:** Scene control/door access/times/documentation
- Log times: discovery, call, entry, cut-down, CPR start, AED on, EMS arrival, pronouncement/transfer.

Every staff member must be trained and authorized to initiate life-saving interventions, including CPR and emergency activation, when a suicide attempt is discovered. Delays in response are a recurring theme in litigation; a clear, practiced plan for immediate action strengthens legal defensibility.

16. Communication and Information Sharing (HIPAA-Compliant)

- **QMHP → Custody:** Observation level, housing/property rules, early-warning signs, triggers to escalate
- **Custody → QMHP:** Observed changes, contraband/ligature prep, peer reports, family calls
- Use **minimum necessary** disclosures for safety; standard **Safety Alerts** in EMR and shift pass-downs

- Family warnings: log caller, content, actions; ensure same-shift QMHP review.

The policy must establish clear channels for timely sharing of suicide risk information among custody staff, medical and mental health professionals, and outside providers as needed. Breakdowns in communication are frequently exposed in litigation; a defined system shows the facility acted to prevent gaps in care and monitoring.

17. Documentation Standards (Non-Negotiable)

- Real-time, **staggered** interval entries; no "straight-line" watch logs
- Record rationales for level/housing decisions and any deviations
- Time-locked electronic logs where available; otherwise, supervisor co-sign each shift
- Cut-down/AED checks documented every shift

All screening results, risk assessments, observation logs, housing decisions, and emergency responses must be recorded promptly, accurately, and in a manner retrievable for review. Courts heavily rely on documentation to assess reasonable care; thorough, contemporaneous records are a key line of defense.

18. Post-Incident Procedures

- **Survivors:** QMHP evaluation ≤24h; adjust level/housing; written Safety Plan; scheduled follow-ups
- **Deaths/serious attempts:** Notify chain, coroner/ME, required agencies; preserve scene/video/records

- **Reviews:**
    - Clinical review (≤72h for survivors)
    - Operational review (≤14 days) with corrective actions/owners/dates
    - Mortality review with root-cause analysis; lessons shared with staff
- **Staff wellness:** Offer confidential support/debriefing
- **Family notification:** Prompt, professional, documented

Following any suicide or serious attempt, the facility should have a structured response plan that includes immediate medical care, scene preservation, staff debriefing, psychological support, and a root-cause review. Demonstrating a systematic, learning-focused response shows organizational commitment and helps defend against claims of systemic disregard.

19. Audits and Continuous Quality Improvement (CQI)

- **Quarterly audits:** screening timeliness/completeness; SRA timing/content; watch compliance (missed/staggered checks); CIWA-Ar/COWS usage; emergency-response times
- Leadership **dashboard** with red/amber/green indicators and action plans
- **Annual program review:** trends in attempts/suicides, near-misses, audit findings; revise training/policy accordingly

Regular, documented audits of housing safety, policy compliance, and training effectiveness, coupled with corrective action plans, show proactive risk management. Courts look favorably on evidence that the facility identifies and corrects deficiencies before tragedy occurs.

20. Governance

- **Policy Owners:** FSPC (clinical lead) + designated custody lead.
- **Review Cycle:** At least **annually**, and after any sentinel event or significant legal/policy change.
- **Distribution/Competency:** All staff acknowledge receipt; competency checks after major revisions.

The policy should clearly define leadership accountability for suicide prevention, including the authority of Qualified Mental Health Professionals (QMHPs), reporting structure, and oversight by senior administrators. Clear governance prevents gaps in responsibility and strengthens the defense that reasonable professional judgment guided decisions.

21. Scaled Implementation for Small/Rural Lockups (Minimum Viable Program)

- **One-to-one** intake screening (simple tool + six to eight critical questions)
- Clear two-level observation (CO/Close) with **staggered** checks and a single-page log
- **Basic withdrawal protocol** (CIWA-Ar/COWS quick sheet; hospital/EMS triggers)
- **Telehealth QMHP** via regional MOU if no on-site clinician
- **Quarterly mini-audit** by sheriff/lockup chief with corrective actions

Recognizing resource limitations, the framework allows smaller facilities to adopt core safety elements in proportion to their size, while still meeting accepted standards. Showing a reasoned, tailored approach protects small agencies from claims of neglect while acknowledging their operational realities.

LEGAL DEFENSIBILITY OF THE SUICIDE PREVENTION POLICY FRAMEWORK

A suicide prevention policy must do more than guide daily practice; it must also **withstand the close review of courts, regulators, and plaintiffs' attorneys.** This framework was developed to help facilities craft policies that are **operationally useful, clinically sound, and legally defensible.**

Clarity is essential. Each provision assigns **specific, understandable duties** to custody, health, and administrative staff. Policies that leave responsibility vague or undefined are frequently cited in deliberate-indifference claims and can erode a defense.

Flexibility protects the agency as standards evolve. The framework is aligned with **NCCHC, ACA, and other recognized guidelines**, yet encourages site-specific adaptation to staffing, design, and population needs. Courts recognize that a well-tailored policy shows thoughtful application rather than blind copying.

Availability and accessibility matter. Policies must be **easily retrievable, integrated into training, and known to staff** at all levels. A document that exists only on paper but not in practice undermines any claim of due diligence.

Prevention and documentation form the core of legal defensibility. Courts examine not only whether preventive systems—screening, safe housing, observation, emergency response—were in place but also whether the facility can **prove** they were used. Logs, watch sheets, training records, environmental audits, and response drills all become crucial exhibits.

The framework encourages **built-in audits, drills, and continuous quality improvement**. Demonstrating that leadership proactively reviews housing safety, drills suicide response, and updates training shows reasonable care and weakens deliberate-indifference allegations.

Finally, **codifying the authority of Qualified Mental Health Professionals (QMHPs)** provides clear, clinical decision-making lines: who initiates, modifies, or ends suicide precautions; who determines housing; and how custody and health staff communicate. Clear clinical authority is a recurring issue in litigation.

By combining **clarity, flexibility, accessibility, prevention with documentation, and due-diligence mechanisms**, this framework allows administrators to build policies that **guide staff reliably and withstand legal challenge**. For attorneys reviewing policies—whether to enforce them or to challenge them—the structure signals that the agency recognized risk, acted on accepted standards, and created a defensible system of care.

BUILDING LEGALLY DEFENSIBLE SYSTEMS

Courts consistently emphasize that a policy is only as strong as its implementation. In litigation, attorneys scrutinize whether the facility's actual practices match the written directives. A beautifully written suicide prevention manual offers little defense if logs are falsified, suicide watch is not performed as documented, or staff lack training to recognize acute risk. Conversely, even a modest policy, when faithfully implemented and well documented, can provide strong protection in court.

Attorneys frequently point to discrepancies such as:

- **Outdated policies** left unrevised for years, despite known deficiencies
- **Paper compliance**—suicide prevention policies existing only to satisfy accreditation requirements
- **Ignored red flags**—risk factors clearly noted at intake but not followed by referral or watch
- **Inadequate-staffing claims**—facilities citing budget limitations while suicides occur under their watch

In my consulting experience, juries and judges often view a facility's failure to "practice what it preaches" as deliberate indifference, leading to substantial settlements or verdicts.

Examples of Strong Policy Language

Courts and accrediting bodies respond positively to policies that are clear, specific, and actionable. The following excerpts illustrate language that has been viewed favorably in litigation:

- *"Only a Qualified Mental Health Professional (QMHP) may discontinue suicide precautions, and such decisions must be documented with clinical rationale."*
- *"All staff shall receive annual training on the recognition of suicide risk factors, warning signs, and emergency intervention procedures."*
- *"Any observed change in inmate mood, affect, or behavior must be communicated immediately to mental health staff and documented in the inmate's record."*

These formulations go beyond vague promises; they establish enforceable standards that leave little room for ambiguity.

Future Directions: Adapting to Changing Realities

Correctional suicide prevention policy cannot remain static. Evolving challenges require adaptation:

- **Staffing shortages**—Policies should anticipate reliance on cross-trained officers and mandate collaboration between custody and mental health.
- **Technology**—Remote monitoring, AI-based flagging of at-risk inmates, and electronic medical-record integration can strengthen early detection but must be embedded in policy and backed by human oversight.
- **Special populations**—Veterans, transgender individuals, and those with co-occurring substance and psychiatric disorders require tailored procedures.
- **Continuous improvement**—Policies should mandate annual revision, incorporating lessons from litigation, case reviews, and updated NCCHC standards.

Policies that remain rigid while suicide rates climb will be seen as relics. Facilities that evolve—guided by litigation lessons, research, and staff input—will not only save lives but also reduce liability.

CONCLUSION

A suicide prevention policy is more than a set of rules on paper; it is the facility's front-line defense against tragedy and liability. The history of correctional-suicide litigation demonstrates that courts consistently look beyond policy language to whether prevention practices are real, enforced, and documented. Case Vignette 10.1, like many others, shows how the absence of a comprehensive, living policy framework creates conditions where vulnerable detainees are left unprotected and facilities are left indefensible in court.

A **legally defensible policy framework**—grounded in NCCHC standards, collaborative responsibility, and lessons learned from litigation—sets the foundation for safer facilities. But policy alone cannot prevent suicide. Its effectiveness depends on consistent staff training, rigorous monitoring, communication across disciplines, and administrative commitment to accountability.

By embedding due diligence, clear roles, and continuous quality improvement into the policy framework, correctional facilities not only reduce the risk of inmate suicide but also strengthen their legal standing when prevention is challenged in court. Ultimately, a strong suicide prevention policy is both a **clinical imperative** and a **legal shield**—ensuring that **when no one is watching**, the institution remains vigilant.

REFERENCES

1. American Correctional Association, *Standards for Adult Correctional Institutions*. Alexandria, VA: ACA, latest edition
2. *Bowring v. Godwin*, 551 F.2d 44 (4th Cir. 1977)
3. *Estelle v. Gamble*, 429 U.S. 97 (1976)
4. *Farmer v. Brennan*, 511 U.S. 825 (1994)
5. National Commission on Correctional Health Care (NCCHC), *Standards for Health Services in Jails and Prisons*. Chicago: NCCHC, 2018
6. U.S. Department of Justice, *Civil Rights of Institutionalized Persons Act (CRIPA)*, 42 U.S.C. §1997 (1980)

CHAPTER 11

TRAINING: A CASE LAW-BASED APPROACH

"Courts do not judge intentions—they judge actions. Training is what turns awareness into legally defensible care and protects those who cannot protect themselves."
—Anasseril E. Daniel

INTRODUCTION

The fundamental goal of suicide prevention training in correctional facilities is to significantly reduce suicidal behaviors—including both suicide attempts and completed suicides—while also protecting institutions from costly litigation. A substantial proportion of suicide cases in custody result in lawsuits that carry multimillion-dollar settlements or judgments. These financial and reputational losses reinforce a central truth: effective suicide prevention training saves not only lives but also institutions. Designing and implementing robust training programs, however, is both time-consuming and resource-intensive. Facilities frequently struggle with budgetary constraints and limited staffing, which can undermine the quality of training provided. Yet, when suicide prevention is neglected or training is inadequate, the costs—human, legal, and financial—far outweigh the investment required. As the World Health Organization emphasized in its *Preventing Suicide in Jails and Prisons: Resource Guide*, staff training serves a dual purpose: reducing the number of lives lost and reducing the number of lawsuits filed against facilities.

Research underscores the importance of comprehensive approaches. Stijelja and Mishara's systematic review and meta-analysis of more than 900 studies found that suicide prevention in correctional settings is most effective when programs address multiple risk factors simultaneously. Key components include systematic screening, suicide risk assessment, enhanced supervision, effective communication among staff, post-suicide administrative reviews, staff debriefing, and timely access to clinical and psychiatric care.

The U.S. Department of Justice has also recommended targeted training strategies, such as the use of cut-down tools, AEDs, naloxone for overdose response, and protocols for post-incident documentation. Lawsuits repeatedly reveal that training deficiencies in recognizing risk factors, applying suicide prevention policies, and executing emergency responses are pivotal in establishing liability.

A new approach is therefore warranted—one that moves beyond traditional awareness training toward a **case law-based model**. This model complements existing strategies by grounding staff education in real legal precedents. Correctional officers, medical professionals, and administrators must learn not only the warning signs of suicide but also how courts have judged failures in recognition, documentation, monitoring, or communication. In this way, training becomes both clinically informed and legally defensible, ensuring that staff understand the life-or-death importance of compliance with policies and procedures.

OBJECTIVES OF SUICIDE PREVENTION TRAINING

- **Reduce suicide risk and deaths:** Equip staff to identify, monitor, and intervene effectively with at-risk inmates, thereby lowering suicide attempts and fatalities.
- **Enhance legal defensibility:** Ensure staff actions align with constitutional requirements and accepted standards of care, reducing liability exposure.
- **Promote consistency in practice:** Standardize how all staff recognize, document, and respond to suicide risk factors.
- **Integrate case-law lessons:** Ground training not only in clinical best practices but also in lessons learned from litigation and court rulings.
- **Strengthen institutional culture of prevention:** Emphasize that suicide prevention is a shared responsibility across all staff categories.
- **Improve emergency-response readiness:** Prepare staff to act quickly and competently in life-threatening situations such as hanging attempts or overdoses.

WHO SHOULD RECEIVE TRAINING?

- **Correctional officers:** As first responders and daily observers of inmate behavior
- **Medical staff (nurses, physicians, psychiatrists):** To integrate suicide prevention into clinical care and treatment
- **Mental health professionals (QMHPs, psychologists, social workers, counselors):** To conduct assessments, manage suicide watch, and provide interventions
- **Supervisory and administrative staff:** To ensure oversight, accountability, and program implementation

- **Support staff (classification officers, intake staff, chaplains, volunteers, contractors):** To recognize warning signs and follow referral protocols
- **New hires:** All incoming staff must receive suicide prevention training as part of orientation.
- **Continuing staff:** All employees should participate in annual refresher courses to reinforce skills and update knowledge of policy, risk factors, and legal developments.

"Suicide prevention in corrections is not optional—it is a constitutional duty and a legal imperative. Every staff member must be prepared to recognize risk, intervene effectively, and act in concert with policy and law to save lives and safeguard institutions."

TRADITIONAL TRAINING APPROACHES

For decades, correctional systems have relied on a **traditional training model** for suicide prevention. While this approach has increased awareness, it has serious limitations, particularly given the continuing rise in suicide rates since 2015.

1. Format and Delivery

- **Orientation-based:** Suicide prevention is typically introduced during staff orientation, often within a larger block of general training.
- **Lecture-driven:** Training is primarily delivered through lectures, PowerPoint slides, or prerecorded videos, with minimal interactive discussion.

- **Policy review:** Emphasis is placed on the written suicide prevention policy, suicide-watch procedures, and documentation requirements.

2. Core Content

Traditional training usually covers the following:

- **Basic definitions** of suicide ideation, attempt, and completion
- **Signs and symptoms of mental illness,** with a focus on mood disorders, psychosis, and substance withdrawal, but at a very general level
- **Risk factors and warning signs,** such as recent bad news, giving away possessions, or withdrawal from peers
- **Myths and facts,** for example: "People who talk about suicide won't actually do it" (a myth), or "Most suicides occur early in detention" (a fact)
- **Emergency-response procedures,** including summoning medical help, initiating CPR, and notifying supervisors
- **Policies and procedures,** with step-by-step guidance on placing inmates on suicide watch and filling out suicide-watch logs.

3. Content Often Missing

Despite covering basic ground, traditional training seldom addresses key realities of suicide in corrections:

- **Rates and prevalence:** Suicide remains the leading cause of death in jails and the third leading cause in prisons, but this is rarely presented to staff.
- **Demographics and timing:** Patterns such as the high frequency of suicides within the first twenty-four to forty-eight hours of

detention or the predominance of hanging as a method are often not explained.

- **Case-law and litigation outcomes:** Staff are not educated about how suicides have led to lawsuits, settlements, and findings of liability, leaving a major gap in prevention knowledge.

4. Audience and Duration

- **Primarily correctional officers:** Though mental health and medical staff may participate, the training is generally aimed at line officers.
- **Short duration:** Most sessions last two to four hours and, occasionally, a full day.
- **Limited continuing education:** After orientation, follow-up training is usually annual and often reduced to a policy review or video refresher.

5. Evaluation and Reinforcement

- **Sign-offs and quizzes:** Staff may complete a short quiz or acknowledgment form, but real-world competency testing is rare.
- **Minimal practice:** Few programs include role-play, scenario exercises, or supervised drills.
- **Weak reinforcement:** Refresher training seldom builds on earlier sessions, resulting in knowledge gaps.

6. Limitations of Traditional Training

While it raises basic awareness, traditional training is **reactive** rather than **proactive.** Common weaknesses include:

- **Overgeneralization:** Suicide risk is presented as a checklist rather than a nuanced, case-by-case evaluation.
- **Limited scope:** Staff rarely learn the *known facts of suicide in corrections*—such as methods, rates, timing, and demographic risk factors—despite their central importance.
- **Lack of integration:** Training does not build collaboration between correctional, medical, and mental health staff.
- **No legal lens:** Lessons from litigation, which could shape more-effective prevention, are omitted.
- **Minimal impact:** Despite widespread use, suicides in correctional settings have continued to rise, suggesting this approach is not achieving its intended purpose.

In summary: Traditional suicide prevention training is an **introductory, policy-centered approach** that focuses on awareness of risk factors and procedures. It covers signs of mental illness and debunks some myths but rarely teaches the *realities of suicide in corrections* or equips staff to integrate legal and clinical perspectives into daily practice.

WHY TRADITIONAL APPROACHES FAIL

Despite decades of reliance on the traditional model, suicide in correctional settings has not abated. In fact, the data show that it is getting worse.

According to the **Bureau of Justice Statistics (BJS)**, suicide rates in U.S. jails began rising sharply after 2015, reversing earlier declines that had been attributed to improved screening and intervention programs. From 2000 to 2014, prevention initiatives—such as intake screening, suicide-watch cells, and staff orientation training—appeared to stabilize suicide rates. However, beginning in 2015, suicides in jails increased by **13 percent**, and the upward trajectory has continued through the most recent reporting periods.

This troubling escalation is striking because it has occurred **despite improvements in screening and intervention.** Most facilities now have written suicide prevention policies, conduct routine intake screenings, and provide staff with at least basic training on warning signs and emergency response. Yet the very outcome these measures were designed to prevent—the loss of life by suicide—remains the leading cause of death in jails and the third leading cause in prisons.

The paradox is clear: **we are training more staff, screening more inmates, and implementing more interventions than ever before—yet the rate of suicide is climbing.** This disconnect signals that the traditional approach, while necessary, is insufficient.

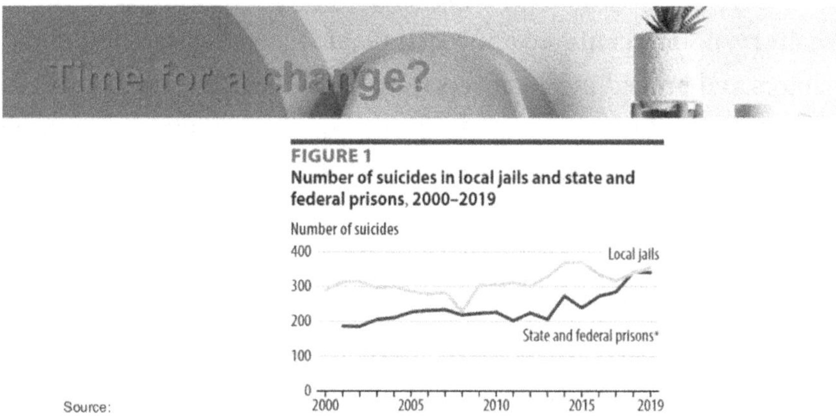

Source:
Bureau of Justice Statistics, Federal Law Enforcement Agency Deaths in Custody Reporting Program
Suicide in Local Jails and State and Federal Prisons, 2000–2019 – Statistical Tables [16]

Relying on brief orientation lectures, generic lists of warning signs, and rote policy reviews cannot match the complexity of the problem. Suicidal behavior in custody is not simply the result of individual risk factors—it is also shaped by institutional practices, environmental hazards, and failures of communication, many of which have been documented and litigated in court. Training that ignores these realities misses the most powerful lessons correctional staff need in order to prevent deaths and protect their institutions from liability.

As the graph of suicide trends illustrates, the **post-2015 escalation in jail suicides** is not an aberration but a pattern. Without a fundamental shift in how training is designed and delivered, the correctional system will continue to face both preventable deaths and costly litigation.

The persistence of high suicide rates despite traditional prevention efforts demands a new strategy. Training must evolve beyond generic awareness and embrace the lessons of actual cases and court decisions. By analyzing how facilities lost—or in cases successfully defended—lawsuits, staff can learn what actions, omissions, and attitudes most often determine outcomes.

CASE LAW AS A TRAINING TOOL

The **case law-based training approach** complements traditional methods by embedding real-world consequences into learning. It highlights not only the human cost of inmate suicide but also the institutional and financial consequences of neglect. In this way, training becomes both clinically relevant and legally defensible, offering correctional staff and administrators a stronger foundation for prevention and risk management.

Author's Early Interest in Case Law-Based Training

The limitations of traditional training became clear to me as early as 2009, when I published an article in the *Journal of Correctional Health Care* titled "Suicide-Related Litigation in Jails and Prisons: Risk Management Strategies." In that work, I examined several appellate cases—*Steele v. Shah*, *Woodard v. Myres*, and *Comstock v. McCrary*—that revealed how courts consistently identified failures in screening, monitoring, communication, and clinical judgment as central to liability.

What struck me was the recurring disconnect: while correctional staff received generalized suicide prevention training, courts were holding them accountable for far-more-specific failures. These included lapses in following policy, neglecting to communicate warnings, or failing to act decisively during crises. The lawsuits made one point repeatedly—**broad-awareness training was not enough**.

This realization marked the beginning of my interest in what I later came to call **case law-based training**. If courts are defining what constitutes negligence and deliberate indifference, then it follows that training programs must draw directly from those rulings. Put simply, training should not only prepare staff to recognize warning signs of suicide but also to understand the legal expectations that shape their duties.

As my consulting practice expanded—covering more than 110 suicide cases—the same lessons appeared again and again. Failures that courts had already ruled upon were being repeated in facilities across the country. It became clear that a new training model was needed.

To close this gap, I developed an **innovative, legal liability-driven training approach** that uses **actual court rulings and case outcomes** to teach staff how their actions (or inaction) are evaluated under constitutional standards. This approach reframes suicide prevention as both a clinical and risk management responsibility, improving staff vigilance and strengthening an agency's legal defense.

Recognizing the originality of this concept, I sought and obtained **copyright protection for the approach itself: *Legal Liability-Driven Suicide Prevention Training*** (U.S. Copyright Office, TX-9-337-876, recorded October 24, 2023, U.S. Library of Congress). The purpose of this step was to ensure that the approach could not be claimed by others as their own. **This chapter represents my first comprehensive effort to translate that protected approach into a structured training curriculum** for correctional settings.

Although the legal literature contains **hundreds of reported inmate-suicide cases**, this book highlights **fifteen carefully selected decisions.** These cases were chosen not for their sheer number but for their **clarity in illustrating recurrent system failures** that drive litigation and for the **practical lessons they offer** to correctional administrators, custody staff, and mental health professionals. Each case addresses a **distinct, high-impact issue**—from flawed intake screening and ignored warning signs to breakdowns in supervision, communication, and emergency medical response—that courts have repeatedly recognized as a basis for liability. By distilling the **essential themes** from these representative cases, this section avoids duplication and provides a **manageable framework for training.**

The **deliberate use of case law** shows why **litigation-based lessons must complement traditional suicide prevention training.** While standard training emphasizes risk factors and general awareness, **case law provides concrete, real-world examples of failures** that courts have scrutinized and penalized. Linking these two approaches ensures that suicide prevention training is **both clinically informed and legally defensible.**

KEY LEGAL PRECEDENTS AND FAILURES

The bullet points below synthesize the **most frequent and critical failures** identified across these fifteen decisions, offering **practical "red flags"** for correctional leaders to incorporate into staff education and policy development.

- **Failure to conduct adequate suicide screening or assessment** (*Comstock v. McCrary*, 273 F.3d 693 [6th Cir. 2001])
- **Ignoring or discounting recent suicide attempts and failing to provide adequate psychiatric reassessment or monitoring** (*Greason v. Kemp*, 891 F.2d 829 [11th Cir. 1990])
- **Abrupt discontinuation of psychotropic medication without evaluation or monitoring** (*Steele v. Shah*, 87 F.3d 1266 [11th Cir. 1996])
- **Failure to respond to obvious and substantial suicide risk factors and to maintain suicide precautions** (*Woodward v. Myres*, 368 F.3d 917 [7th Cir. 2004])
- **Overreliance on an inmate's denial of suicidal ideation despite clear risk indicators and history** (*Williams v. Mehra*, 186 F.3d 685 [6th Cir. 1999, *en banc*])
- **Inadequate monitoring and failure to maintain observation despite known risk** (*Gordon v. Kidd*, 971 F.2d 1087 [4th Cir. 1992])
- **Failure to train staff in recognizing and responding to suicidal behavior despite known risk** (*Freedman v. City of Allentown*, 853 F.2d 1111 [3d Cir. 1988])
- **Failure to communicate critical risk information to staff and launch the suicide protocol** (*Estate of Ryan L. Clark v. County of Green Lake*, 255 F. Supp. 2d 890 [E.D. Wis. 2016], aff'd *sub nom Clark v. Walker*, 860 F.3rd (7th Circuit 2017)])
- **Improper placement in segregation/isolation despite known suicide risk and failure to maintain protective observation** (*Hott v. Hennepin County*, 260 F.3d 901 [8th Cir. 2001])
- **Failure to act on explicit family warnings of suicidal intent and serious mental illness** (*Sanville v. McCaughtry*, 266 F.3d 724 [7th Cir. 2001])

- **Falsification or inaccuracy in suicide-watch logs after missed rounds and delayed response** (*Estate of Clay v. Marion County Sheriff's Office*, No. 1:15-cv-01723, 2017 WL 979024 [S.D. Ind. Mar. 14, 2017])
- **Failure to restrict obvious means of suicide and provide a safe environment for a known at-risk detainee** (*Hare v. City of Corinth*, 74 F.3d 633 [5th Cir. 1996, *en banc*])
- **Delay in psychiatric referral or treatment despite clear indications of need** (*Ketchum v. County of Alameda*, 811 F.2d 1243 [9th Cir. 1987])
- **Failure to perform timely life-saving measures once a suicide attempt was discovered** (*Colburn v. Upper Darby Township*, 946 F.2d 1017 [3d Cir. 1991])
- **Systemic policy failures—absence of adequate procedures and staff training to address known suicide and safety risks** (*Farmer v. Brennan*, 511 U.S. 825 [1994])

TWENTY CRITICAL ACTIONS TO PREVENT SUICIDE AND AVOID LIABILITY

The following twenty action points synthesize the **most frequent failures** identified in both landmark court cases and forty real-world suicide vignettes. They define what every correctional facility and staff member must know—and do—to protect lives and reduce legal exposure.

1. **Thorough Suicide Screening at Intake**—Use validated tools plus records/history review; avoid perfunctory or check-box assessments.
2. **Reassessment after Any Self-Harm or Crisis Event**—Each self-injury, attempt, or acute psychiatric episode must trigger a full mental health review.

3. **Do Not Rely Solely on Inmate Denial**—Never clear or downgrade precautions based only on "I'm not suicidal" when other risk indicators exist.
4. **Triggered New Screening During Custody Changes**—Segregation, legal setbacks, PREA allegations, or bad news should prompt renewed evaluation.
5. **Reliable Communication and Risk Handoffs**—Ensure risk info travels across shifts, housing units, intake, and medical/mental health.
6. **Respond to Family or Outside Warnings**—Treat calls or records from family/community providers as actionable clinical data.
7. **Safe Housing and Ligature Mitigation**—Audit and remove tie-off points; place high-risk individuals only in suicide-resistant cells.
8. **Control of Hazardous Items and Medications**—Manage razors, plastic bags, cords, and **keep-on-person (KOP)** medications; avoid unsafe issue.
9. **Observation Standards and Active Monitoring**—Follow required check intervals; actively watch video feeds; intervene on concerning behavior.
10. **Accuracy and Integrity of Watch Logs**—Maintain truthful documentation; falsification and gaps are legal liabilities.
11. **Timely, Adequate Emergency Response**—Enter immediately, provide CPR/bleeding control, and summon EMS without delay.

12. **Medication Continuity and Safe Psychotropic Changes**—Avoid abrupt discontinuation; continue community prescriptions when safe; monitor closely after changes.
13. **Recognition and Management of Withdrawal**—Monitor alcohol/opioid withdrawal with scoring tools; provide MAT when indicated; avoid isolating untreated patients.
14. **Prompt Psychiatric Referral/Escalation**—Do not delay consults when screening, staff observation, or collateral info shows acute risk.
15. **Training for All Staff on Suicide Recognition and Legal Duties**—Custody, medical, and mental health staff need to spot red flags and understand deliberate-indifference risk.
16. **Legally Defensible Policy Framework**—Policies must define roles, authority, audits, observation levels, and clinical decision processes to survive litigation.
17. **Governance and Continuous Quality Improvement**—Leadership should oversee audits, drills, policy updates, and data-driven prevention improvement.
18. **Cautious Use of Segregation/Isolation**—Avoid placing at-risk inmates in restrictive housing unless essential and with enhanced precautions.
19. **Post-Incident Review and System Learning**—After suicides/attempts, analyze failures, update policy, and retrain staff.
20. **Clear Documentation of Clinical and Operational Decisions**—Record rationale for watch changes, housing, medication, and response actions—critical in defending care.

Together, these action items establish a **training priority matrix**: what staff must know, what they must practice, and what they must document.

METHODOLOGY OF TRAINING EXECUTION

- **Case-Based Scenarios**: Each training session begins with a vignette (from real cases or anonymized composites), followed by small-group discussion on "what went wrong" and "what should have happened."
- **Legal-Lens Integration**: Trainers present the **court's ruling** from landmark cases to connect daily practices with constitutional obligations.
- **Skill-Based Drills:** Observation logs, suicide-watch procedures, emergency cut-downs, and role-play for communication/reporting.
- **Cross-Disciplinary Collaboration**: Training conducted jointly by custody, mental health, and medical staff, reinforcing collaborative responsibility.
- **Evaluation and Feedback**: Post-training assessments include scenario-based testing, documentation exercises, and team evaluations.
- **Continuous Reinforcement**: Short refresher sessions and debriefs after actual incidents to embed lessons into practice.

A **case law-informed training methodology** incorporates actual rulings, settlements, and case examples into training exercises so staff can see the *real-world consequences* of lapses in screening, documentation, communication, and emergency response. By studying cases, staff internalize both the *human cost* (preventable inmate deaths) and the *legal cost* (lawsuits, settlements, liability).

Key features of this methodology include:

- **Integration of Case Law:** Each training unit begins with a short case summary and court outcome.
- **Link to Policy:** Staff identify which specific policies were violated or ignored.
- **Role-Specific Scenarios:** Officers, nurses, and QMHPs apply lessons to their own duties.
- **Skills Drills:** Staff practice responding to scenarios (e.g., hanging attempt, withdrawal crisis).
- **Legal-Lens Reflection:** Training concludes with the legal and ethical takeaways—how to avoid both tragedy and liability.

DRAWBACKS OF CASE LAW-BASED TRAINING

While case law-based training offers unique advantages in grounding staff education in real-world consequences, it is not without limitations. Correctional administrators and trainers must recognize these potential drawbacks to ensure the approach complements, rather than replaces, traditional training strategies.

1. Reactive rather than proactive focus

Case law reflects events that have already led to tragedy and litigation. Training built primarily on court rulings risks being reactive—focusing on what went wrong—rather than proactive in fostering innovation and prevention beyond existing precedents.

2. **Variability in applicability**

Court decisions are often fact-specific, shaped by the details of a particular facility, jurisdiction, or inmate. What a federal court deemed constitutionally inadequate in one setting may not translate neatly to another. Overgeneralizing rulings could cause confusion or the misapplication of lessons.

3. **Legal complexity and accessibility**

Legal language can be difficult for front-line correctional officers to grasp without careful translation into clear, actionable guidance. Without careful adaptation, staff may become overwhelmed or disengaged by the technicality of legal analysis.

4. **Potential chilling effect**

Overemphasis on litigation risk may shift training culture toward fear of lawsuits rather than genuine concern for inmate safety and well-being. Staff may become defensive or overly cautious in documenting actions, potentially detracting from therapeutic engagement with inmates in crisis.

5. **Lag in reflecting emerging risks**

Case law often trails behind evolving correctional realities. For instance, new patterns of substance use (such as synthetic opioids or novel psychoactive drugs) may not yet be reflected in rulings, leaving gaps if training relies exclusively on published legal outcomes.

6. Resource demands

Developing effective case law-based modules requires trainers to stay current with litigation, interpret rulings accurately, and integrate them with operational policy. Smaller jails and lockups—often those with the highest vulnerabilities—may lack the expertise or resources to implement such specialized training effectively.

TOWARD A HYBRID, LEGALLY DEFENSIBLE TRAINING MODEL

Although the **case law-driven approach** offers powerful, reality-based lessons, it has not yet been empirically tested as a stand-alone training method. This limitation is understandable: case law is inherently **reactive**, developing only after tragedy and litigation, and it does not lend itself easily to controlled, prospective study. Yet decades of court decisions have created a **rich, practical body of knowledge** about where suicide prevention efforts fail and how those failures are judged under constitutional standards. These lessons can—and should—be **applied proactively** in staff education.

Until more is known about the effectiveness of a purely case law-based curriculum, the most responsible and defensible path is a **hybrid training methodology**: one that integrates traditional, evidence-based suicide prevention content (clinical risk factors, screening, monitoring, safe housing, emergency response) with the **concrete, cautionary lessons** derived from landmark lawsuits and real-world case failures. This blended model maximizes both **clinical soundness and legal defensibility**. It prepares staff to detect and respond to suicide risk in line with accepted mental health standards while also equipping them to avoid the operational and documentation lapses that courts consistently interpret as deliberate indifference. By marrying clinical data with the hard legal lessons learned from litigation, facilities can move beyond check-the-box training toward an approach that truly **saves lives and shields staff and agencies from avoidable liability.**

Key Features of the Hybrid Model

1. **Foundation in Best Practices**

   Begin with established suicide prevention principles outlined by NCCHC, ACA, APA, and WHO, ensuring staff are grounded in recognized standards of care.

2. **Case-Law Integration**

   Use selected cases, as noted above, to illustrate failures, consequences, and how policies were judged in court. Each legal example is distilled into plain-language lessons tied directly to daily tasks.

3. **Scenario-Based Application**

   Blend clinical knowledge with legal lessons in practical, facility-specific scenarios (e.g., intake screening, responding to threats, documenting suicide watch). These exercises allow staff to practice decision-making in ways that reflect both **clinical responsibility** and **legal accountability.**

4. **Tiered Training Delivery**
   - **Correctional officers** focus on identifying risk factors, observation, documentation, and emergency response.
   - **Health staff** emphasize clinical assessment, treatment, and communication with custody.

- **Administrators** learn to evaluate policy compliance, ensure quality improvement, and manage litigation risk.

5. Feedback and Reinforcement

Post-training debriefings and supervisory feedback ensure that lessons are internalized and applied consistently. Hybrid programs are also reinforced with **annual updates** reflecting both emerging research and new legal rulings.

6. Simplicity and Adaptability

Training materials are designed to be modular—easily adapted for small lockups or large prison systems—without requiring excessive resources. Facilities can scale the program to match staff size, inmate population, and available expertise.

Training Steps

Step 1. Establish Core Learning Objectives

- **Objectives should explicitly include:**
  - Recognizing suicide risk factors and protective factors
  - Responding to acute risk situations
  - Understanding how courts evaluate staff actions and policies
  - Documenting observations and interventions in a legally defensible manner

Step 2. Present Traditional Training Foundations

- **Core curriculum topics:**
  - Suicide risk factors (static and dynamic)
  - Warning signs and observable behaviors
  - Basic mental health conditions (mood, psychotic, anxiety, PTSD, substance use)

    - Myths and facts about suicide in correctional settings
    - Facility policies, including intake screening, suicide-watch procedures, and referral protocols.
- **Use clear examples from daily operations to ground abstract material.**

Step 3: Present Case Law-Based Learning Modules

Once staff understand the clinical baseline, the curriculum shifts to **legal-reality training**. Each module presents a **landmark court decision** or a **real-world vignette**:

- A concise case narrative is presented—the facts, the sequence of events, and what staff did or failed to do.
- Participants identify **operational breakdowns** (e.g., *Comstock v. McCrary* shows the danger of superficial screening; *Colburn v. Upper Darby Township* illustrates the need for immediate life-saving action).
- The **legal outcome** is explained in plain terms: how courts defined "deliberate indifference," which failures mattered most, and what damages or institutional consequences followed.
- The holding is translated into **operational expectations**—what staff must do differently to avoid the same outcome.

Once staff have absorbed both the clinical foundation and the lessons from case law, the next step is to bring these together in applied practice.

Step 4. Integrate through Applied Scenarios

The culmination of hybrid training lies in integration. Staff should be engaged in scenario-based exercises that mirror real-world events, where they are asked to recognize warning signs, apply appropriate levels of observation, and anticipate both clinical and legal consequences of their decisions. These applied sessions allow participants to test their responses in a safe environment, highlight the importance of communication between custody and clinical staff, and demonstrate how failures identified in case law translate into practical risks. By weaving clinical standards and legal precedents into these exercises, facilities cultivate a culture where suicide prevention is understood not only as a healthcare responsibility but as a constitutional duty. This final step reinforces the principle that prevention is proactive and that every decision made in daily practice must withstand both clinical scrutiny and legal accountability.

GOVERNANCE, CQI, AND SUSTAINABILITY

Leadership plays a critical role in sustaining this training. Administrators should:

- **Audit** suicide-watch documentation, cell safety, and staff compliance.
- **Conduct regular drills** and post-incident reviews.
- **Update policies** based on lessons learned and legal developments.
- **Track data** on suicides, attempts, and near misses to guide continuous improvement.

Such governance demonstrates **due diligence** and strengthens the facility's defense against deliberate-indifference claims. Correctional suicide prevention training can no longer be a **check-the-box exercise.** Every death in custody brings not only human tragedy but also legal and public scrutiny. By combining **clinical data with lessons from litigation**, facilities can teach staff exactly where failures occur and how to prevent them. The hybrid, case law-informed model outlined in this chapter empowers officers, clinicians, and administrators to **recognize risk early, respond decisively, and document defensible care**. Facilities that embrace this approach save lives, protect staff, and stand on the strongest possible ground when challenged in court.

CONCLUSION

Training is the single most powerful tool correctional systems possess to turn suicide prevention from a policy on paper into a **living, life-saving practice**. For too long, training has been **generic, fragmented, and disconnected from the urgent realities behind cell doors**. This chapter calls for a decisive shift. It shows why traditional approaches fail, how decades of court decisions illuminate the same preventable errors, and how those hard lessons can reshape the future.

A **hybrid, case law-informed training model**—grounded in clinical science, strengthened by the unmistakable warnings of litigation, and brought to life through real-case scenarios—gives staff the clarity and courage to act. It moves beyond awareness to **operational mastery**, empowering officers, nurses, and mental health professionals to recognize risk early, intervene effectively, and document care that withstands both clinical scrutiny and constitutional challenge.

Every suicide in custody is a profound human loss and a public reckoning. Facilities that adopt this model send a clear message: **we will not repeat the failures of the past.** They create a culture where vigilance is standard, accountability is embraced, and lives are saved. This is the future of correctional suicide prevention training—one that protects the vulnerable, honors professional duty, and stands strong when the world asks if enough was done.

REFERENCES

1. Carson, E. Ann. *Mortality in Local Jails, 2000–2019—Statistical Tables.* Bureau of Justice Statistics, U.S. Department of Justice, December 2021
2. Daniel, Anasseril E. "Suicide-Related Litigation in Jails and Prisons: Risk Management Strategies." *Journal of Correctional Health Care* 15, no. 1 (2009): 58–72 https://doi.org/10.1177/1078345808326629
3. Stijelja, Stella, and Brian L. Mishara. "Preventing Suicidal and Self-Injurious Behavior in Correctional Facilities: A Systematic Literature Review and Meta-Analysis." *eClinicalMedicine* 51 (2022): 101560. https://doi.org/10.1016/j.eclinm.2022.101560
4. World Health Organization. *Preventing Suicide in Jails and Prisons: Resource Guide.* Geneva: WHO, 2006.
5. U.S. Department of Justice, Office of the Inspector General, *Evaluation and Review of Suicide Prevention Practices in Federal Bureau of Prisons Facilities.* Washington, DC: DOJ, 2024

CHAPTER 12

LEGAL LIABILITY AND RISK MANAGEMENT

"Effective suicide prevention demands more than compliance; it requires leadership willing to translate lessons from tragedy and litigation into proactive, defensible systems."
—Anasseril E. Daniel

INTRODUCTION

S*uicide in custody* is not only a public-health crisis but also one of the most frequent sources of litigation against correctional facilities in the United States. Every in-custody suicide forces institutions to confront two intertwined realities: the human tragedy of a preventable death and the legal consequences that follow. Lawsuits arising from inmate suicide regularly allege deliberate indifference, medical negligence, or systemic failures in suicide prevention policies. The financial stakes are high—settlements and judgments often reach millions of dollars—but the reputational and operational damage to a correctional system can be even greater.

This chapter builds on themes explored earlier in the book. Chapter 2 traced the contours of suicide-related litigation, highlighting claims of deliberate indifference and medical negligence. Chapter 3 examined common problems that lawsuits expose—poor documentation, denial of ideation, and falsification of records—while Chapter 5 detailed the vulnerable-inmate profiles that often appear in litigation. Together, these earlier sections reveal how the same risk factors that drive suicide also shape liability. The lessons converge here, where prevention and risk management meet.

ESTATE OF RYAN CLARK V. COUNTY OF GREEN LAKE (LATER APPEALED AS *CLARK V. WALKER*)

To translate legal principles into practical risk management, this chapter begins with *Ryan Clark v. County of Green Lake*—an illustrative case that underscores how deficiencies in suicide prevention policy implementation, staff communication, and emergency response can transform clinical risk into constitutional liability and costly litigation. This case later proceeded on appeal as *Clark v. Walker*, with the Seventh Circuit affirming key aspects of the District Court's analysis; together, these decisions provide a clear road map for understanding both the operational failures that lead to tragedy and the legal standards that shape liability.

Ryan Clark committed suicide five days after being booked into the Green Lake County Jail in Wisconsin. He had a long history of **alcoholism, depression, multiple prior jailing episodes, suicide attempts, and self-harm behavior**. At intake, his **blood alcohol level was .27** (more than three times the legal limit), and the **Spillman intake risk assessment** scored him at **"maximum suicide risk."** Although the jail had a **suicide prevention protocol** that required special housing, mental health referral, and closer surveillance, **those protocols were**

never initiated. Instead, Clark was placed in a regular holding cell, not in the suicide prevention cell or on special watch.

Over the ensuing days, Clark prepared a ligature, tied it to parts of his bedding, and hanged himself. Surveillance video showed his preparation took about thirty minutes, though no staff intervened. An officer later discovered his body, but, by then, he could not be revived.

The estate of Clark sued under 42 U.S.C. §1983, alleging that corrections officer Bruce Walker and nurse Tina Kuehn acted with **deliberate indifference.** In the district court, summary-judgment motions by Walker and Kuehn were denied, leaving material-fact questions about their knowledge and responsibilities. On appeal, the Seventh Circuit affirmed the denial of qualified immunity, holding that inmates have a clearly established right to be free from deliberate indifference to suicide risk, and that the facts in Clark's case raised triable issues about the defendants' state of mind and failure to act.

Because Kuehn was a private-contract nurse, the appellate court also ruled that she could not claim qualified immunity. The case underscores that even where a protocol exists, failure to **activate** or **follow** it—especially when the risk is plainly indicated—can itself constitute constitutional liability.

BROADER IMPLICATIONS OF *RYAN CLARK*: RISK MANAGEMENT STRATEGIES

The *Clark* case carries profound lessons for correctional health, risk management, and policy design. Below are key implications to guide institutional reforms:

1. **Protocol existence is not enough**

   Clark shows that having a suicide prevention policy on paper is inadequate if staff do not **trigger it**. A facility must build **active**

triggers (e.g., high-risk scores, intoxication, past behavior) that force initiation of watch protocols.

2. **Clear assignment of responsibility is essential**
   The appeal emphasized ambiguity over **who had duty to initiate** the protocol (officer vs. nurse). Risk management must define precise **roles and accountability**, so no "someone else's job" gaps emerge.

3. **Risk classification cannot be left to intuition or discretion alone**
   Clark's case illustrates how even an automatic risk score (Spillman "maximum") was disregarded because officers believed intoxication always produced that score. Training and policy must ensure **discretion is informed and constrained by supporting data**, not assumptions.

4. **Communication and handoffs matter critically**
   Neither Walker nor Kuehn notified housing staff or those on watch about Clark's risk. Risk management must require **verbal and written communication of suicide risk**, especially at shift changes, housing moves, or status changes.

5. **Surveillance must be meaningful**
   Video footage recorded Clark's preparation, but no one observed or acted. Thus, video monitoring alone is insufficient—**staff must be assigned to watch feeds and intervene** when behavior is risky.

6. **Rapid identification and intervention protocols**
   The fact pattern suggests Clark had thirty minutes of preparation and was discovered after the fact. A robust system must include

immediate cell checks, rescue protocols, and **emergency-response drills** to reduce the window of unobserved time.

7. Documentation and audit trail as defense

In litigation, absence of logs, failure to follow protocol, or missing notes become powerful evidence. Facilities must enforce **honest documentation**, routine audits, and oversight to maintain institutional integrity.

8. Qualified immunity does not shield failure to act

Clark confirms that even personnel with official status (or private contractors) cannot hide behind immunity if the constitutional right is clearly established and the failure is obvious. Risk management must treat suicide prevention as **constitutional safety**, not optional care.

9. Tailored training that links law to practice

The *Clark* case shows that staff must internalize not just "what to do," but **why failing to act has legal consequences**. Training should use *Clark* (and similar cases) to reformulate policy into **legally defensible practices.**

10. Continuous review and post-incident learning

The discursive facts in Clark's case—e.g., failure to initiate critical steps—should feed into **post-incident analysis, audits, policy revision, and retraining.** A death, while tragic, must become a catalyst for system improvement.

RISK MANAGEMENT STRATEGIES FROM CASE LAW AND CLINICAL PRACTICE

The *Ryan Clark v. County of Green Lake* decisions crystallize how predictable suicide risks turn into constitutional liability when systems fail. Yet *Clark* is only one example. Across the **forty real-world cases** analyzed in this book and the **fifteen landmark court decisions** examined in Chapter 11, the same failures recur: superficial screening, ignored warnings, unsafe housing, poor handoffs, inadequate monitoring, medication disruption, and slow or chaotic emergency response. Effective risk management must, therefore, combine **lessons from litigation** with **sound clinical, operational, and policy principles.**

1. Build Reliable Screening and Risk Assessment Systems

- **Key Lesson:** *Clark* and many other cases show that intake screening is often completed but ignored.
- **Strategy:** Require **automatic-activation triggers** when high-risk indicators appear (e.g., prior attempts, intoxication, acute mental illness).
- **Integration:** Use structured tools, but require **clinician review** and re-screening after key events (segregation, bad news, withdrawal).

2. Strengthen Early Custody Protections

- **Key Lesson:** The **first two weeks** are the most lethal.
- **Strategy:** Implement heightened observation and mental health contact for **new admissions, intoxicated detainees, and those with withdrawal or crisis reactions**.
- **Integration:** Practical checklists (Chapter 9) guide staff actions during this vulnerable window.

3. **Clarify Roles and Authority**

    - **Key Lesson:** In *Clark*, no one acted on the "maximum risk" score; in other cases, watch discontinuation was left vague.
    - **Strategy:** Define **who can start, stop, or escalate suicide precautions**. Require supervisor sign-off and clear **QMHP authority**.

4. **Ensure Communication and Handoffs**

    - **Key Lesson:** Courts repeatedly fault facilities for lost or ignored risk information.
    - **Strategy:** Mandate **verbal and written handoffs** at shift change, housing moves, and clinical-status updates.
    - **Integration:** Embed standardized risk-transfer forms and **shift-commander review**.

5. **Maintain Safe Housing and Eliminate Ligature Points**

    - **Key Lesson:** Unsafe fixtures (beds, vents, sprinkler heads) feature prominently across cases.
    - **Strategy:** Systematically **audit and repair** cells; do not label cells "suicide resistant" without documented inspection.
    - **Integration:** Apply Chapter 8's detailed **ligature-mitigation protocols**.

6. **Observation Must Be Active and Verifiable**

    - **Key Lesson:** Cameras and checks fail if **nobody watches** or logs are falsified.
    - **Strategy:** Assign observation posts, use **unpredictable rounds**, and audit logs regularly.

- **Integration:** Training from Chapter 7 on **monitoring and emergency response** reinforces this.

7. **Guarantee Medication Continuity and Safe KOP Policies**

   - **Key Lesson:** Abrupt discontinuation (*Steele v. Shah*) or unsafe self-administration has fueled litigation (*Andrews v. Wayne County*).
   - **Strategy:** Review **KOP policies**, ensure high-risk medications are controlled, and maintain continuity of psychotropics and MAT during incarceration.

8. **Manage Intoxication and Withdrawal Safely**

   - **Key Lesson:** Several cases—including *Clark*—involved **substance use and withdrawal.**
   - **Strategy:** Combine **withdrawal protocols** with suicide risk assessment, and trigger **psychiatric referral** for complex cases.

9. **Build Rapid Emergency Response Capability**

   - **Key Lesson:** Courts scrutinize delays in rescue and EMS activation (*Colburn* and multiple vignettes).
   - **Strategy:** Train all staff in **cell entry, ligature cutting, CPR, bleeding control, and EMS activation**; conduct surprise drills.

10. **Demand Honest, Timely Documentation**

    - **Key Lesson:** Falsified or incomplete watch logs devastate defense (*Estate of Clay*).
    - **Strategy:** Require **real-time logging**, supervisor spot-checks, and electronic timestamping to deter after-the-fact entries.

11. Train with Clinical and Legal Integration

- **Key Lesson:** Standard "risk factor" training fails to change practice.
- **Strategy:** Adopt the **hybrid case law-based model** from Chapter 11: real cases, court outcomes, and operational checklists tied to the **Twenty Critical Actions.**

12. Build Governance and Continuous Quality Improvement

- **Key Lesson:** Courts examine leadership's diligence.
- **Strategy:** Appoint a **Suicide Prevention Coordinator** or committee.
- **Integration:** Perform **mortality reviews**, track trends, update policy and training, and document corrective action.

ROAD MAP FOR FACILITY IMPLEMENTATION

A comprehensive suicide prevention program must be **systematic, auditable, and leadership-driven.** Facilities can follow this practical road map:

1. Gap Analysis and Audit

- Compare current policy and practice with **NCCHC/ACA standards** and the **lessons from *Clark* and other cases.**
- Identify weak triggers, vague authority, unsafe cells, or poor documentation.

2. Policy Refinement and Legal Review

- Update policies to be **clear, flexible, and defensible** (Chapter 10).
- Have them reviewed by legal counsel for both enforceability and liability exposure.

3. **Hybrid Training Rollout**
    - Deliver the **clinical and case-law training model** from Chapter 11.
    - Include *Clark* and other sentinel cases to reinforce **constitutional duty** and **practical prevention.**
4. **Scenario Drills and Simulations**
    - Test intake screening, watch discontinuation, emergency rescue, and log accuracy.
    - Track **time-to-response** and adherence to protocol.
5. **Audits and CQI**
    - Monthly **policy-compliance audits**, random **log reviews, ligature audits**, and **mortality reviews.**
    - Use data to drive policy updates and refresher training.
6. **Leadership Oversight and Governance**
    - Empower a **Suicide Prevention Coordinator** or team to track metrics, oversee training, and report to senior leadership.
    - Document **due diligence** to defend against deliberate-indifference claims.
7. **External Review and Accreditation**
    - Seek **outside consultation** or NCCHC/ACA survey feedback.
    - Close identified gaps with documented corrective action.

Why This Framework Matters

No single lawsuit or standard defines suicide prevention; the **pattern of failure is consistent across decades.** *Clark* highlights one vivid path to tragedy and liability, but the larger body of case law and clinical experience forms a **map for prevention.** Facilities that integrate these strategies create not just compliance but also a **culture of safety and legal defensibility**—protecting detainees, staff, and the institution itself.

DOCUMENTATION

A correctional facility's credibility in both preventing suicide and defending itself in litigation often hinges on the strength of its documentation practices. Courts consistently scrutinize not just whether policies existed, but whether staff followed them and created an adequate written record of their actions. In suicide-related lawsuits, a facility can rarely defend itself with vague assurances of compliance; instead, contemporaneous records of screenings, housing decisions, supervision checks, medical evaluations, and emergency responses become the central evidence.

Proper documentation demonstrates diligence. When officers record their rounds accurately, mental health staff chart evaluations comprehensively, and supervisors review logs routinely, the paper trail establishes that the facility took the inmate's safety seriously. Conversely, when logs are falsified, left blank, or contain suspiciously identical entries, they provide powerful evidence of deliberate indifference. Courts have repeatedly held that such deficiencies undermine a facility's defense, even if policies looked sound on paper.

A comprehensive risk management approach, therefore, treats documentation not as bureaucratic burdens but as essential safeguards. They serve the dual function of protecting incarcerated individuals from harm and protecting the facility from the devastating consequences of litigation.

> *"In suicide cases, the record speaks louder than testimony—logs, notes, and reports often decide whether a facility is seen as diligent or indifferent."*

TRAINING AS RISK MANAGEMENT

One of the clearest lessons from decades of suicide-related litigation is that **training is not optional; it is a cornerstone of risk management.** Courts have repeatedly found that correctional facilities that fail to train their officers and clinical staff in suicide prevention expose themselves to liability. The rationale is straightforward: suicide in correctional settings is both foreseeable and preventable when staff are equipped with the skills to identify risk and intervene appropriately.

Much case law underscores this point. Policies exist on paper, but staff has not been consistently trained on suicide warning signs, mental health symptoms, or emergency-response protocols. As a result, front-line officers do not recognize inmates' escalating distress, nor do they take the steps that might interrupt the chain of events leading to death. The courts often highlight these training deficiencies as evidence of systemic failure.

Effective training goes beyond classroom lectures or check-the-box annual refreshers. It must be **practical, scenario-based, and grounded in case law and real-world outcomes.** Training that incorporates lessons from lawsuits—what courts have said about failures in monitoring, documentation, housing, and emergency response—gives staff a tangible sense of the consequences of inaction. When correctional officers see that ignoring a suicide threat is not only a moral failure but also a legal liability, the urgency of suicide prevention becomes real.

In this way, **training becomes both a shield and a compass.** It shields facilities from costly litigation by demonstrating that they exercised due diligence in preparing their staff. It also serves as a compass, pointing staff toward behaviors and practices that save lives. By integrating legal rulings, institutional lessons, and clinical best practices, suicide prevention training transforms from a bureaucratic requirement into a powerful instrument of risk management.

LEADERSHIP AND OVERSIGHT

If training is the engine of suicide prevention, **leadership and oversight are the steering wheel.** Even the best-trained staff will falter if the organizational culture fails to prioritize suicide prevention. Litigation repeatedly shows that systemic failures occur when leadership treats suicide as an isolated clinical issue rather than a shared institutional responsibility.

In the *Clark* case, leadership shortcomings were evident in the lack of accountability for suicide-watch procedures. Officers were not adequately supervised to ensure that required checks were carried out, and documentation was inconsistent. The court recognized this lack of oversight as a form of institutional neglect, noting that policies without enforcement are little more than hollow promises.

Strong leadership begins with clear communication from the top. Wardens, sheriffs, and administrators must set the expectation that suicide prevention is integral to facility safety, not an optional add-on. Oversight mechanisms—such as unannounced audits, review of video surveillance, and continuous quality-improvement programs—are necessary to confirm that policies are implemented in practice. Without these checks, even well-crafted policies risk becoming irrelevant in daily operations.

Oversight also extends to the quality and training of staff. In the *Clark* case, correctional officers failed to recognize obvious signs of crisis and did not follow basic procedures. Supervisors who overlook such patterns or fail to discipline repeated neglect indirectly reinforce dangerous practices. By contrast, facilities that investigate incidents promptly, document findings clearly, and hold staff accountable through retraining or discipline are far more likely to withstand legal scrutiny. Courts often look for evidence of a system that is responsive rather than reactive, one that learns from mistakes rather than repeating them.

External-oversight mechanisms add another layer of protection. Consent decrees, Department of Justice investigations, and accreditation reviews by organizations such as the National Commission on Correctional Health Care (NCCHC) or the American Correctional Association (ACA) often serve as catalysts for reform. While sometimes perceived as intrusive, these interventions can provide both the framework and the political will to implement long-overdue improvements. In fact, compliance with external standards and accreditation requirements is frequently cited in litigation as evidence that a facility has taken reasonable steps to prevent suicide.

Leadership must foster a **culture of prevention rather than reaction.** Instead of waiting for lawsuits or media scrutiny to prompt reform, proactive leaders review near misses, conduct psychological autopsies after suicides, and share lessons with staff. Such practices not only strengthen risk management but also demonstrate to courts, families, and the public that the institution takes its constitutional duty seriously.

Ultimately, **leadership and oversight provide the credibility that courts and communities look for.** A facility that can show that its leaders actively monitor compliance, enforce accountability, and allocate resources for suicide prevention stands on stronger legal ground. Without these elements, training and policy remain fragile, and preventable tragedies are far more likely to occur.

ACCOUNTABILITY

Accountability is the cornerstone of any defensible suicide prevention system. The death of Ryan Clark, like so many others, exposed not only individual failures but also a deeper absence of institutional oversight. Correctional leaders cannot assume that written policies or posted procedures are sufficient. The courts have repeatedly emphasized that liability arises when staff disregard clear risks and when administrators tolerate a culture where suicide prevention is treated as optional rather than essential.

True accountability begins at the top. Wardens, sheriffs, and superintendents must ensure that suicide prevention policies are not static documents but living instruments that guide practice. This requires regular audits, unannounced checks, and meaningful reviews of compliance with monitoring, screening, and housing protocols. Where lapses occur, corrective action must follow. Without such follow-through, even the most carefully drafted policies become meaningless, and facilities risk being found deliberately indifferent under the law.

Finally, accountability must include transparency with families and the public. When a death occurs, facilities that communicate openly, conduct thorough psychological autopsies, and share findings with oversight bodies demonstrate both integrity and responsibility. This transparency not only helps families process their grief but also signals to courts and communities that the facility takes its duty of care seriously. Secrecy, denial, or attempts to minimize the event almost always exacerbate liability and erode public trust.

In short, accountability and oversight are not afterthoughts but integral elements of risk management. A facility that builds a culture of supervision, demands compliance with policy, welcomes external review, and commits to transparent communication is far less likely to repeat the failures seen in Ryan Clark's case—and far better positioned to defend itself when tragedy does occur.

INTEGRATING RISK MANAGEMENT INTO DAILY OPERATIONS

For suicide prevention and liability reduction to be effective, risk management cannot remain a policy stored in a binder or a response limited to crisis moments. It must be embedded into the daily fabric of correctional operations. Risk management in this context means constant vigilance, structured communication, and routine practices that align staff behaviors with both constitutional obligations and professional standards of care.

In practical terms, this begins with intake. Every new detainee should be viewed through a risk management lens: screening for suicide risk, mental illness, and substance use must be treated as a front-line responsibility, not a formality. From that point forward, officers and mental health staff should integrate suicide risk considerations into routine duties. Regular cell checks, for example, are not only a matter of custody but also a core part of suicide prevention. When staff understand that each observation round is an opportunity to detect warning signs, risk management becomes part of their daily rhythm rather than an added burden.

Communication is equally central. Inmates are often observed by multiple staff categories—correctional officers, nurses, counselors—yet information about risk can be lost if it is not shared systematically. Daily briefings, logbook entries, and electronic health records should all reflect suicide risk factors and current precautions. A culture that emphasizes collaborative responsibility ensures that no single officer or clinician carries the weight alone.

Training reinforces this integration. Policies and procedures must be practiced until they are second nature. Staff should know instinctively when to escalate concerns, how to conduct emergency responses, and the boundaries of their authority—for example, that only a qualified mental health professional can discontinue suicide precautions. Risk management succeeds when these standards are not theoretical but ingrained in daily routines.

Finally, leadership plays a decisive role. Administrators must model accountability, emphasize prevention as a core mission, and track compliance through audits and continuous quality improvement. When supervisors routinely ask, "How did today's operations mitigate suicide risk?" they send a message that prevention is inseparable from safety, liability reduction, and professional duty.

CONCLUSION

Legal liability in suicide cases is not driven by the presence or absence of a policy alone but by **how consistently a facility turns policy into action.** Courts have made it clear: when staff fail to activate suicide watch, ignore clear risk indicators, miscommunicate vital information, or delay rescue efforts, those lapses are judged as **deliberate indifference.** The *Ryan Clark v. County of Green Lake* decisions, together with decades of case law and real-world tragedies, illustrate that **predictable failures invite constitutional claims and costly settlements.**

This chapter provides a **practical risk management road map:** clear authority and communication channels, reliable screening and reassessment, safe housing and medication continuity, robust emergency response, honest documentation, and leadership-driven quality improvement. Combined with **case law-informed training,** these elements transform suicide prevention from a compliance exercise into a **legally defensible, clinically sound, and ethically imperative system.**

Facilities that embrace this approach can move beyond fear of litigation toward **confidence in their prevention efforts**—protecting both the lives entrusted to their care and the integrity of the organization itself.

"Risk management in corrections is not a legal strategy after a suicide—it is a daily commitment to preventing the next one."

REFERENCES

1. *Estate of Ryan Clark v. Green County*, No. 20-cv-842 (W.D. Wis. filed 2020)
2. National Commission on Correctional Health Care, *Standards for Health Services in Jails*. Chicago: NCCHC, 2018

CONCLUSION

THE DUTY THAT NEVER ENDS

In these pages, we have traveled through the realities of suicide in custody—from the human cost to the legal repercussions; from the vulnerabilities of certain detainees to the gaps in screening, monitoring, and supervision that too often end in tragedy. We have examined the **critical first two weeks of incarceration**, when risk is at its peak, and explored how **training and sound risk management strategies** can save both lives and careers.

These lessons have not come from theory alone. They are drawn from more than **twenty-five years of working inside housing units**, reviewing massive case files, testifying in depositions and trials—and, most importantly, **listening to those most affected**: the families of the deceased, the correctional officers who carry the weight of these losses, and the administrators who bear the responsibility of prevention.

If there is one unshakable truth I have learned, it is this: **suicide prevention in corrections is not a single program or a well-written policy—it is a culture.** That culture is built one decision at a time, in moments when **no one is watching**, by staff at every level who understand that **their actions matter**.

The legal complaints, failures, and problem areas outlined in this book are **not a catalogue of blame**; they are a **blueprint for change**. Every intake interview, every observation round, every exchange among custody, medical, and mental health staff is an opportunity to act wisely and to do better than the last time.

The challenge is great—and so is the responsibility. My hope is that you leave this book not only with **knowledge** but also with a renewed commitment to act decisively when you are the one standing between a person in crisis and an irreversible outcome. In corrections, the question is not *if* you will be tested; it is *when*. In that moment, the preparation, vigilance, and integrity you practice every day will be your most powerful tools—not only to prevent suicide but also to **protect the reputation and future of your facility**.

In the end, the strongest legal defense is a **well-run facility**, where prevention is more than policy—it is the way you do business, every day, without fail.

APPENDICES

INTRODUCTION

The appendices provide practical tools that complement the main text of *When No One Is Watching: Preventing Suicide and Avoiding Lawsuits—Insights from 25 Years as a Correctional Expert.* While the chapters present case analyses, legal perspectives, and prevention strategies, these materials are designed for immediate use by correctional administrators, medical and mental health staff, and line officers. They translate key concepts into actionable frameworks that can be implemented in daily operations, training, and policy development.

TABLE OF APPENDICES

1. **Appendix A:** Screening Checklist
2. **Appendix B:** Static and Dynamic Risk Factors, and Protective Factors
3. **Appendix C:** Hybrid Training Checklist
4. **Appendix D:** Risk Management Checklist

APPENDIX A

SUICIDE PREVENTION CHECKLISTS

Purpose and Use

This checklist has been developed as a practical tool for intake and ongoing screening of suicide risk in correctional settings. It is designed to be brief, structured, and legally defensible, with clear "Yes/No/Explain" options for documentation. Certain items, when endorsed, automatically trigger placement on suicide watch and referral to a Qualified Mental Health Professional (QMHP).

Adaptability

The checklist is intended for use in lockups, jails, and prisons of all sizes. While it reflects standards set forth by the National Commission on Correctional Health Care (NCCHC), facilities may adapt language or procedures to align with state regulations, institutional resources, and accreditation requirements.

Training Requirement

All staff who conduct intake or wellness checks must be trained in how to administer and document this checklist. Training should emphasize that accurate completion and timely referral are critical not only to inmate safety but also to institutional-liability management.

Legal and Ethical Context

Use of this checklist demonstrates due diligence by showing that staff consistently applied a structured tool to identify risk. It reinforces the principle of collaborative responsibility among custody, medical, and mental health staff. The checklist does not replace clinical judgment but serves as an essential foundation for immediate decision-making and referral.

APPENDIX A

Suicide Risk Screening Checklist

To be completed at intake by booking or medical staff. Any "YES" to a trigger item requires ***immediate placement on suicide watch*** *and referral to a Qualified Mental Health Professional (QMHP).*

ITEM	SCREENING QUESTION	YES	NO	EXPLAIN (DETAILS, CONTEXT, OBSERVATIONS)
1	Have you ever attempted suicide? **(Trigger item)**	☐	☐	
2	Are you thinking about killing yourself right now? **(Trigger item)**	☐	☐	
3	Do you have a current plan or means to harm yourself? **(Trigger item)**	☐	☐	
4	Have you experienced recent loss, humiliation, or major stress (e.g., court, sentencing, family)?	☐	☐	
5	Are you currently experiencing severe withdrawal symptoms from drugs or alcohol? **(Trigger item)**	☐	☐	
6	Do you have a history of mental illness (e.g., depression, schizophrenia, PTSD, bipolar)?	☐	☐	
7	Have you been recently hospitalized or treated for psychiatric reasons?	☐	☐	

ITEM	SCREENING QUESTION	YES	NO	EXPLAIN (DETAILS, CONTEXT, OBSERVATIONS)
8	Are you prescribed psychiatric medications? If yes, are you currently taking them?	☐	☐	
9	Have you ever been placed on suicide watch in this or another facility?	☐	☐	
10	Are you withdrawing from or recently intoxicated with substances (alcohol, opioids, methamphetamine)?	☐	☐	
11	Have you expressed feelings of hopelessness, helplessness, or being "done" recently?	☐	☐	
12	Is there observable behavior suggesting risk (tearing sheets, isolating, agitation, self-injury, giving away possessions)? **(Trigger item)**	☐	☐	

Instructions for Use

1. **Administration**

    - Conduct at intake or booking for all detainees.
    - Ask each question directly; note both verbal answers and observed behavior.
    - Ensure privacy to encourage honest responses.

2. **Trigger Items**
    - Items **1, 2, 3, 5, and 12** are considered **automatic triggers**.
    - Any "YES" to these requires:
        - Immediate placement on suicide precautions/suicide watch
        - Referral to a Qualified Mental Health Professional (QMHP)
        - Documentation of the action taken

3. **Documentation**
    - Every screening must be documented in the inmate's medical/mental health file.
    - "Explain" column should be completed whenever risk is identified or if clarification is needed.
    - Documentation must include actions taken (e.g., referral, housing assignment, watch initiation).

4. **Collaboration**
    - Screening results must be communicated promptly to custody, medical, and mental health staff.
    - Suicide prevention is a **collaborative responsibility**: all staff must act consistently with policy and training.

5. **Training**
    - Staff must be trained to recognize signs of mental illness, suicide risk factors, protective factors, and emergency management procedures.

- Only a QMHP may discontinue suicide watch or downgrade precautions.

6. Review

- Facilities should periodically review screening results and outcomes as part of their Continuous Quality Improvement (CQI) program.
- Adapted from NCCHC Standards (2018) and clinical/legal-consultation experience (Daniel, 2022). For inclusion in correctional suicide prevention policy and practice manuals.

APPENDIX B

RISK FACTORS: STATIC AND DYNAMIC

Static Risk Factors (Fixed/Historical)

1. Recent (within one year) near-lethal suicide attempt
2. Prior placement on suicide watch in the same institution
3. Actively symptomatic mental disorder (e.g., schizophrenia, bipolar disorder, major depression)
4. First-time arrest for a serious or stigmatized offense, particularly sex offenses
5. Pre-trial status (not yet adjudicated)
6. Active substance abuse involving alcohol, fentanyl, or methamphetamine
7. Placement in solitary confinement or restrictive housing
8. Veteran status with post-traumatic stress disorder (PTSD)
9. History of suicide in a first-degree relative

Dynamic Risk Factors (Variable/Incarceration-Based)

1. *Active suicidal ideation with intent or plan*
2. Recent self-injurious or preparatory behavior (e.g., hoarding medications, making a ligature)
3. Acute mental-status change, including depression, anxiety, or agitation
4. Recent significant behavioral change, such as isolation or withdrawal

5. Acute intoxication or withdrawal (alcohol, fentanyl, methamphetamine)
6. Recent adverse legal development (new charge, unexpected sentence, or parole denial)
7. Sexual victimization within the facility
8. Acute loss of external support system (family, partner, or community contact)
9. Denial of or delay in psychiatric treatment

Protective Factors (Buffers Against Risk)

1. *Strong religious or spiritual beliefs, particularly when suicide is viewed as morally unacceptable*
2. Stable marriage or committed supportive relationship (unless troubled)
3. Presence of young children or dependent family members
4. Strong parental attachment, particularly with a mother
5. Broader social connectedness within or outside the facility
6. Future-oriented thinking and identifiable post-release plans
7. Engagement in purposeful activities, programs, or work assignments

Note: *The presence of protective factors does not eliminate risk. They may buffer against vulnerability, but correctional staff must always assess suicide potential in the overall context of risk. Neglecting critical risk factors remains a frequent basis of liability claims in suicide-related litigation.*

APPENDIX C

SUICIDE PREVENTION POLICY CHECKLIST

This checklist integrates **traditional suicide prevention principles** *with a* **case law-based approach**. *It is designed to be practical, modular, and easily adaptable for correctional facilities of any size.*

1. Foundations of Suicide Prevention

- ☐ Review signs and symptoms of common mental illnesses.
- ☐ Learn myths and facts about suicide in corrections.
- ☐ Understand baseline suicide statistics in jails, prisons, and lockups.
- ☐ Recognize facility-specific vulnerabilities (e.g., cell design, staffing, rural limitations).

2. Screening and Intake Procedures

- ☐ Administer standardized suicide screening tool at booking.
- ☐ Document all responses thoroughly.
- ☐ Ensure that "Yes" responses on critical questions (e.g., prior suicide attempt, active ideation) **trigger immediate referral** to Qualified Mental Health Professional (QMHP).

3. Risk Factor Recognition

- ☐ Identify static factors (history, demographics).
- ☐ Identify dynamic factors (acute stressors, intoxication, recent legal setbacks).

- ☐ Integrate awareness of protective factors as part of balanced assessment.

4. **Housing, Supervision, and Monitoring**

- ☐ Assign housing consistent with risk (suicide-resistant cells when indicated).
- ☐ Conduct irregular but frequent checks; never predictable.
- ☐ Ensure clear documentation of supervision rounds.
- ☐ Confirm that QMHP is the only staff authorized to discontinue suicide watch.

5. **Communication and Collaboration**

- ☐ Train all staff on the principle of **collaborative responsibility** (custody, medical, mental health).
- ☐ Emphasize safe and lawful information sharing consistent with HIPAA.
- ☐ Require immediate communication of any observed risk behaviors to supervisors and mental health staff.

6. **Emergency Response Training**

- ☐ Practice cut-down tool use and airway management.
- ☐ Train in CPR, AED, and naloxone administration.
- ☐ Ensure that officers know how to transmit clear, descriptive radio communication during crises.
- ☐ Review post-incident evidence-preservation protocols.

7. **Case Law-Based Lessons**

   - ☐ Review selected precedent cases (e.g., *Estelle v. Gamble, Farmer v. Brennan, Ryan Clark v. Green County*).
   - ☐ Emphasize how **policy failures, poor documentation, or inadequate training** led to findings of deliberate indifference or negligence.
   - ☐ Apply "What would a jury see?" lens to each policy and practice.

8. **Post-Incident Review and Learning**

   - ☐ Conduct psychological autopsy under direction of chief mental health staff.
   - ☐ Consider independent external investigation when appropriate.
   - ☐ Implement staff debriefings to process emotional impact and reinforce lessons.
   - ☐ Integrate findings into **continuous quality improvement** (CQI) and training updates.

9. **Policy Familiarity**

   - ☐ Train staff not only on suicide prevention but also on the **facility's own written-policy framework**.
   - ☐ Require competency testing or signed acknowledgment of understanding.

10. Ethical and Legal Awareness

- ☐ Highlight staff duties of confidentiality balanced with duty to protect.
- ☐ Review due-diligence principles and liability risks.
- ☐ Reinforce that adherence to policy and professional judgment is staff's strongest defense in litigation.

SUMMARY:
The hybrid model ensures staff acquire **clinical awareness, operational competence, and legal literacy**. *By merging traditional prevention knowledge with the lessons of litigation, facilities can reduce suicides, strengthen defenses in lawsuits, and build a sustainable culture of safety.*

APPENDIX D

RISK MANAGEMENT CHECKLIST

This checklist is designed to help correctional administrators, mental health professionals, and custody staff integrate suicide prevention into daily operations and minimize legal liability. Each item represents a key element identified from case law, litigation reviews, and consultation experiences. Facilities are encouraged to adapt the checklist to their policies and procedures, ensuring ongoing compliance with standards of care.

1. Policies and Procedures

- ☐ Comprehensive written suicide prevention policy consistent with **NCCHC standards** is in place and reviewed annually.
- ☐ Policies address intake screening, housing, monitoring, emergency response, staff training, and post-incident review.
- ☐ A suicide prevention coordinator is designated and accountable.

2. Staff Training

- ☐ All staff (correctional, medical, mental health, administrative) receive **initial and annual training** on:
    - Signs and symptoms of mental illness
    - Suicide risk factors (static and dynamic)
    - Protective factors
    - Suicide prevention policies and emergency protocols

- ☐ Training includes **hands-on exercises** (cut-down tools, CPR, AED, naloxone use)
- ☐ Documentation of training is maintained

3. **Intake and Screening**

- ☐ Standardized suicide-screening tool is administered at intake.
- ☐ Screening results are documented and immediately communicated to appropriate staff.
- ☐ Positive screens trigger **mental health referral and housing precautions.**
- ☐ Prior suicide attempts and acute risk indicators automatically require placement on suicide watch until cleared by a QMHP.

4. **Communication and Collaboration**

- ☐ Custody, medical, and mental health staff share relevant information under **HIPAA allowances for safety.**
- ☐ Daily shift briefings include updates on at-risk inmates.
- ☐ Suicide-watch logs are reviewed regularly for accuracy and compliance.

5. **Housing and Environment**

- ☐ Suicide-resistant housing is available (cells free of tie-off points, with tamper-resistant fixtures).
- ☐ Safety audits are conducted **quarterly**; deficiencies are corrected promptly.
- ☐ Inmates on suicide precautions are housed in safe cells, never isolation for punishment.

6. Monitoring and Supervision

- ☐ Inmates identified at risk are observed at intervals consistent with policy (e.g., fifteen minutes or continuous).
- ☐ Only a **QMHP** may discontinue suicide precautions.
- ☐ Monitoring logs are reviewed for completeness and accuracy.

7. Emergency Response

- ☐ All staff are trained and equipped for emergency intervention (cut-down tools, CPR, AED, naloxone).
- ☐ Protocols are in place for contacting **EMS/paramedics** immediately upon discovery of a suicide attempt.
- ☐ Drills are conducted regularly; response times are documented.

8. Post-Incident Procedures

- ☐ A psychological autopsy is conducted by mental health leadership.
- ☐ Independent or external review is considered in serious cases.
- ☐ Incident reports should include staff actions, timelines, and corrective measures.
- ☐ Debriefing is provided for staff and inmates affected.

9. Documentation

- ☐ All actions (screening, monitoring, interventions) are documented contemporaneously.
- ☐ Logs and medical notes are reviewed by supervisors for accuracy.
- ☐ Documentation is maintained for litigation defense and quality improvement.

10. Continuous Quality Improvement

- ☐ An annual review of suicides and attempts is conducted.
- ☐ Trends are analyzed to identify systemic issues.
- ☐ Policies are revised in light of lessons learned.
- ☐ Results are shared with staff for transparency and accountability.

CLOSING NOTE

These appendices are not meant to be exhaustive but to serve as working tools that align with the evidence, case law, and litigation lessons discussed throughout the book. By integrating these checklists, digests, and structured references into practice, correctional leaders can strengthen suicide prevention efforts, reduce legal exposure, and promote safer environments for incarcerated individuals and staff alike.

ACKNOWLEDGMENTS

This book is the product of more than twenty-five years of work as a correctional psychiatrist and expert witness. Along the way, I have been fortunate to collaborate with dedicated correctional officers, mental health professionals, attorneys, and administrators who have trusted me with their questions, frustrations, and hopes for a safer system.

I am especially grateful to the families and legal teams who consulted me to review their cases. Their courage in pursuing accountability, even in times of immense grief, has contributed to systemic changes in some facilities.

On a personal note, I thank my colleagues, friends, and loved ones who encouraged me to turn decades of consultation into a single resource. Without their support and faith in this project, *When No One Is Watching* would not have been possible.

ABOUT THE AUTHOR

A*nasseril E. Daniel, MD*, is a psychiatrist and nationally recognized expert in correctional mental health and suicide prevention. In a career spanning more than fifty years, Dr. Daniel has cared for thousands of individuals with severe mental illness and has worked closely with correctional teams to improve care and reduce preventable deaths. His approach combines clinical expertise, legal insight, and a deep commitment to dignity and humane treatment for people in custody.

Over the past twenty-five years, Dr. Daniel has focused his work inside, consulting on suicide prevention systems and serving as an expert witness in complex litigation. He is the author of *Suicide in Jails and Prisons: Preventive and Legal Perspectives* (2022) and has published widely in journals such as the *Journal of the American Academy of Psychiatry and the Law* and the *Journal of Correctional Health Care.* His innovative case law-driven suicide prevention training approach is protected by a 2023 U.S. copyright registration.

Known for his humility and collaborative style, Dr. Daniel believes that lasting change is achieved when correctional staff, mental health professionals, and administrators work together. His lifelong mission remains clear: save lives, reduce suffering, and help create safer, legally defensible correctional systems.

Contacts:
aedaniel@aol.com
anasserildaniel@gmail.com

INDEX

A

ACA (American Correctional Association) standards of care, 209, 214
ACEs (adverse childhood experiences), 88
acute risk, 215
AEDs (automated external defibrillators), 161
alcohol abuse, 111–112
ambiguous suicidality, 74–76
arrest-and-booking process, 144–145
assessment, 3–4. *See also* screening; SRA (suicide risk assessments)
  CIWA-Ar (Clinical Institute Withdrawal Assessment of Alcohol, revised), 111
  lawsuits, 46–48
  mental-status examination, 46
  NSSI (non-suicidal self-injury), 72–77
  questionnaires, 125–126
audits, 225, 268
  accountability and, 273
  audit trail, 263
  CQI, 178, 225, 268
  deliberate indifference and, 221
  gap analysis, 267
  leadership and, 271
  safety audits, 168, 292

B

bipolar disorder, 105
bleeding-control kits, 161

C

C-SSRS (Columbia Suicide Severity Rating Scale), 132
case law-based model of training, 234, 241–243, 248–251
case vignettes
  1.1 Mental illness, 5–7
  2.1 Failure to provide lifesaving measures, 27–29
  3.1 Superficial screening, 43–44
  3.2 Group screening, 45–46
  3.3 Ignored records, 49–50
  3.4 Delayed psychiatric care, 52–53
  3.5 Withdrawal protocol initiation, 53–54

3.6 Ignored family warnings, 57
3.7 Risk information withheld, 58–59
3.8 Communication failure
59-61
3.9 Records falsification, 61–62
4.1 Denial of ideation, 71–72
4.2 Self-injury/ambiguous suicidality, 74–76
5.1 Stigmatized charges, 89–90
5.10 Intoxication and withdrawal, 114
5.2 Solitary confinement/parole denial, 92–93
5.3 Sexual assault, segregation, mental illness, 94–96
5.4 Transfer, medication disruption, single-cell placement, 96–97
5.5 Past attempt ignored, 99–100
5.6 Veteran with PTSD, 102–105
5.7 Major depressive disorder, 106–107
5.8 Schizophrenia, 108–110
5.9 Substance and intoxication and withdrawal, 112–113
6.1 SRA absence, PREA follow-up failure, delayed emergency response, 133–135
6.2 Cursory evaluation, 136–138
6.3 Inadequate SRA, suicide watch removal, transfer, 138–140
7.1 Holding-cell neglect, 145–146
7.2 Plastic-bag asphyxiation, 146–147
7.3 Solitary confinement suicide, 154–155
7.4 Delay in lifesaving measures, 162–163
7.5 Delay in lifesaving measures, 163–164
8.1 Sprinkler head anchor point, 168–170
8.2 Razor suicide, 172–173
8.3 Intercom failure, 174–175
8.4 Angela White, 178–181
8.5 Bradley Farm v. Missouri Board of Police Commissioners and Securus Technologies, Inc., 182–185
9.1 Lockup suicide, 193–195
9.2 U.S. Marshals transfer, 196–198
9.3 Drug Withdrawal, 201–202
10.1 Death in lockup without policy, 211–212
case-level failures, 4
causes of action
Eighth Amendment, 32, 37–38
Fourteenth Amendment, 32, 37–38
medical malpractice, 32
Monell claims, 33, 37–38
negligence, 32, 35–37
wrongful death, 33
CDC (Centers for Disease Control and Prevention)
definitions, 66–67
cells. *See* environmental risks
checklists, 17
risk management, 291–294
suicide prevention policy, 287–290
Suicide Risk Screening Checklist, 281–284
CIWA-Ar (Clinical Institute Withdrawal Assessment of Alcohol, revised), 111

claims for relief, 33
clinical evaluation, 216, 219–220
close observation (Q10-15), 216, 220
CO (constant observation), 74, 158, 216
collateral information, 131, 137–138
communication, 3, 265
  accuracy, 54–55
  HIPAA, 223–224
  practice points, 56
  record keeping, 55–56
  screening and, 126
  staff, 16–17
  suicidal ideation statements, 77–78
  training, 55
compassion, 23–24
confidentiality, 23
  group screening, 44–45
core practices, 161–162
COWS (Clinical Opiate Withdrawal Scale), 28, 201
CPR (cardiopulmonary resuscitation), 161
CQI (continuous quality-improvement) programs, 15, 178, 225, 268
criminal justice process
  suicide vulnerability and, 88–89
crisis intervention, 157–158
CSUs (Crisis Stabilization Units), 158–159
custodial responsibility, 37

D

deinstitutionalization of the mentally ill, 7
deliberate indifference, 6–7, 32–33, 35, 140, 186, 194
  audits and, 221
  case law-based training, 242
  documentation and, 269
  due diligence and, 22, 268
  environmental risks, 168, 171, 174
  kites delay, 152–153
  legal compliant and, 29
  Monell claims, 37–38
  monitoring failures, 144, 147–148
  policy and practice, 213
  protocol absence, 53
  records review, 50–51
  standard, 12
  standard of care and, 208
  withdrawal treatment, 203
demographics, risk factors, 86–88
depressive disorders, 105–107
direct observation, 131, 144, 147, 157, 265
cell visibility, 168, 173–174
observation levels, 220–221
documentation, 266, 269–270
  absence, 133
  accuracy, 54–55
  due diligence, 22, 24
  emergency response, 223
  falsification of records, 61, 136
  kites, 152
  litigation, 27–28
  monitoring and, 147
  practice points, 56
  risk stratification, 132
  SRAs (Suicide Risk Assessment), 130–131
  standards, 224
  training, 55, 217
drug withdrawal management, 28, 36, 53–54

bridge medication, 51
COWS (Clinical Opiate Withdrawal Scale), 201
death during withdrawal, 105
fentanyl withdrawal, 112–113
MAR (Medication Administration Records), 159
MAT (Medication-Assisted Treatment), 160
medication discontinuation, 50
methamphetamine, 114
opiates, 112–113
rescreening, 218–219
suicidal ideation, 69
suicide risk during, 200–204
untreated, 52
due diligence, 24
training and, 20–22
dynamic risk factors, 116–117, 285–286
static, 132–133

E

early stages of incarceration, 189, 264
drug withdrawal, 200–204
lockups, 192–199
psychological state of detainee, 191–192
Eighth Amendment, 32, 37–38
emergency response, 28, 223, 266
emotional impact of suicide, 17–19
empathy, 160–161
environmental risks, 167
cell components, 168–171
cell design, 173–174
cell visibility, 168
facility-issued razors, 171–172
intercoms, 174–176
issue-return systems, 172
KOP medications, 176–178
ligature materials, 170–171
ligature mitigation, 221
suicide-resistant house design, 168
telephone cords, 181–182
ethics, 22–24
evaluation. *See also* screening
clinical, 219–220
CQI (continuous quality improvement), 15
delayed, 51
telehealth, 97
timing, 47–48
expert witnesses, 34–35

F

falsification of records. *See* documentation; records
family
information disclosure, 57–59
legal responses, 19–20
reactions, 19–20
fentanyl withdrawal, 112–113
first two weeks, 189
Fourteenth Amendment, 32, 37–38

G

general-population housing
CSUs (Crisis Stabilization Units), 158
mental health issues and, 109
governance, policies, 226, 267

H

healthcare, correctional, 11–12
HIPAA, 23, 223–224
housing, 221, 265

- cell components, 168–171
- cell design, 173–174
- cell visibility, 168
- intercoms, 174–176
- restrictive, 222–223
- suicide-resistant, 168
- U.S. Marshals Service, 199

I

ICE (Immigration and Customs Enforcement), 191–192
identification and screening issues, 42–46
institutional consequences of suicide, 18
institutional factors, 91–92
institutional liability, 13
intake screening, 218
interim precautions, 219
intervention
- crisis intervention, 157–158
- CSUs (Crisis Stabilization Units), 158–159
- MAT (Medication-Assisted Treatment), 160
- medication management, 159

intoxication and withdrawal. *See* withdrawal management
issue-return systems, 172

J

JIMS (jail information-management systems), 126

K

kites. *See* MSRs (Medical Services Requests)
KOP (keep-on-person) medication programs, 176–178, 222, 266

L

lawsuits, 41–42
- assessment issues, 46–48
- communication issues, 54–62
- documentation issues, 54–62
- identification and screening issues, 42–46
- mental health care issues, 48–54
- psychiatric care issues, 48–54

leadership
- oversight, 268
- prevention program implementation, 271–272

legal complaints, 29
- causes of action
  - Eighth Amendment, 32, 37–38
  - Fourteenth Amendment, 32, 37–38
  - medical malpractice, 32
  - Monell claims, 33, 37–38
  - negligence, 32, 35–37
  - wrongful death, 33
- discovery, 34–35
- evidence gathering, 30–31
- expert witnesses, 34–35
- jurisdiction, 30
- parties, identification, 30
- statement of facts, 31–32
- venue, 30

Legal Liability-Driven Suicide Prevention Training, 242–243
legal representation, 29
ligature mitigation, 221, 265
lockups, 192–195
- policies and, 211–212

scaled implementation, 226

M

man down response, 161
manuals, 15–16
MAR (Medication Administration Records), 159
MAT (Medication-Assisted Treatment), 160
medical emergencies, medication withdrawal, 53–54
medical malpractice, 32
medication management, 23, 50–51, 222, 266
  bridge medication, 51
  high risk, litigation risk and, 180–181
  KOP (keep-on-person), 176–178
  MAT (Medication-Assisted Treatment), 160
  withdrawal management, 53–54
mental health care issues. *See also* PTSD (post-traumatic stress disorder)
  deinstitutionalization, 7
  delayed care, 51–54
  failures, 48–49
  general-population housing, 109
  intake screening, 122–123
  medication and, 50–51
  mood disorders, 104–106
  personality disorders, 105
  psychological states, 110
  psychotic disorders, 105, 107–108
  records consult, 49–50
  schizophrenia, 107–110
  substance-use disorders, 105
  threat disclosure from family, 58
methamphetamine withdrawal, 114
Monell claims, 33, 37–38
monitoring, 143–144
  arrest-and-booking process, 144–145
  by correctional officers, 148–149
  by mental health professionals, 149–152
  deliberate indifference, 144, 147–148
  direct observation, 147
  holding cell neglect, 145–146
  MSRs (Medical Services Requests), 149, 152–154
  solitary confinement, 154
  U.S. Marshals Service, 198
  video surveillance, 155–157
mood disorders, 104–106
MSRs (Medical Services Requests), 47–48, 149, 152–154

N

NCCHC (National Commission on Correctional Health Care) standards, 14–15, 209
  Suicide Prevention Policy Framework, 214
negligence, 32–37
NIH (National Institutes of Health) definitions, 66
NSSI (non-suicidal self-injury), 65, 72–76, 215

O

observation levels, 220–221
operational diligence, environmental risks, 168
opiate withdrawal, 112–113

P

pathways to prevention, 4
PBDS (Performance-Based Detention Standards), 199–200
personal representative, 30
personality disorders, 73–74, 105
policies, 11. *See also* Suicide Prevention Policy Framework
  deficiencies, 214
  development problems, 212–213
  failures, reasons for, 213–214
  governance, 226
  implementation, 210–212
  refinement, 267
  written, 207
post-incident procedures, 224
PREA (Prison Rape Elimination Act), 94, 134
prevention program implementation, 267–272
prisoner, xiv
professional organizations, 13
protective factors, 123, 286
  social support, 115–116
psychiatric care issues
  delayed care, 51–54
  failures, 48
  medication and, 50–51
  records consult, 49–50
  threat disclosure from family, 58
psychological states, 110
  early stages of incarceration, 191–192
psychotic disorders, 105, 107–108
PTSD (post-traumatic stress disorder) among veterans and soldiers, 101–105

Q

Q10-15 (close observation), 216, 220
Q30 (Enhanced Routine), 216, 220
QMHP (Qualified Mental Health Professional), 220
questionnaires for screening and assessment, 125–126

R

re-screening, 218–219
records
  communication and, 55–56
  falsification, 5–7, 61–62
resident, xiv
responsibility of administration, 216–217
risk factors, 2
  criminal justice process, 88–89
  demographics, 86–88
  depressive disorders, 106–107
  drug withdrawal, 200–204
  dynamic, 116–117, 123, 285–286
  environmental (*See* environmental risks)
  ignored, 129
  institutional factors, 91–92
  interfacility transfers, 96–97
  intoxication and withdrawal, 112–115
  prior attempts, 98, 99–100
  protective, 286
  schizophrenia, 109
  sentencing hearing, 90–91
  sexual victimization during incarceration, 93–96
  solitary confinement, 91–93
  static, 116, 123, 132–133, 285

stigmatized charges, 91
stratification, 132
risk management, 22
checklist, 291–294
daily operations integration, 274–275
documentation and, 269–270
strategies
case law, 264–267
Clark, Ryan, 261–263
clinical practice, 264–267
training as, 270–271
roles of administration, 216–217, 265

S

SAD PERSONS, 132
scenario drills, 268
schizoaffective disorder, 107–110
screening, 3, 28, 121, 264. *See also* assessment
communication and, 126
escalation and, 218–219
evidence-based policies and, 122
failures, 124–125
group screening, 44–46
intake, 218
mental health intake, 122–123
MSRs (Medical Services Requests), 47–48
outcome and next steps, 123
purposes, 124
questionnaires, 125–126
referrals to mental health professionals, 126–127
self-injury, 122
superficial screening, 43–44
timing, 47–48, 123
training, 127–128
triggered re-screening, 218–219
U.S. Marshals Service, 198
withdrawal management, 123–124
self-injury, 74–76
screening and, 122
staff attitudes, 80–81
sentinel events of suicide, 70
sex offenders, 89–90
sexual victimization, 93–96
SI (suicidal ideation) definition, 215
social support, 115–116
solitary confinement, 91–93, 154–155
special-needs populations, 99
SRA (suicide risk assessments), 46–47, 56, 121, 264
absence, 133
as core standard of care, 140–141
behavioral observation, 131–132
C-SSRS (Columbia Suicide Severity Rating Scale), 132
clinical judgment, 130
collateral information, 131, 137–138
definition, 216
documentation, 132
dynamic factors, 132–133
evaluator qualifications, 140–141
history taking, 131
inadequate, 135–136
legal standards, 130
level of risk, 129
mental-status examination, 131
probabilistic clinical judgement, 130
records review, 131
risk stratification, 132
SAD PERSONS, 132
solitary confinement, 154
static factors, 132–133

structured clinical interview, 130–131
training, 140–141
staff
collaboration, 16
communication, 16–17
coordination, 16–17
emotional impact of suicide, 17–18
ethics, 22–23
psychological impact of suicide, 17–18
self-injury, attitudes, 80–81
support systems, 18
staff training. *See* training
standard of care
ACA (American Correctional Association), 209
history, 208–210
negligence, 35–36
SRA as core standard, 140–141
statement of facts, 31
impact statement, 31–32
static risk factors, 116, 285
statute of limitations, 30
stigmatized charges, 89–91
structural vulnerabilities, 7
substance abuse, 111–112. *See also* drug withdrawal management; withdrawal management
substance-use disorders, 105
suicidal behavior, 65, 66, 69–71
suicidal ideation, 66
communicating, 77–78
denial, 71–72, 76–77
intentionality, 68–69
NSSI (non-suicidal self-injury), 72–76
suicide attempt, 69–71
definition, 215
method of choice, 78–80
suicide plan, 66
suicide prevention development history, 208–210
suicide prevention policy checklist, 287–290
Suicide Prevention Policy Framework, 214–230
suicide watch
denial and, 76
premature discontinuation, 138
suicide, definition, 67, 215
support systems, staff, 18
systemic problems, 3
Monell claims, 38

T

telephone cords, 181–182
tourniquets, 161
training, 11
as risk management, 270–271
broad-awareness training, 242
case law-based model, 234, 241–243, 248–251
communication, 55
CQI, 255–256
critical actions, 245–248
documentation practices, 55
due diligence, 20–22
evaluator qualifications, 140–141
governance, 255–256
hybrid model, 251–255, 268
Legal Liability-Driven Suicide Prevention Training, 242–243
legal precedents, 243–244
objectives, 235
persons receiving, 235–236

- screening, 125, 127–128
- SRA (suicide risk assessments), 140–141
- staff training, 3
- suicide prevention, 13
- sustainability, 255–256
- timing, 217–218
- traditional training model, 236–241
- U.S. Marshals Service, 199

transfers between facilities, 96–97

U

unspecified mood disorders, 105
USMS (U.S. Marshals Service), 196–199
PBDS (Performance-Based Detention Standards), 199–200

V

veterans and soldiers, 101–105
video surveillance, 155–157
vulnerable persons, 85–89
- special-needs populations, 99
- veterans and soldiers, 101–102

W–Z

withdrawal management, 111–115, 221–222. *See also* drug withdrawal management
- death during withdrawal, 105
- early incarceration period, 190
- early signs, 145
- kites, 152
- MAR (Medication Administration Records), 159
- MAT (Medication-Assisted Treatment), 160
- medication management, 159
- protocol, 175
- re-screening, 218–219
- screening and, 123–124

withdrawal protocol, 54
written policies. *See* policies
wrongful death, 33

www.ingramcontent.com/pod-product-compliance
Lightning Source LLC
LaVergne TN
LVHW020412220926
848484LV00016B/2541/J